Advance Praise for
Straight from the Horse's Mouth

"Amelia Kinkade, through her wise words, has washed away any left-brain scientific skepticism concerning animal telepathy that had been engrained in me through my veterinary medical education. This book is a true gift to the animal kingdom that offers hope to improve communication with all species. It's a must-read for all animal lovers! Read it and share it with all sentient beings! *Straight from the Horse's Mouth* will single-handedly revolutionize animal communication."

ALLEN M. SCHOEN, D.V.M., M.S., author of *Kindred Spirits* and
Director, Veterinary Institute for Therapeutic Alternatives (VITA)

"*Straight from the Horse's Mouth* is a tribute to the power of intuition to facilitate the reality of interspecies communication. In a compassionate, warm, and humorous style, Amelia Kinkade shows us how to listen deeply and hear the needs of the animals we love."

JUDITH ORLOFF, M.D., author of *Dr. Judith Orloff's
Guide to Intuitive Healing* and *Second Sight*

"I have read many books by animal communicators, but nothing like Amelia Kinkade's *Straight from the Horse's Mouth*. I set the book down thinking, 'Wow, I think I COULD do this!' Well written, funny, enlightening, and immensely practical. Read it!"

SUSAN CHERNAK MCELROY, author of *Animals as Teachers and Healers*

"A healthy change is in the wind, and Amelia Kinkade is the major motivator. *Straight from the Horse's Mouth* is a call to action, a challenge to us all to pay more attention to animal psychics. It is a classic in the field that will make a significant difference in how we view and treat our animal kin."

MARC BEKOFF, professor of biology, University of Colorado, Boulder,
author of *Strolling with Our Kin,* and editor of *The Smile of a Dolphin:
Remarkable Accounts of Animal Emotions*

Straight from the Horse's Mouth

How to Talk to Animals and Hear Them Talk Back

Amelia Kinkade

Thorsons

Thorsons
An Imprint of HarperCollins*Publishers*
77–85 Fulham Palace Road,
Hammersmith, London W6 8JB

The Thorsons website address is:
www.thorsons.com

First published in hardback in the USA
by Crown Publishers 2001
First published in paperback by Thorsons 2001

1 3 5 7 9 10 8 6 4 2

© Amelia Kinkade 2001
Foreword copyright © Bernard S Siegel, M.D.

Designed by Cynthia Dunne

Amelia Kinkade asserts the moral right to
be identified as the author of this work

A catalogue record of this book
is available from the British Library

ISBN 0 00 712349 3

Printed and bound in Great Britain by
Creative Print & Design, Wales

To everyone who ever called me in times of need—
and their owners.

Contents

Acknowledgments

I've read a thousand of these pages. Page one. "A special thanks to . . ." "This book never would have been made were it not for . . ."

But I've always wondered, is a book really a collaborative effort? Wasn't the writer alone hunched over a notebook, scribbling away quietly in the candlelight, night after night, year after year? Ah . . . well, now I understand. Alone, yes, but there were whispers in my ears keeping me company. The echo of loving words kept my pen moving:

> "You can do it. The animals need you." —Denise Landau Rorty
> "Just keep going. God will guide you." —Linda Sivertsen
> "Don't listen to criticism. Your work is important." —Carol Cellucci

These women lifted me up on the wings of their love. But there were other gypsy women who kept me airborne. Jo Fagan, at Jane Dystel Literary Management, helped me take flight and taught me that authors don't fly solo, but in precision formation.

My wingman is my editor, the brilliant Betsy Rapoport, who doesn't believe in standard-issue fluffy-winged angels—but is one. Her hawk eyes and razor-sharp instincts helped me fly straight.

Beside us sails Stephanie Higgs, an editorial assistant whose warm heart and keen wit help keep my wings level. Pamela Stinson-Bell and Sona Vogel, my production editor and copy editor, made my flight path clear and true.

Sailing on my left is my brother, Brendan, who dares to fly not ahead nor behind, but wingtip to wingtip with his wild little sister.

Gliding effortlessly just ahead is Dr. Marc Bekoff, the voice and champion of all animals everywhere. Behind but not forgotten is my teacher John Larkin, who taught me how to psychically soar. My reverend, Dr. Tom Johnson, is the warm summer wind beneath my wings.

And blazing above us all is the incomparable Dr. Bernie Siegel, who let us catch a comet by the tail and sent a dazzling spray of diamonds in his wake.

Lucky for us, the masterful photographer Shel Secunda joined our flight pattern to capture a freeze-frame of the magic midair. Art director Laura Duffy sent it skyward with her wonderful cover.

Thank you all for the flying lessons.

And thank you, Crown Publishers, for freeing us into the infinite sky.

The others to whom I am indebted are the animals themselves.

Miso, the purring wonder, and Anka, the generous shepherd, who so patiently posed with me for the jacket cover of this book.

Rodney-Oscar, the cat who taught me that love is not the slave of space and time and that miracles are not something you "believe in," but something you witness with your own eyes.

And finally, I thank the love of my life, who recently graced the angels with his presence: This book is for you, Mr. Jones. No matter what your proximity in heaven or on earth, you are the sunlight in my universe.

Author's Note

I have written this book with the desire to help you learn to communicate with your nonhuman loved ones. This book isn't intended to be a substitute for medical care or the expert diagnosis of a trusted veterinarian, but it is my hope that you will be able to cooperate in harmony with a veterinarian who is compassionate, intuitive, and willing to treat both you and your animals with the utmost respect. Please take care to cross-reference your intuitions with professional opinions and diligently seek feedback from outside sources.

I have disguised the names and identifying characteristics of my clients and their animal friends to protect their privacy. However, some of my most treasured client/friends have generously granted me permission to use their real names in their stories. I have also included the real name of my most beloved veterinarian: the late great Dr. John Craige.

Foreword

"Boo Boo, Where Are You?"

I happily agreed to take care of his animals and home while our son Jeff was away refurbishing our old vacation house on Cape Cod. After all, I already fed the chickens and gathered their eggs, then walked and fed the dogs and yard cats every morning anyway before I worked out on his exercise equipment. Indoors was Boo Boo, his house cat, who had had her front claws removed and who had her routine, too. We basically worked out together and shared the equipment, so Boo Boo received plenty of attention while I exercised.

The first morning after our son left, Boo Boo didn't greet me at the sliding door as she usually did when I came to visit. I thought she probably had been accidentally locked in somewhere, but after opening every door and cabinet and searching every inch of the house, I found no sign of Boo Boo. I called Jeff, figuring she must have snuck out while they were moving things to his truck. He mentioned that whenever she went out, she always stayed near the house. I searched every acre of the property and the basement, calling her name over and over. No answer or sign of Boo Boo. I left her food dish and litter outside, but they went untouched.

A week went by with no sign of our beloved Boo Boo. I was certain she had been carried off by some predator, since she had no claws to protect her or help her to climb a tree. We were all depressed. The only hopeful sign was that it looked as if someone was raiding the food bowl of Eanie and Meanie, the outdoor cats. Could it be Boo Boo? (Meanie was just what her name implied, mean toward everyone. Even the dogs stayed away from the yard boss.)

I had to go to San Francisco for the Kinship for All Life Conference sponsored by the SPCA, so off I went with a heavy heart. Jeff's friend watched over the house and animals while I was away. He also reported no sign of Boo Boo. While at the conference, I met Amelia Kinkade, an animal communicator and intuitive. I briefly shared what had happened at home, and we discussed the possibility of her helping locate Boo Boo.

It broke my heart to return to Jeff's empty house and work out or sit and read the paper with no Boo Boo to demand love and attention and keep me company. For the next week, Jeff's dog Cybil and I toured the yard every day, calling out for Boo Boo with no luck.

Amelia and I began to e-mail, and I kept bringing up Boo Boo and my feelings of loss. Amelia agreed to try to help me by visualizing what Boo Boo was experiencing, even though she lives in California and we are across the continent in Connecticut. Amelia asked for a photograph of Boo Boo, but each time I entered the house I was so heartbroken and lonely I'd forget to look for one. She began to give me clues but I still did not have my heart in it, believing Boo Boo was long gone.

Then one day an extensive e-mail arrived from Amelia describing Jeff's house, where she said Boo Boo was hiding, and what the little cat was going through. I had given her no details about any of the things she mentioned. I couldn't believe her accuracy in describing the house; she correctly said it was up on a hill, with a fountain (which is in the pond to aerate the water), a sprinkler system, and a Dumpster in the yard for garbage, on land scattered with pinecones. She told me that Boo Boo was hungry, fearful, and could see the full moon, so she had to be alive.

Amelia described two dogs in a penned-in area (Cybil and Bruiser, a recent addition to the household) and a black cat with white paws (Meanie), who had driven Boo Boo under the house, threatening her and refusing to let her out to eat when she was hungry, effectively holding her prisoner. Amelia also got my wife's and son's first names and the name of our veterinarian, Michael, whom she said Boo Boo wanted to see.

With this and more information, I went right back to the house, choked with emotion, convinced that Boo Boo was there. I circled the property, continually calling Boo Boo's name. After fifteen minutes I heard a cry coming from beneath the long wooden staircase that leads from the house down the side of a hill. I lay down and peered into the darkness. There was Boo Boo! I cried with joy, but she was too frightened to come to my outstretched hand. I ran into the house and got some food for her and enticed her to come toward me. I finally managed to pull her out; it was a tight fit. She was fearful and angry, and she hid immediately as soon as I got her inside. She eventually came out when she realized she was safe. She was covered with sores. I cleaned them and applied antibiotic ointment.

She had lost a pound or two, and even though we returned to our exercise routine, she still wasn't her totally playful self yet. I knew, because each evening she used to hide four play balls under the exercise equipment, which I would have to find each morning before we began our workout. Three weeks after finding her, I could find only three of the four balls, so I looked under the treadmill and, sure enough, I found that Boo Boo had hidden the missing ball. We were back to normal again.

I still grow tearful as I share this and can't thank Amelia enough. I have always been open-minded, but now I am a believer. With Amelia's training, I can now communicate with our cats and house rabbit. I hear what they are thinking, and we talk without words to each other. The rabbit, Smudge Bunny, now lets me pick her up in the front yard (prior to this only my wife had that honor), and the cats (Miracle, Penny, Dickens, and Gabriel) allow me to clip their nails, brush their teeth, and comb out their knots without complaint because I can now tell them what I'm doing and why. Now if I could just use this technique to read my wife's mind! Ah well, that will probably take some graduate work with Amelia. Women are a tough species to communicate with. Amelia may be an exception.

Bernie Siegel, M.D.
Author of *Love, Medicine & Miracles*
and *Prescriptions for Living*

Prologue

My Promise to You

I firmly believe a hundred years from now a book about mental telepathy will be as necessary as a book about how to eat with a fork. Telepathy will be nothing more than a simple tool that everyone uses.

This is not a book of outrageous stories about supernatural abilities you do not possess. This is a book of outrageous stories about natural abilities all humans possess. Everything I do, you can do, too. Use my words as a guide to empower yourself and learn real, lasting skills to practice every day for the rest of your life.

Ten years ago I did not know psychic communication was possible, yet for the last decade I have found myself conversing with thousands of animals. Until my first encounter with an animal communicator, my ability was like an underground stream, coursing silently just under the skin of my psyche. No sooner was I introduced to the concepts of nonverbal communication than this wellspring exploded out into the light like a geyser. Through years of research I have built upon that initial epiphany, fine-tuning it, analyzing it, developing techniques, terminology, and methods for psychic communication. I have designed exercises for other animal lovers to access pictures and emotions sent by their animals, formulate words, investigate physical conditions, locate missing animals through Gestalt, and even contact departed friends on the Other Side.

I now conduct workshops where I have the honor of teaching other people how to exchange telepathic information with animals. I see breakthroughs so frequently that I know, without the shadow of a doubt, that nonverbal communication is a *learned skill*.

When my intuitive ability surfaced, my practice escalated quickly. I appeared on a flurry of television talk shows and received the honor of inclusion in *100 Top Psychics in America* (Paulette Cooper, Simon & Schuster) within the same year I started practicing professionally. I could barely meet the public's demands. My phone rang off the hook at odd hours of the night with animal lovers calling from all over the United States, Canada, England, Australia, Argentina, and Brazil. The callers' needs varied dramatically—some wanted to solve their companions' medical problems, some needed to locate lost animals, while others wanted to speak to their friends who had passed on—but the intention was all the same: contact. My clients did not question that psychic communication was possible—what they all wanted to know was *how*?

Many people crave this connection. Animals are the keys to our own souls; and in order to deliver them from suffering and extinction, communion with our own souls is the last vestige of hope. Our modern society has strayed so far from our identification with the earth, with animals, nature, and our innate spirituality, we have apparently forgotten our way back home.

Use this book as a roadmap. These pages are my travelogue through rocky uncharted territory, where I stumbled and laughed and wailed at the gods as I fought my way through the psychic jungle, hiking under the moonlight—utterly alone. You will not take this journey alone. This book is my gift to you and your animals; and with it, I make this promise: If you dare open your mind to new possibilities and court the magical powers within, you will experience the miracle of psychic contact with fellow living beings—and your animal friends will experience the comfort and relief of psychic contact with *you!*

This first chapter is the story of my introduction to interspecies communication, my first experience with an animal psychic, and the tale of Rodney, the cat who made it all possible.

Straight from the Horse's Mouth

1

The Reluctant Psychic

*In his strange, not-quite-human way, [Adam] is
constantly reminding me that real magic doesn't
come from achieving the perfect appearance,
from being Cinderella at the ball with both glass
slippers and a killer hairstyle. The real magic is
in the pumpkin, in the mice, in the moonlight;
not beyond ordinary life, but within it. . . . It is a
quality of attention to ordinary life that is so loving and intimate it is almost worship.*

—Martha Beck, *Expecting Adam*

▓ Rodney Speaks ▓

I was as skeptical as any sane person would be that morning,
fourteen years ago, when I loaded Rodney, my cat, into his carrier to take him down to the holistic veterinary clinic where a

psychic was seeing animals. I was having some problems with Rodney that my regular vet couldn't help, and I figured, why not give the psychic a shot? It seemed a little odd and I felt a little foolish, but what did I have to lose? No matter what, it was sure to be good for a laugh.

I thought at the time, as some of you may think now, that the psychic business is either a hokey sideshow act or a solemn, mystical affair, full of incense-burning gypsies and weird witches with crystal balls. Boy, was I in for an eye-opener.

Gladys, the psychic, wore no heavy eyeliner, no gold hoop earrings or jangling charm bracelets. She was less gypsy fortune-teller and more midwestern grandmother. Were those ketchup stains on her shirt? I was perplexed.

When I extracted Rodney from his carrier and put him down on the cold metal table in front of her, he didn't howl like a triggered car alarm or jump off the table, his usual reaction at the vet's. Instead, he sat perfectly still and quietly scrutinized Gladys. He actually seemed startled to see her. She returned his gaze.

"What are you doing?" I whispered to her.

"I'm talking to him," she replied flatly.

You've got to be kidding! I wanted to yell. *No incantations? No sweeping arm movements? No speaking in tongues?* My curiosity won out over my skepticism.

"What does he say?" I whispered.

"I asked him what his favorite food is and he says chicken."

Good guess, I thought. True, Rodney gobbled up quite a bit of fresh chicken, but what cat doesn't like chicken? Any ninny could have figured that out.

"Now I am asking him what his favorite spot in the house is," she said. Again, Gladys did nothing more than look at the little cat, who returned her gaze, nonplussed.

The answer must have come to her quickly: "He says he likes to sit on the back of an orange chair that overlooks a window. A chair in the den."

"That's exactly right," I gasped. When Rodney was inside the house, he planted himself on the back of the peach-colored armchair in the den.

"The window in the den overlooks the yard with the little white dog," Gladys said.

"What dog?" I asked.

"Across the street from your building is a little dog behind a fence. Rodney likes to go over there and tease that little dog. He walks back and forth in front of the fence to make the dog bark."

I cast a fish-eyed glance at him. There was, indeed, a small white terrier behind a fence across the street, but I never dreamed Rodney went over there. "You torment that dog, do you?" I snarled at him.

"He's very full of himself," she continued. "He says women are always commenting on the pretty yellow markings on his head. He loves women. He's been told that he's quite handsome."

My jaw made a nasty clattering sound as it hit the linoleum floor. My boyfriend's secretary had been visiting our condo only the weekend before, and she had made a huge fuss over Rodney. She had praised the three little stripes on his head and used the very word *handsome*.

I took a deep breath and cut straight to the punch: "So why does he go door to door caterwauling?" I asked.

"He only howls at the windows where there are other cats. He thinks that if he calls them, they will be able to come out and play. He's lonely."

The answer was so obvious, I felt pretty foolish. Not once had it occurred to me that he was meowing not at the neighbors, but at the neighbors' *cats*.

"But . . . but . . . how can I make him stop before we get kicked out of the condo? I can't bear to keep him cooped up inside, but when I let him out, he screams," I whined.

"Get another cat. He's lonely. He doesn't want to be the only cat," she snapped. She had no way of knowing Rodney was the only cat at home; nonetheless, I wasn't thrilled with her prescription. One cat seemed to be more trouble than I bargained for—the little furry foghorn had already got us booted out of our last apartment; now the homeowners association in our new condo threatened to give me and my pint-sized Pavarotti our walking papers . . . *again*. How was I supposed to consider a second cat?

"Did you know your neighbors feed him?" she continued.

"What? What neighbors?"

"The neighbors with the two little girls. He goes in their house. Several of your neighbors let him in to be fed." I knew the neighbors with the two little girls, but I had no idea they were having my cat over for dinner.

"That's why he hasn't seemed very hungry lately."

I cast a wary glance in his direction. Rodney had settled into a squat on the cold table. He was calm, he was smug, and there was no mistaking the expression on his little furry face: He was smiling. He was finally getting the best of me, as he always thought he should. By this time, the strangeness of the communication had worn off and I was asking questions freely, like a foreign ambassador with a really fast translator:

"Ask him why he pees on my clothes," I said.

"He doesn't want you to go away and leave him alone. Peeing on your clothes is the only way he can express his anger." This was too true to be believed. I had a promotional modeling job that sometimes took me away for weekends, where I'd wear a specific uniform. When I got home Sunday night and emptied out my suitcase, I'd pile all my travel clothes on the floor, mingling my uniform with a week's worth of other dirty laundry. Then I'd get distracted by other chores. Later I'd find the pile strewn all over the floor. Rodney would have singled out my uniform from the pile of laundry and peed *only* on it. Eventually I learned not to leave my laundry on the floor, so he resorted to peeing directly into my freshly packed suitcase. That way I wouldn't discover until I unpacked my bag in Palm Springs that everything I brought was soaked and my uniform reeked to high heaven.

"He seems to know the uniform I wear when I go away. How could he possibly know what clothes I wear to work?" I asked.

"He just does," she replied.

"Why does he freak out every time I leave? He even seems to be afraid of the dark. Ask him why he has screaming panic attacks at three A.M. Ask him where he came from," I urged.

"He says he lived in an industrial part of Van Nuys, where there were a lot of strays. Men would put food out in the alley for the cats. There were piles of cardboard boxes and machinery and a lot of grease on the ground. He got shut up in the warehouse at night and was very cold and hungry. Howling was the only way he could get fed."

"So, he really *is* afraid of the dark? And he gets claustrophobic?" I asked.

"Only at night, he says."

"Poor little guy," I cooed, and patted his head. This explanation shone a whole new light on our dilemma. It couldn't have made more perfect sense. I had found him in the North Hollywood pound, on feline skid row. The little operatic kitten had serenaded me even as I'd entered the room. When I'd peeked in his cage, his nose was so obtrusive, I felt as though I were looking down the barrel of a shotgun. He wasn't my type. I was looking for Marlon Brando in fur, not Woody Allen. But when I'd lifted him up, he made an unprecedented move. He'd wrapped his minuscule arms around my neck, like two possessed pipe cleaners. Reaching his tiny face toward mine, he had kissed me on the lips. It was the most deliberate kiss I've ever received in my life. That's how the little orange salesman closed me. Oh sure, he was just a loudmouthed, needle-nosed redhead, a common model I call the Honda Civic of cats, but he had a certain *je ne sais quoi.*

"What does he think of me?" I asked.

"He loves you. He says he loves his mother."

Lately he had been showing some aggressive behavior around my boyfriend. If Benjamin touched me in front of him, Rodney would frantically attack him and run out of the room. So I had to ask: "What does he think of my boyfriend?"

Her response was: "He's very jealous. He thinks he should have you all to himself. Sometimes he wishes your boyfriend would just go away." *Ah,* I thought, *I sometimes feel that way myself.*

After I paid the psychic the $35—a measly price for turning my world upside down—I reached out to put the little cat back in his carrier, noticing that my relationship with him had already changed. I was more careful with him than usual. He wasn't just a little noisy pet anymore. He was an intelligent creature with distinct thoughts and feelings of his own, a creature who could observe and act on his observations, a creature who could *reason.*

In the car, for the duration of the ride home, the air was thick between us. I had never seen Rodney so smug and pleased, truly tranquil for the first time. He had finally had his say, and I had witnessed the most miraculous event of my life—I had found a human being who could talk to a cat. Frogs and whistles! What a world! Everything I ever believed had been changed in an instant.

Gladys had handed me a flyer on the way out for a workshop in animal communication she was offering that weekend. The first half of the class was to be a lecture on how interspecies communication works; during the second half, we'd practice on each other's animals, with the guardians there to verify information.

⚞ The Class That Changed My Life ⚞

We met outdoors in a sunny backyard furnished with picnic tables. Although it was a breezy spring day in Los Angeles, I spent the first two hours sweating and fighting the chorus of naysayers in my head. Even as I listened to Gladys, the demons of doubt rode me like a flock of scavenger birds on a rhinoceros's rump. Today I had given them a lot to talk about: *What if I'm the only one who can't do it? I will make such a fool of myself. This is all impossible, anyway! Why am I sitting here listening to this nonsense? Even if Gladys really can do it, I'll never be able to learn.*

I fought my demons: *So I'll make a fool of myself, so what? It wouldn't be the first time. I'll probably never see any of these people again, anyway. I might as well try.*

But while I was a nervous wreck, Rodney was calm and collected.

It didn't take long to notice that I was the only student who had brought a cat. The other six women who had brought their animals had brought dogs. Rodney waited quietly in his carrier by my feet under a picnic table.

The first volunteer was a big chow-type dog. The exercise went something like this: The teacher would call out a series of questions we were supposed to mentally ask the dog, and we'd write down the very first answer that flew into our heads.

The morning's lecture had been about telepathy, sending and receiving mental pictures. I had tried to absorb the idea, but it all seemed so abstract. I could have listened all day, but what could I *do*? I was tense.

The test questions were fairly rudimentary, the first being "What's your favorite food?" Gladys instructed the class to pretend we *were* the dog, while envisioning an empty food bowl in front of us. Then, with our mind's eye, we were to visualize what we'd like the bowl to be filled with.

The answer hit me like gangbusters. I heard the words inside my head: *Spaghetti and meatballs!* I struggled to make a mental picture of a dog's bowl, but I could see nothing but a dinner plate piled high with spaghetti and meatballs.

A few moments of silence followed before Gladys asked the students what we "got."

Everyone else produced the more practical answers like beef, chicken, and kibbles. My demons of doubt started to pick me apart: *I must have just made it all up in my mind! I had to be wrong. Why was my answer so ridiculous when everyone else was so obviously right?* I sank down low in my seat. Finally Gladys asked me what I "got." I mumbled sheepishly, "Spaghetti and meatballs."

The dog's guardian squealed. "Yes! That is exactly right! Spaghetti and meatballs is her favorite food! She ate a whole plate of it last night!"

That was nothing, my demons jabbed, *just a lucky guess.*

The next question was "What is your favorite toy?" I heard the voice again in my head—not the teacher's, not the demons'—this was a new voice introducing itself inside my brain, but I heard it distinctly. It was a woman's voice that said, *I like to wear my red-and-white-striped hat.* Instantly I saw in my mind's eye a candy-striped visor. I wrote it down.

The next question was "Do you have a job?" Gladys had said that many dogs, like Seeing Eye dogs, were able to talk about their jobs.

The female voice said, *Yes, now that Mother and Father are divorced, my job is to protect Mother and her house.* I scribbled it down, chagrined and disbelieving even as I wrote it. In response to the next question—"Were you ever in love?"—the female voice answered emphatically, *Yes, but I had to leave him when we moved.*

At this point, during a pause in Gladys's instruction, I took the liberty of asking questions of my own.

"Where did you live?" I mentally asked her. Immediately I saw a mental snapshot of a trailer home with a huge pine tree in front. Pinecones appeared on the ground only inches from my eyes, as if a camera had moved in from a long shot to a close-up. My nose tingled with the fresh scent of pine needles. With this, I heard the voice elaborating on her own: *He lived next door.*

"Show him to me," I asked. Instantaneously I saw a flash of a big black Doberman, accompanied by a pang of sadness in my chest.

"Do you miss him?" I asked. *Yes,* she said. The teacher interrupted our repartee with another instruction.

"Ask her if she has ever had puppies." I didn't need to. The dog answered the question before I asked.

No, I never got to have children. Mother got me fixed. I saw in my mind the scar on her abdomen, from her own point of view, as if I were looking down at my own belly. I felt a sharp pain in my pelvis, followed by terrible soreness. The voice continued, *I wanted to have children with my boyfriend.* Again she showed me the black Doberman next door. *I take care of the neighborhood cats instead.*

Even as I wrote, wrestling with the outlandish impossibility of this conversation, I felt the feeling of sadness intensify.

Despite the rebuttal from my demons (*You're making all this up. This is nothing more than your imagination!*), the sadness engulfed me. My abdomen ached, my eyes welled with tears, and my left hand scribbled like a mad fiend. My silent interrogation had provoked a stream of answers so rapidly, I could barely get it all on the paper. I skipped whole words and pieces of sentences as I scrawled out several tear-streaked pages. Dabbing my eyes with one hand and writing with the other, I stole a glance to either side to see how the other students were doing. The first thing I noticed was that no one else had spontaneously burst into tears. The second thing I noticed was that the other women were jotting down one or two words at most. When Gladys called us to stop, I was still frantically taking dictation from the voice, while struggling to swallow the embarrassing lump in my throat.

Even if I could have rationalized a fictitious conversation and let my demons chalk it all up to my wild imagination, I was not prepared for physical pain, much less fits of strong emotion. The feelings of loneliness and heartache were almost overwhelming.

Letting all the other women volunteer their answers, I saved my comments for last. I was still prepared to make a complete ass out of myself when I started reading my notes to the dog's mother. My heart was pounding so hard, I could barely find my voice, but as I spoke, she confirmed everything I said:

"Yes, she wears a red-and-white visor. Yes, there was a pine tree in front of my former home in the trailer park! Yes, the neighbor's dog was indeed a big black Doberman! Yes, he was her best friend! Yes, I had to leave him behind in the divorce—"

This couldn't be happening! It was too easy! It was too good to be true! I silenced my demons and continued to read my notes aloud.

When I said the dog had wanted to have puppies with the Doberman, her guardian's eyes misted over. She felt her dog's pain.

"Tell her 'I'm sorry,' and 'I'm sorry I took her away from her boyfriend,'" she urged.

Taking a moment to try to tell the dog, I experienced for the first time the frustration I would feel a thousand more times in years to come. I was trying to explain to an innocent animal why we humans do the things we do.

The impossibility of the conversation melted away. I succumbed to being responsible—responsible even for having the ability to talk to animals. I had jumped in with both feet. There would never be any going back.

The next dog was as easy to communicate with as the first—different, but easy. The dogs were as unique in personality as any two women you might chat with in a supermarket checkout line. I could hear their voices with equal intensity, but their vocal patterns and accents were distinct. Their senses of humor were different, as were their levels of intimacy. I was buzzing with elation. I couldn't believe I could do this! It was so fantastical, so marvelous!

And with every dog the class improved, too. In the beginning we had received a variety of answers to the same questions with several of the answers correct. (A dog could like chicken *and* beef.) However, as the class progressed, there were more and more unanimous answers. We were all "doing it." The confirmation made it undeniable. Nonetheless, I was worried that once I went home, this fairy-tale ability would disappear as magically as it had appeared.

Then it was Rodney's turn. I opened his carrier and held him up in my arms where everyone could see him, noting that when people were communicating with him, his behavior was *different*. He didn't try to weasel out of my arms and jump to the ground. He looked confidently, expectantly, from face to face, like a comic on a Vegas stage who had done the same show night after night for years—he knew his material was gonna kill 'em.

He was right. As soon as the class made contact, everyone started to laugh. "He's so full of himself!" "What an ego!" the women cried out. "He's a total egomaniac! He says that he's the most beautiful cat on earth!" one woman said, chuckling. "He says people are always telling him how beautiful his markings are!" another woman exclaimed. Yep, I thought, that settles it. They were tuning in to the right cat.

One student cried, "He says he's the only orange-striped cat in the world!" He *was* the only orange cat in the building and apparently in the entire neighborhood. If he had never seen another orange cat, I could understand how he could make that deduction. A trip to an Abyssinian cat show might really have burst his bubble.

I suggested the group ask Rodney what he felt for my boyfriend. The answer was almost unanimous: "He's very jealous." "He doesn't want to share his wife." "He wants your boyfriend to move out." "He wishes your boyfriend would go away." There were those words again: *Go away.* This really cracked me up. After our long lively conversation with Rodney, Gladys dismissed the class. Rodney had been the finale. We all stumbled toward our cars, dazed and in awe of how dramatically our perception of reality had been changed.

As I drove home, my mind was in a whirl:

If people can talk to animals, if I can talk to animals, if animals can talk—the ramifications of it were innumerable.

*If animals can talk, I can go to the zoo and—*I shuddered.

*If animals can talk, then the cows in slaughterhouses are—*I broke into a cold sweat.

*Do I really want this much responsibility? They can tell me when they're sick. I like that idea. But if all animals can think and feel pain, that means all those animals in all those cages—*My eyes blurred with tears.

The horror of animal experimentation came crashing down on me so hard, the world didn't seem like such a magical place anymore. The world didn't even seem like a world I could bear to live in anymore.

At that moment, the most incredible joy I had ever felt in my life came saddled with the most unbearable anguish. I could communicate with animals, but I would never be able to escape the agony they suffer at human hands. I would begin to feel what they feel, to think what they think, to suffer along with them when they experience the feelings of confusion, betrayal, rage, and helplessness at our incomprehensible cruelty.

For every gift there is a price. The greater the gift, the higher the price tag. So for this most glorious of gifts, God was asking that I barter with my most precious possession: my innocence.

⬛ Developing the Gift ⬛

Now, at this point in my life, I was a twenty-four-year-old, burned-out professional jazz dancer and struggling actress. I was about as numbed out as a person can be without falling down. Oh sure, I'd had my share of fluky psychic experiences; but in retrospect, I now view my early twenties as a time when I was desperately trying to tune down my sensitivity and succeeding dramatically. In fact, I had been so oblivious to the feelings of animals, my ex-roommate's cat had died on my couch and I hadn't even *noticed*. But the animals woke me up. The animals taught me.

I had grown up on a diet of dance and metaphysical books. Dancing six days a week, sometimes eight hours a day, had taught me how to concentrate in silence. I had learned how to observe and communicate without words; to listen and respond instantly; to commit completely to the moment; to meditate in motion; not to shirk pain but to breathe through it; to work through sweat, illness, agony, and injury to build self-esteem through the most powerful force in the universe—grace. When I wasn't dancing, I was reading. I spent years backstage in one theater or another, squinting in the half-light, hunched over the writings of Edgar Cayce, Jane Roberts, Taylor Caldwell, and Ruth Montgomery. I was fascinated by psychics, I dated psychics, I read about psychics, but I always thought my own psychic ability was nonexistent. If you had told me ten years ago I would ever work as a professional psychic, I would have fallen down laughing.

However, I was so steeped in metaphysical philosophy, wherever I

lived, I was always the first nominated to be the local witch or reluctant ghostbuster. Perfectly normal, unsuspecting people would call
me when they had a little psychic snafu they would never dare mention to anyone else. One innocent friend called to tell me there was a
poltergeist in her garage causing her plastic baby dolls to levitate in
midair. Who'd she call to exorcise the bogle? Me, of course. Another
extremely conservative girlfriend called to complain that her new
boyfriend confided that he could change into a wolf. She dropped
him immediately and who'd she set him up with? Well . . . me, of
course. Another friend called to vent that he'd met a man who
claimed to be from the Pleiades—not a spirit from another planet
incarnate into an earthling infant body, but an alien *directly* from the
Pleiades. (I didn't even flinch. Half of Los Angeles claims to be from
another planet.)

Incidentally, I never saw the baby dolls picnicking midair or the
shape-shifter morph like *An American Werewolf in London,* nor could
I convince the alien to show me where he'd parked his spaceship; but
whenever there was a freak poltergeist or a werewolf or alien loose out
on the town, I was usually the first to be consulted. Why? All my
friends might as well have been speaking in unison: "I didn't know
who else to call. No one else would believe me."

Well, the shoe's on the other foot now, folks. It's finally my turn.
This book will test your limits. Let's see if *you* have the nerve to
believe *me.* I know these stories sound utterly fantastical, but in order
to fabricate stories of this magnitude, I'd have to be a creative genius,
and believe me when I tell you—that ain't the case. I have only
changed the names and identifying characteristics of some humans
and their animals to protect their privacy.

A single animal workshop opened the floodgates of magic for me—
gates that must have been about to burst after many years of transcendental meditation. I have always had an appetite for meditation.
Having spent years in a weekly meditation class focused on opening
the third eye, I have been an avid first-thing-in-the-morning meditator
my entire life. Because telepathy is virtually impossible without
extensive training in meditation, this book is a compilation of medita-
tive techniques I believe led up to my discovery that I could hear animals. I will share with you the techniques that primed my psychic
pump. Telepathy is a spiritual *discipline,* not a sideshow act or parlor

trick. It can't and shouldn't ice a half-baked cake. The psyche must have the form and substance to hold it up, and the intention can never be coercion. If you hope to learn telepathy to better dominate animals, the animals simply won't respond the way you want them to.

As soon as I returned home from that initial workshop, I practiced fanatically with my cat, soon to become cats. In order to fulfill Rodney's request, I visited a no-kill shelter where a glamorous black-and-white coquette named Betty selected me. Rodney was smitten, and all his problems evaporated in her company. Within the year I found the infamous Mr. Jones eating salmon out of a Dumpster behind one of L.A.'s finest fish restaurants. (He's always had the world's most impeccable taste.) Mr. Jones was soon to become my passion, my master teacher, and my assistant: whenever I couldn't get a clear picture about another animal, I would just ask Mr. Jones. (After you learn to communicate with one animal, he may be able to answer your questions about any other animals.) Over the course of writing this book, I lost Rodney. Betty stayed in the custody of my ex, but I acquired Oscar, Billie, Cyrus, and Ella, as I will describe in the final chapter.

In the beginning, communication with my own cats was a struggle. My emotions blocked my circuitry. However, soon after that break-through workshop, I began to have vivid dreams of Rodney standing on my chest, speaking to me out loud in English. His mouth moved as he spoke, like one of the animated models from *Wallace & Grommit*. Eventually I could ask him questions before I fell asleep at night, only to dream he stood on my chest and answered me in English.

I also began to dream of all sorts of other talking animals: giraffes, badgers, elephants, and llamas. Something was opening in my psyche—hatching, perhaps—something exotic and fragile and terri-bly wacky. My dreams became a veritable Toon-Town. In my dream-state, as my animals conversed with me, they began to shape-shift into human forms. Loony as it all sounds, and as hard as I tried to fight it, information started coming: medical information, psychologi-cal information, accurate information—frighteningly accurate. I com-mitted myself to learning how to trust the process. Clearly, if the universe were to bring me this spectacular new skill, I would have to undergo a huge transformation in order to accommodate it.

Since that initiation, I've spent over a decade counseling animals and their people while teaching interspecies communication. There are many wounds mankind has yet to mend, yet the thrill of making contact and the love of communion with animals is a reward beyond measure. On this road less traveled, I have found more magic in myself and in the world around me than I ever dreamed possible. I will share with you some of the amazing conversations and revelations I've experienced over the years. But first I'd like to explain how the telepathic process works so that you can begin to awaken your own abilities.

In Chapter 2 I will introduce you to several new concepts and guide you step by step through a series of exercises designed to penetrate the communication barriers that keep us distant from animals and each other. In order to harness these new skills, you may need to abandon many of your lifelong belief systems. Your transformation may happen quickly, as it often does with my students, or your psychic senses may open slowly, unfolding like the petals of a rose. Trust your process. This is an exercise in faith.

At the end of this chapter I will outline a set of techniques that can help you build a bridge between you and your animal. You will begin to discover his or her needs, wishes, likes, and dislikes.

In the following chapter on clairsentience, we will focus on your animal's feelings, the possibility of emotional trauma, and tactics for solving behavioral problems. In the chapter on clairaudience, we will explore techniques that encourage you to hear your animal's thoughts in spoken words. Through the exploration of Gestalt therapy, we will discover where animals hurt and what they need physically and nutritionally. Finally, we will delve into exercises where I teach you how to not only track living animals who are stolen or lost, but communicate with the souls of animals who have departed this earth.

The easiest and most available ability is telepathy, or ESP, the exchange of pictures from one mind to another. But first you will need a working understanding of the nature of thought, so before we actually practice with animals, I invite you to explore with me the following nine steps.

2

Clairvoyance: Mind to Mind

Imagination is more important than knowledge.

—Albert Einstein

Step One: Understanding Telepathy

Thoughts have more substance than we ever imagined. The idea that thoughts have power is a concept that our culture is coming to accept.

That some people can perceive these thoughts in their natural state is also becoming accepted as more than science-fiction fantasy. Here in America, every time we turn on the television or visit the bookstore, we are inundated with psychic phenomena and stories of angels, ghosts, and mental telepathy.

The idea that might be new to you is that we all—each and every one of us—have psychic powers. We all are capable of telepathy; and not only is it within our reach genetically and physiologically, we are already telepathing with each other now—constantly—every day.

Who hasn't had the experience of hearing the telephone ring and knowing who was on the other end of the line before even picking up the receiver? Or thinking about an old friend or acquaintance for the first time in years and not being able to shake the image of that person from your mind, only to have them call "out of the blue" or run into them "by accident" later that same day? Or altering your course while driving a car—for whatever inexplicable reason—like making a sudden lane change, deciding to take a different route to work for no apparent reason—only to discover later that you inadvertently avoided an accident or a roadblock or even saved your own life?

This instinct has been flippantly dubbed "women's intuition." The powers of the mind are as available and as prevalent in men as they are in women. It's a shame that the realm of instinct is often dismissed as something frivolous and unreliable.

When you know beyond the shadow of a doubt that there is something wrong with your child, even though he is out of sight and beyond the range of hearing, only to find that your suspicion was right . . .

When you know that something has happened to one of your friends or family members even though there is no conscious way for you to know, and your suspicion gets confirmed . . .

Are you using your psychic senses? Are you using the powers of mental telepathy? For some reason, it may seem like a difficult fact to admit. We may feel more comfortable calling it "intuition," "instinct," or just a "gut feeling." So often people say, "I just *knew* it! I don't know how, but I knew it." Sadly, I frequently hear this phrase made as a negative statement. So often I hear people say, "I *knew* I shouldn't have bought that stock!" or "I *knew* I shouldn't have eaten that fish!" These laments are always followed by self-condemnation: "But I didn't listen to my intuition," or "I didn't trust my first instinct."

If you've ever moaned, "I just *knew* . . ." you are a candidate to answer these questions: How did you know? What was talking to you? Your intuition? Your Higher Self? Your guardian angel? Was it God himself? Or were you picking up on other people's *thoughts*? Were you responding to the images generated by other people's minds?

There is nothing new about any of these concepts. There is not one among us who is *not* psychic. Each and every one of us has within reach the ability to telepath; and I believe with all my heart that this innate power will be as common in our society in the next century as electricity has become in the last century.

What does all this have to do with learning to communicate with animals? These misunderstood laws of nature apply to our communication with animals as well as our communication with each other. In order to telepath with any living being, you must first have a working understanding of thought-forms and how they function.

I have presented you with the possibility of telepathy between human beings first because it is more prevalent and these skills are valuable in learning to communicate with nonverbal humans such as coma victims or babies, but the principles of telepathy with animals are exactly the same. There is no distinction between the two: communication is communication. But what exactly is it?

❈ Step Two: Redefining Communication ❈

In our culture, we have adopted a rather lazy shorthand that says communication is nothing but the exchange of words. This is deceptive. We must remember that the words we use to describe people, objects, places, feelings, and events in our lives are not actually the people, objects, places, feelings, and events. Words are nothing more than *symbols* for the more tangible objects in our worlds. Language is only one aspect of communication. Communication is the raw exchange of emotion and pictures among living things. We don't talk *instead* of telepathing—we talk *while* telepathing.

Let's say you bought a new couch and are trying to describe what it looks like—you hold in your mind an image of the couch and several details about it: its color, fabric, size, weight, softness.

Sometimes when you're engaged in the act of describing something in a conversation, the person you're speaking to will suddenly get a flash of insight. No matter how well or how poorly you're describing the couch, your friend may suddenly "see" the picture in his mind of what you are trying to get across. Your friend may suddenly exclaim, "Oh! *I know* what you're talking about!" Then he might paraphrase your description in a way that makes sense to him or compare the object you are describing with something that seems *more familiar* to him. (Remember those magic words: *more familiar.*) We use words only until we have successfully transferred the pictures in our minds.

No matter what we are describing to each other with language, we constantly hold in our minds a series of pictures, sometimes accompanied with strong emotions. Language does not encompass communication. Communication is something much deeper.

▨ Step Three: Perceiving the Film, ▨ Not the Sound Track

Have you ever had the gut feeling that someone was lying to you? Even if the person was a very skilled liar, and her story should have been believable, deep in your gut you just *knew* what she was saying wasn't the truth. How did you know? That person's film and sound track didn't match up. The pictures in her mind weren't in sync with her words.

Does this mean that you had direct access to that person's inner filmstrip, to her *thoughts?* You might say that you *sensed* that the person was lying to you. But what senses were you using?

There is a sixth sense in all of us that is no more mysterious than our sense of sight or smell. Its sole purpose is to transmit and receive thoughts. It can perceive, measure, register, and analyze thoughts or pulses of energy emanating from other living beings, including animals.

▨ Step Four: Recognizing Thought-Forms ▨

What are thoughts, really? I am aware of two different kinds of thoughts. The first type of thought is a replica of the person who sent it. This is an emanation generated by a particular intent, whose mission is to act upon that person's intent. These thoughts, therefore, carry with them the emotional content of the person who sent them. They have an intention and a life span. This is precisely why positive thinking works. Unfortunately, it is also why negative thinking works. Fears are nothing more than dark thoughts we have brought to life.

Whatever we think, be it positive or negative, will take on a life of its own, for a time, and go forth into the world to create.

When you think this type of thought, you are generating a shadowy replica of yourself and releasing it out into the world around you. This self-replica can speak and act on the emotion or desire that created it. Eventually this thought-form will become fainter and fainter until it fades into oblivion, unless you reinforce it with more desire and replenish its form and intention.

You may use the workings of a radio station as an analogy. A signal is sent out on a certain frequency. That signal may be strong or faint and can be reinforced by adding more energy to the output. Anyone with a radio that can receive that particular channel can pick up the signal. The human brain works in a similar fashion. Whether we realize it or not, we are all generating thought-forms and sending out signals.

My first direct experience with these kinds of thought-forms was in a dream I had fifteen years ago. I was dating a psychic at the time, but I personally had no awareness of my own psychic ability. He had a hell of a time trying to convince me that thoughts were real.

I was napping in the middle of the day, deeply enmeshed in a dream. Suddenly my dream was interrupted by my "boyfriend," who walked into my bedroom and put his arms around me. I was jolted awake, or so I thought, until I turned around and was surprised to see my body sound asleep in my bed! Here in this place between waking and dreaming, I sat with my "boyfriend" at the foot of my bed. Even though I was as conscious as I had ever been in my waking reality, I could *not* be awake because I could see my body bundled in the bed; nor could I be asleep because my friend had abruptly interrupted my dream and brought my awareness back into my bedroom. He slipped his arms around me from behind and kissed my back right between the shoulder blades. I could see and feel his body as strongly as if he were actually there in person. Not only did his body have weight and mass, but there was warmth to his touch. Then I heard his voice out loud in my ear, saying, "Wake up. It's time to wake up."

A few seconds later the phone rang and my "boyfriend" flew out of the room. The sound of the telephone propelled me back into my body, and I was truly jolted awake. When I picked up the receiver, my boyfriend was on the other end of the line.

"Did you get my thought?" he asked. I was dumbfounded.

"You were just here!" I argued.

"No, it wasn't really me," he said. "I just sent you a thought. I asked you to wake up."

After that startling initiation, I started to become sensitive to other people's thoughts and more aware of the thoughts I was sending out.

The second type of thought-form is not a replica of the person who sent it. It is merely an image of an inanimate object. We are constantly conjuring pictures in our minds and launching them out into the world. We also fire off emotional thought-forms, jam-packed with desire. People and animals send out both replica thought-forms and object thought-forms. One of my best examples of this mental game of catch came from my ex-boyfriend Benjamin. One day I had a terrible craving for cheese popcorn. I was also in need of some double-A batteries for my miniature tape recorder. I was busy that day and irritated by the thought of having to make a trip to the store just to buy the batteries and maybe the popcorn.

Even though I made no mention of it to Benjamin, he came home from work that night with the cheese popcorn and the double-A batteries. No other groceries or other treats—just the popcorn and the batteries.

He said he'd pulled off the road on the way home and stopped at a convenience store just to buy these two items. When he got home he said to me, "I thought you might need these." I asked him how he knew that I had been wanting them all day. His reply was, "I just couldn't get them out of my mind. I knew that I didn't need them, so I assumed the thoughts must have been coming from you." Over a seven-year span, our telepathy became so strong that I could see his shadow replicas walk into the room saying things like "I have to work late tonight" or "I had Chinese food for lunch." Sometimes this shadow was so dim, I couldn't see him, but I felt his presence— a warm, tingling buzz in the air—and even stronger was the smell of his cologne.

We all have this power of direct connection, and we have it by necessity. If there is an earthquake, tornado, flash flood, or natural disaster that prevents us from using the telephone, we can rely on our internal communication lines. If our ancestors had not used their intuition to find safe water, food, and homestead sites, none of us would be here now. Psychic ability is our birthright as human beings.

※ Step Five: Honoring Our Innate Ability ※

Native Americans believe that there is no *super*natural. Incorporating and relying on the intuition is as "natural" as trusting the skeleton to support one's body or the stomach to digest one's food. The aborigines of Australia are the most ancient and isolated indigenous people on earth, uncorrupted by the outside world. If they did not use their psychic senses to find water in the endless expanse of Australian desert, they would have died of thirst thousands of years ago.

I believe that even we clumsy, hapless, machine-addicted Westerners have all of our psychic senses intact until we reach the age of about four or five, when we have it socialized out of us by critical adults and the onslaught of "education." I've never known a child who did not have "invisible friends" or could not see "the pretty lights," or remember past lives, hear the thoughts of animals, or blatantly telepath with family members and friends. When children receive enough criticism or patronizing comments on their "wild imaginations," they conclude that they're irrational and eventually learn to keep the information to themselves. Over time, they learn to dismiss the transmissions entirely.

Studies of the pineal gland, which is located between the eyes and is given the attributes of the "third eye," show that the gland begins to atrophy when a child reaches the age of seven or eight and continues to dwindle down as the child matures. Science has found no use whatsoever for the little pinecone-shaped gland; all they know is that whatever it *was* doing, it *stops* doing by the time we all hit puberty. Then, of course, the body becomes obsessed with what is happening only from the waist down!

※ Step Six: Operating from ※ the Right Side of the Brain

In *Drawing on the Right Side of the Brain*, Betty Edwards describes the left hemisphere of the brain as the side that houses all the analytical skills, the critical mind, the powers of deductive reasoning, and the ego. The "I" that we all know ourselves to be, roosts in the left hemisphere of our brains.

An estimated 70 percent of people have their communication skills housed in the left side as well, but I suspect that mine are in my right side (albeit crouching down low), which might explain why I receive telepathic transmissions in spoken English words. This ability is called *clairaudience*.

When the left-brain verbal skills are silenced, the right-brain visual skills take over and can result in a pleasant respite where one can experience freedom from judgment. There is no judgment in the right side of the brain; there is only raw experience, the same brand of raw experience that young children may enjoy all the time.

This same altered state of consciousness is achieved in any kind of artistic endeavor where there is enough mastery to turn off the mind and allow the body to be "on automatic." I've heard the same state of bliss described by professional basketball players and transcendental meditators. It also seems to apply to ice skaters, sculptors, skiers, jugglers, football players, and even chefs, to name only a few. Many jazz musicians refer to this place reverently as getting "in the pocket" or "in the groove." In the world of professional dance, some choreographers call it *arriving*.

In *The Inner Game of Tennis,* Timothy Gallwey tells us the focus of the player must always be kept on what is about to happen rather than judging what just happened. In this manner, the mind is kept so alert in the present moment that there is no time to judge the last shot, even if it merits praise. Dancers, athletes, artists, airplane pilots (we hope), and racing car drivers learn to stay in the moment. Only in the present moment can we find a state of perfect concentration without judgment.

Another theory of what stimulates psychic activity is that the key is not in the brain at all, be it the right or the left side. The key is to shut off the brain as completely as possible and retreat into the silence of the heart. The heart is the only place where we can escape our mental chatter and quiet the mind long enough to truly *listen*.

This is a concept that is virtually unheard of in the Western world but is universal to all the Eastern religions that involve seeking enlightenment through meditation. We will explore this technique in the section of this book on clairsentience, the art of receiving emotion from other living beings.

※ Step Seven: Learning Patience with Ourselves ※

There is a system of techniques in learning to telepath, a system with a very concrete structure. Once you learn the techniques and practice them so often that they sink into your body, you can turn off your brain and enjoy a state of suspended grace.

Nonverbal communication is an art like all other arts, and in time, the ability to access the right side of the brain will become a habit, not an accident. Telepathy is extremely artistic, because it is the ability to think pictorially—to send and receive pictures you have crafted in your mind as if on a painter's canvas.

Riding a bicycle is a right-brain activity, but the first few times you did it successfully required all your left-brain concentration and attention. Now it probably requires so little attention that you do not have to consciously think about it at all. Even walking was once a treacherous endeavor. With practice, psychic communication may become that old hat to you. When that day comes, you will be able to walk your dog while you telepath with him or her without having to concentrate on remembering either skill.

※ Step Eight: Staying Out of Our Own Way ※

We human animals think an estimated forty thousand thoughts a day (although I know a few folks who I'd swear have only two or three thoughts on a good day.) When an animal or even another person tries to phone in, he will always receive a busy signal. The main agenda of the human brain seems to be to send out as many messages as possible and look busy at all costs.

Those are forty thousand impulses generated by your own personal radio station reaching out into the world around you. If your thoughts were visible to the naked eye, we could see them going out, out, out, out, continuously—all day, every day.

In order to telepath, you will learn to stop sending signals out. You will learn to turn the disc jockey off, clear your channels, and begin to *receive.* The sixth sense is subtler than the other five. The third eye will flutter and wake from its sleep only when it is surrounded with perfect peace and quiet.

You will discover that you are not your thoughts. When you become so detached from your own thoughts that you can experience yourself in total silence, you will find a greater *you.* You can call it *the spirit, the soul, the Higher Self, the witness, the observer,* or *the immortal divine essence.* The *you* that is not your thoughts has supernatural powers. The new you will function in a greater capacity than you have ever thought possible.

■ Step Nine: Honoring Our Own Divinity ■

I find that the paradigm of the Mother Goddess, even if you call her Mother Nature, works more effectively for psychic communication than the notion that God is male, that He created us, abandoned us, and is now living somewhere else. The idea that the world is part of God/Goddess's body and we are therefore a part of Mother Earth is a more workable abstraction for telepathic communication. If you cut your finger, it automatically proceeds to heal itself. Is that not proof that there is divinity within you that is absolutely beyond your comprehension? No division exists between us and the Goddess inside us or outside us, or between humans and the Goddess's other creatures. We are living in the Goddess's body, and the Goddess is alive and well in ours.

Please explore the following meditation in a spirit of playfulness with your animal. If you approach it as a monumental task, your fears and worries may block your circuitry. Keep in mind that the key word in mastering this meditation is *effortlessness.* You may want to stick to questions whose answers you don't know, but then again, your animal's answers may surprise you. Practicing with your friends' animals might be more productive in the beginning, because you won't have as many preconceived notions, and your friends can help verify your information. Have a journal handy, which I will refer to as your Paws and Listen notebook. (You will soon become familiar with my affinity for bad puns.) Jot down all your perceptions or, if you are more comfortable speaking, have a tape recorder ready.

▓ Techniques of Interspecies Communication ▓

I shut my eyes in order to see.

—Paul Gauguin

Clairvoyance Exercise
Exchanging Pictures with Your Animal

1. *Relax your body*. Find a place where you can feel completely relaxed and safe. Wear loose-fitting, comfortable clothing. Turn off the telephone, close the shades, and ensure that you will be completely undisturbed. You may want to be in the same room with your animal friend, or you may prefer to be out of doors, seated comfortably in your yard, balcony, or horse stall. Either way, you may wish to go where your animal friend already is rather than try to bring your animal to you. The proximity of your animal is irrelevant. You can be as close or as distant from him as you like. Sit on a pillow on the ground or in a chair with your spine as erect as comfortably possible. This posture allows the energy to move up and down your spine freely. Don't lie down because you may become too drowsy to concentrate. Make sure that your animal is relaxing comfortably as well, or at least playing contentedly.

2. *Focus on your breathing*. Take three deep breaths, filling your lungs completely and emptying them completely on the exhale. Visualize all the tension in your body pouring out as you exhale. Relax your body completely. Bring your attention to your heart and to the smooth rhythm of your breath.

3. *Enter the silence*. Close your eyes and, with your eyelids shut, gently look up. This eye movement will raise your attention to your third eye. Visualize your thinking process as a film that is being shown in a theater. See the curtains on either side of the stage slide closed on your thinking process. A huge white scrim may also drop from the ceiling. Now the show is over. There are no more thoughts allowed on the stage. If words try to return to the stage, gently catch them and usher them off. Allow the blank stage to start glowing with a beautiful white light. The light will become more and more brilliant as you enjoy resting in this place without words.

4. *Visualize your message.* Visualize the object you would like to convey to your friend by seeing it on the stage. Let's begin with your friend's food bowl. Visualize the bowl as the animal's usual food bowl or bag. Picture the empty bowl in the center of the stage and allow it to take shape in your mind. See it clearly. Make the image distinct and the edges crisp. Notice its size, depth, girth, and weight and any details that would help describe it. Most important, see the color of the object vividly in your mind.

5. *Reach out with love.* Without opening your eyes, move your attention to your animal and concentrate on loving your friend. Talk to her silently for a moment. Think the thought "I love you." Then ask her politely, "May I see what you see?" If you open with "I love you," your request will rarely be denied.

In the unlikely occurrence that you feel resistance, try the technique again later. We are always courteous and never impose.

Now, if you are feeling a warm flow of acceptance between the two of you, imagine you are slipping into the animal's body through a door in the top of its head. From this perspective, you *are* the animal. You can actually see out of her eyes.

6. *Ask a simple question.* The question should be one that can be answered pictorially. For our purposes, we will ask "What do you like to eat?" Picture the empty food bowl you conjured on the stage now sitting right in front of you. Remember that because you are looking out your animal's eyes, you will see the dish from her perspective—if your friend is short, for example, you will be very close to the bowl. Think for a few seconds about your stomach and how terribly hungry you are. Feel your mouth salivating in anticipation of taking a big mouthful of the most delicious food in the world. Now project the thought that the bowl or dish is piled high with this food.

7. *Quick! Catch the thought!* Retreat back into the silence and receive the picture. What kind of food is it? The answer will come to you as fast as lightning! The transmission is almost simultaneous. Before you have even finished asking the question, you may have already received the answer.

8. *Trust your first instinct.* The first image that flies into your mind is the right answer. No matter how outlandish the image may seem, there could be some information coded in the answer that the animal is projecting to you. (If you are speaking to a dog and he sends you the picture of a big juicy steak, there should be little doubt in your mind that you have connected successfully with your dog. If you receive something that does not make

immediate sense, don't doubt yourself and dismiss the transmission. The animal might be trying to express to you that it has a vitamin or mineral deficiency or that it needs more greens, grains, or fibre. If you received the image of a bunch of carrots from a horse, you may have simply contacted the horse, but if you receive the image of a bunch of carrots from a dog, he may be trying to tell you he needs more beta-carotene or fibre in his diet.)

Now is not the time to analyze the message. Simply take whatever comes and accept it at face value. You will try to decipher it with your critical mind later. Think of this now only as a game of charades.

In the event that you received an image you cannot tolerate, like that of a dead partridge or a freshly killed mouse, try to be sympathetic. (I will talk in depth in future exercises about courage and listening without judgment.) At this point, you may taste the food in your mouth from your animal's perspective. Don't worry if it's something you would never eat. No matter what it is, if it is your animal's favorite food, and you are experiencing your animal from the inside out, the food will taste absolutely delicious.

If you did not receive an image, fill the food bowl with what you *think* the animal might like, and the animal will correct the image for you. Your bowl of kibbles may transform into a chicken breast. Stay here and enjoy the experience of being your animal as he eats, or you might want to be adventurous and ask one or more of the following:

WHAT IS YOUR FAVORITE TOY? See your human form from the outside, throwing a toy to your friend. From your animal's perspective, run after this object with wild abandon. Enthusiastically pick it up with your mouth. What is it? What color is it? If you didn't receive an answer immediately, send your friend a picture of what you think her toy looks like, and if you are wrong she will correct it by sending back what the toy actually looks like.

WHERE DO YOU LIKE TO SLEEP WHEN I'M NOT HOME? See your animal preparing to bed down in his favorite place. From his perspective, feel yourself growing sleepy and look down at the ground or out at the surroundings. What do you see from this point of view? What color is the bedding, rug, towel, nest, or branch that he's relaxing on? What is the texture? What does it feel like under his body? What is its temperature? (You may send the picture of a green rug, and he may correct it with a picture of a blue bedspread.)

WHO'S YOUR BEST FRIEND? Be prepared. This may not be you. See your animal running, crawling, or flying toward the one other animal she enjoys the most. This feeling of love and excitement is the trigger in finding out whom she loves. Therefore, we are not picturing an object as much as we are creating a feeling. (We will explore the exchange of feelings in the chapter on clairsentience.) An easier way to ask this pictorially might be to ask:

WHO GIVES YOU TREATS? If you picture the treat being dangled in front of the animal's nose, he will send you the picture of the person who is doing the dangling. You may be surprised to find that your neighbors are feeding your dog.

WHAT'S YOUR FAVORITE TREAT? Send a picture of what you think her favorite treat is, and let her correct it for you. Often, this is a zinger. You might discover that her favorite treat is the neighbor's cat food or the French fries she stole off your table last night.

WHO TAKES YOU FOR A RIDE IN THE CAR? From your animal's perspective, go for a ride in the car. Sit where he sits. See what he sees. Remember that he is not your height, so he sees the world from a much lower perspective. Now look over and see who is driving the car and talking to "you" and patting "your" head.

WHERE IS YOUR FAVORITE PLACE TO GO IN THE CAR? Send the feeling of anticipation and, as your animal, climb out of the car. See the world around you from her perspective. Are there birds? Trees? Water? Other animals? What is on the ground? What does it smell like?

WHAT DID YOU DO TODAY? This is a good question to ask if the two of you are apart all day. Send a picture of what you thought he did—sleep in his bed, sit by the window—and he may send back pictures of gnawing on the couch, drinking out of the toilet, tormenting the neighborhood animals, or whatever. Have a sense of humor. If he gets punished after telepathing with you, he won't confide in you anymore.

If you can't get a clear answer to one of your questions, don't force it or get discouraged. Cheerfully go on to a new question. Remember that this is a game of psychic charades. If you didn't receive any picture in return, you can always try again some other time; and if you receive images that you can't comprehend, in all likelihood they will make sense to you later.

9. *Make a gracious exit.* When you've finished your visit, thank your friend for sharing her thoughts and desires with you, no matter what she offered up.

Tell her that you are grateful that she so generously let you into her body and that you'd like to practice this form of communication with her more in the future. Thank her for the conversation and ask her to be patient with you. (Don't think for a moment that animals don't understand *every word we say*.)

10. *Come home to your body*. You may want to practice re-entering your body the same way that you entered your friend's body, through a portal in the top of your head. Focus on your breathing and bring your attention back to your heart. Become aware of the feelings and desires inside your own body, and remind yourself that the sensations you just experienced inside your friend are not your sensations. Your friend has his own body and you have your own body. Although you sometimes share your experiences, you are both separate and unique.

Visualize your friend surrounded in a field of white light as though he were wearing a protective armor of moonbeams. Now, surround your body in your very own suit of moonbeam armor. Let communication through, but keep your identities divinely separate. Even this communion needs healthy boundaries.

11. *Act on your animal's desire*. Whatever your friend requested, make sure that when you have completed your meditation, you give your friend what she asked for. Whether or not you believe you successfully made contact, your animal will *know* you made contact and will be *waiting* for you to fulfill your promise. Don't make promises you cannot keep. That will just teach your animal to distrust you and not want to telepath with you. Always follow through with action as soon as possible after making a telepathic communication. This will encourage your animal to communicate with you in the future, and you will prove yourself to be a trustworthy friend. If you cannot grant your friend's wish (say, for a bowl of partridge or mouse), create the best substitute you possibly can, like a piece of warm, partially cooked chicken.

If you exchanged pictures of favorite treats or toys, go get them and give them to your friend to show her that you received her thought. If you exchanged pictures of a ride in the car, a frolic in the park, or a trip to Grandma's, make that picture a reality. I make the point again, because it is so important to remember: *Always follow up on your conversation with action*. Lavish attention on your friend and praise her profusely for sharing her thoughts with you.

All this positive reinforcement will come in mighty handy when you start to ask questions about sensitive subjects. At this point you are building trust. You must have an animal's trust before you can investigate negative situations, such as medical problems or behavioral difficulties.

You wouldn't ask personal questions of a new human friend (that is, if you have any tact), and you certainly can't open a conversation with an animal by saying something that will hurt his feelings or make him defensive.

I always open with "What's your favorite food?" because most animals, like most people, enjoy discussing what they like to eat. If I opened with "Do you have cancer?" chances are that could be the end of the conversation. (Surprisingly, most animals do know the names for their health problems; I don't know whether they get this from listening to their vets or from a deeper "knowing.") Sometimes, even after you have established a rapport with an animal, he will be put off by nosy questions and shut down communication anyway. You may find animals don't always *want* to answer you. You will also inevitably discover that animals lie (and pull your leg). When asked questions like "Who sprayed my shoes?" "Who chewed up the table leg?" animals may pass the buck like small children. Whenever I ask my five cats "Who started the fight?" I will hear a chorus of *"Not me!"* (Then they laugh.) So in the beginning, be polite and have a sense of humor. Remember to observe these starting points:

1. Build trust first.
2. Investigate problems later.

If you completed this exercise with one of your animal friends and successfully made contact for the first time in your life:

12. *Yell "Hoo-dee-hoo!"* This is where you jump out of your chair and do a football victory dance. Do a jig. Do one of Steve Martin's wild-and-crazy walks around the room. Yell and scream and dance. Finding your psychic ability is no small affair. You did something daring! You flew in the face of convention and discovered that you have mystical, magical, wonderful powers! This is cause for a great celebration!

In all seriousness, this positive reinforcement will help coax psychic channels open with every joyous celebration.

⬛ Some Surprising Answers ⬛

There's always a lot of laughter in my workshops. In one of my earlier workshops, my cat Rodney worked as my assistant, verifying a series of questions for my students. I had written the answers (or at least what I *thought* were the answers!) on flash cards and piled the cards facedown on my lap, so that the answers would be unequivocal. When asked his favorite food, the class gave me accurate answers that I never would have guessed. Clearly, they were not merely reading *my* mind, because I had written "White chicken chunks" on the flash card. One student said, "Cake icing," while another blurted out, "Cheese-fish!" They had no way of knowing Rodney had vandalized my last birthday cake by licking off an entire row of icing roses. Nor could they have guessed that during my last cocktail party I had reached my hand into a bowl of fish-shaped crackers and found the crackers soaking wet. Much to my chagrin, Rodney had licked the cheese off of every single "fish."

On a television pilot for Tammy Faye Bakker, I telepathed with her adorable dog via photograph, a technique I will explain in depth in later chapters. When I asked the dog to show me his favorite food, he sent the picture and flavor of chocolate. Asked his favorite activity, he said he spent his time sitting in something red. Tammy confirmed that only the week before, she had let the dog finish her chocolate sundae, and she always carried him around in a big red purse on her shoulder. (Despite the rumors that dogs are blind to particular colors, this has not been my experience. Dogs and cats have described to me every color of the rainbow. A pug mentally showed me her green-and-purple floral bedspread.)

Understand, however, that the game of charades can be rather subjective. The animals will relay pictures to you as best they can, but the interpretation is up to you. Don't be quick to dismiss what you get as *wrong* or *just your imagination.* Correct translation may take some creativity on your part. Here are a few more examples of "picture talk" where the information was correct but the translations threw me for a loop.

※ Bill's Bulldogs ※

I made a house call a few years ago to meet a couple of bulldogs who made an indelible impression on me. They spoke to me about many things, which I shared with their human guardian, Bill, a powerhouse in the movie industry. As I rambled on and on, Bill sat listening absolutely stone-faced without giving me so much as a nod of confirmation. "What a tough room," I mumbled under my breath.

When I asked Bill's bulldogs to tell me about their favorite activity, they raved to me about a shallow stream of water. They showed "Daddy" taking them to a shallow pool where they waded and splashed knee-deep in the water. The water appeared to be running from a fresh spring, so I assumed that it was a stream or a pond that was fed by a small waterfall. But here is where I got stumped: The dogs kept sending pictures of colorful fish in the water. I told Bill the dogs loved the pond with the fish and wanted me to tell him to take them there again soon. Even as I said it, I wondered where in Southern California Bill could take his dogs to a pond that was filled with brightly colored tropical fish.

At the end of the reading, Bill told me that he intentionally did not react to anything I said because he did not want to lead me one way or the other. But then he pulled out a photo scrapbook and showed me a picture of his bulldogs standing in a baby pool (the *pond*). Bill had inflated it in his backyard and filled it with the garden hose (the spring). The plastic pool was *printed* with *brightly colored* fish!

※ The Iguana and the Grapes ※

I got a call from a lovely and conscientious client, Peggy, who complained that her rescued iguana, Stan, had completely stopped eating. Peggy was in a panic because Stan appeared to be starving himself to death. I had been a professional animal communicator for several years by the time I received this call, but I had never talked to a reptile, and frankly I knew less than nothing about iguanas. Because I had no knowledge of their diets or habits, or any of their requirements, I thought this would be a great opportunity for me to communicate blindly.

Peggy had taken Stan to several vets who apparently knew even less about iguanas than I did. Poor Peggy had been unable to get a diagnosis on him and what few suggestions she had been given weren't working. Stan simply would not eat.

I had seen Stan at Peggy's home while making a house call to talk to her cats, but I had made no attempt to talk to him. In all honesty, Stan gave me the heebie-jeebies. But because I had met him before—face to little green face—when this call came, I attempted contact over the phone.

I started, "Stan, I understand you aren't eating. What would you like to eat?" With this question I pictured that Stan was happily eating something delicious. I heard the words *Banana candy! Banana candy!* I saw in my mind's eye little chunks of dried banana. Peggy confirmed that the only food Stan would eat was called Monkey Chow, comprising dried bananas. I was so relieved. I had actually made contact with an iguana!

When asked what else we could do to improve his overall health, Stan sent me a shiver of coldness and a feeling of claustrophobia. His legs ached to run. He wanted to be out in the sunshine where he could walk freely, not have his motion checked in the cramped aquarium. I thought nothing more of his request to walk freely and foolishly discounted it. After all, what iguana wouldn't rather be outside walking in the sunshine?

"What can we do about your health, Stan? What's wrong with you? Are you so unhappy about your living conditions that you want to starve yourself to death?"

With that, Stan sent me a profound feeling of love for his human mother and told me his life with her was much better than it had been before she came into it. Peggy agreed she had rescued him from a terrible situation and that for a time he'd been eating, content. Stan was even becoming more tame and affectionate, allowing her to pick him up—but then suddenly he had changed. I tried one more time:

"Stan, why won't you eat?" Here's where my interpretation went awry. When Stan showed me the inside of his stomach, I saw bunches of gelatinous marbles covered with thin skins in his belly.

"Have you tried grapes?" I asked Peggy. "He's showing me green grapes. You might try feeding him some grapes." (The Monkey Chow was a treat, not something Stan could thrive on.)

The next day Peggy called to say Stan wouldn't eat the grapes.

Baffled and disappointed, I gave up. For the next few days, I moped and muttered to myself about reptiles being too difficult to understand.

Thank God, shortly after our conversation, Peggy finally found a vet who knew something about iguanas, and received an accurate diagnosis. Excited, she called to tell me the news:

First of all, Stan was a girl! This was a fact none of the other vets had seen, and obviously Stan failed to mention it to me. Second, Stan was pregnant! The vet said Stan's infatuation for her new guardian had caused her to create a false pregnancy. Not only was Stan a pregnant female lizard, Stan was a pregnant female lesbian lizard.

Furthermore, the vet said iguanas have extremely long pregnancies (lasting for months) during which they refuse to eat. They lay their eggs while *walking!* Because Stan was so full of eggs and she couldn't walk very far in her cramped cage, she was about to pop.

Peggy said that Stan had finally managed to walk around the cage, squeezing out a few eggs, and guess what they looked like: small green grapes! So you see, Stan's information was crystal-clear. She had held up her end of the conversation beautifully. She had told me, "I'm in love with my mother. I've got a belly full of grapes, and I need to take a walk." I was the one who fouled up by misinterpreting the information.

I have since consulted an iguana expert, Joleen Lutz, who runs a rescue organization, Winged Iguana. Joleen gave me the real scoop on female iguanas and false pregnancies: The females get pregnant once a year (in love or not), and the gestation period lasts about a month, during which time they refuse to eat. The eggs actually crowd their stomachs so severely that they are unable to eat, which may explain why Stan told me the eggs were *in her stomach*. Joleen said, "Iguanas lay eggs whether they are fertile or not, just like a chicken. Some iguanas are great mothers and are picky about where they lay their eggs, while other mothers will just drop them anywhere." (It reminded me of some actresses I know.) If you'd like to contact Winged Iguana to seek out help for your iguana friends, you will find the telephone number in the resource section in the back of this book.

3

Clairsentience: Heart to Heart

The country creates the family. People, for the most part, don't create their own values; the culture gives values—that's the purpose of a culture.

—Sapphire, *Black Wings and Blind Angels*

Clairsentience: Clear-Feeling

In the following paragraph, Brenda Ueland helps describe a love beyond words:

When Van Gogh was a young man in his early twenties, he was in London studying to be a clergyman. He had no thought of being an artist at all. He sat in his cheap little room, writing a letter to his younger brother in Holland, whom he loved very much. He looked out his window at a watery twilight, a thin lamppost, a star, and he said in his

35

letter something like this: "It is so beautiful, I must show you how it looks." And then on his cheap ruled notepaper, he made the most beautiful, tender, little drawing of it. . . . But the moment I read van Gogh's letter, I knew what art was, and the creative impulse. It is a feeling of love and enthusiasm for it, and in a direct, simple, passionate and true way, *you try to show this beauty in things to others*. The difference between van Gogh and you and me is that while we may look at the sky and think it is beautiful, we don't go so far as to show someone else how it looks. One reason may be that we don't care enough about the sky or other people. But most often I think it is because we have been discouraged into thinking what we feel about the sky is not important.

Substitute the word *animals* for the word *sky* and you will immediately understand clairsentience. Our culture has trained us that the feelings of animals are unimportant—so unimportant that we eventually fail to recognize them at all; and I do say *trained* because it is with great diligence that adults must repeatedly shame the compassion out of children: the innate love, the inner knowing, the built-in clairsentience we all had from birth.

Last Thursday, sketching at the zoo, I happened upon a very sad gibbon, hugging his knees high up on a branch and staring pensively into space. Just as I spotted him, a swarm of children clustered around me, storming toward the glass partition.

"Look! He's sad!" cried a little boy of about eight years, pointing up at the hunkering gibbon.

"Yes, he's so sad!" agreed another little boy. When their adult chaperone stalked up behind them, I held my breath. I thought for a split second she, too, felt the truth, because she apparently validated their perceptions by asking the group, "Why do you think he's sad?"

They all chimed in, "I don't know why, but he sure is sad!"

Suddenly the adult snapped, "Well, he looks perfectly happy to me!"

He didn't look perfectly happy; he couldn't have looked perfectly happy by anyone's standards. But instantly the children were sheepish—they had been shamed and made wrong. Why had she suddenly turned on them like that? Was the truth too painful to bear? How long would it be, I wondered, before those children's clairsentience was shattered and they grew up convincing themselves they couldn't trust their own observations?

It is the natural state of the human animal to feel the feelings of the other animals around it; but in our society we have become desensitized. We've been told that compassion for animals is *babyish,* sentimental, trite, fanciful, an immaturity to be *outgrown.* Our perceptions of their feelings are imaginary, we're told, our natural identification with them false. The adults told us we were projecting *our* feelings *onto them.* We were convinced that compassion is weakness, communication is impossible, and to continue it past childhood is insane behavior. Even when humans treat animals badly, they rarely lock us out. We lock ourselves out.

In order to perceive the feelings of others, we must first awaken to our own feelings, to the trust we once felt, and to the feelings of the lost children within us. Only in recovering our lost innocence can we communicate with animals. Like van Gogh picking up a paintbrush for the first time in an effort to show his brother the sky—because he loved his brother and he loved the sky so much—maybe I can paint a new picture of animals for you. Maybe together we can paint a new world. But first, let's blow those walls we've built around us to high heaven. Here are some dynamite ideas.

> Animals' feelings matter.
>
> It's okay to love them.
>
> It's okay to feel their feelings.
>
> You can learn to talk to animals.
>
> Your perceptions of animals are remarkably clear.
>
> No one's going to call you a baby, a sissy, or a nut case for feeling an animal's pain.

All right, I lied. People might make fun of you, but let that be their problem. When I first started practicing as an animal communicator, I was a member of an improvisational comedy troupe comprised primarily of salty old character actors. Every so often, one of these stand-up comedians would leave a message on my phone machine:

"Amelia, my roundworms are turning square."

"Amelia, my tapeworm won't eat."

"Amelia, my giraffe, Lamont, is having trouble with his retractable neck. I can't fit him in the trunk of my car."

I took their ribbing in stride, but when the chips were down and one of those guys had an animal in trouble, guess whose phone was ringing at 2:00 A.M.?

Your love for animals is the purest love you know how to give, and clairsentience is an act of love—love in action. Feeling the feelings of animals doesn't make you a sentimental lunatic. It makes you a human being, the kind of human being God had in mind.

When we look up at the animals with awe, with reverence, the way van Gogh looked up at his celestial sea of stars, we alter our perspective. We may see them—truly *see* them—for the first time. Animals are here to teach us how to live: to be in the moment, to live utterly without fear, to love without reservation.

There's another reason we shut out our own innate clairsentience, and it isn't that we don't or can't feel—it is because we feel far too much. An obviously clairsentient woman approached me after a seminar last week to tell me she really wanted to learn how to be a professional animal communicator, but any mistreatment of animals throws her into such a blind rage, she doubts she could stand the pain.

"Join the club," I said.

"You don't understand! I'd murder their owners! I feel for them so much I can't stand it if they're in any pain!" she argued hotly.

"Yes!" My voice rose higher to match hers. "You can't stand the pain! But neither can they! At least you have a choice! *They* don't have any choices! It's not really *your* pain! They have to endure whatever pain they're in because people like you won't stand up for them!"

"But I can't do what you do. I'm not clairsentient!" she persisted.

"You *are* doing it! If you weren't clairsentient, you wouldn't feel this way!"

"But I don't see pictures, I don't hear words—"

"No, but you *feel feelings* and that is *enough*," and then I had to ask, "If not you . . . *who*?"

What a Catch-22. What a travesty that the very people who care most about animals are often the ones who can't stand to care. These sensitive souls are precisely the ones who have the greatest gift. I explained to this woman that I spent years crying myself to sleep—I used to tune in to all the animals in all the laboratory cages on this planet—I even quit working as an animal communicator for a while, convinced that I, too, could not stand the pain or control my rage. Over time, I stopped the incessant crying and admitted that my river of tears would not save one furry little head. A little voice inside me never gave up: "If not you . . . *who?*" Is this worth making a fool of yourself over? Is this worth risking being wrong? If it isn't, I don't know what is.

I ended my conversation with this woman by explaining there are also little victories, daily joys, opportunities to intervene when you *can* make a difference, and these accomplishments are what make it all worthwhile. Does the pain get any less intense? Well, no. But it does get more manageable. Buddha said that anger is like a hot ember you hold in your hand with the intention of throwing it at another, all the while getting burned by the anger. You can learn to drop the hot embers of anger and suffering before they burn your hands. The pain and rage won't get any cooler, but you will learn how to let go of them quicker. Education is our only hope. Start slowly. Build gently and use your common sense.

Are you one of the sensitive ones? Because animals can't speak for themselves, only you can give their feelings a voice. Because animals are in a bad way on this planet, they need you now more than ever. If your strength is clairsentience, your challenge is not merely to embrace animals' physical feelings and emotions. Your challenge is to create a space where you feel safe to feel all these feelings. You may fear that animals' feelings are like a tidal wave that will drown you and rip you apart. If you are extremely emotional, your lessons may incorporate not just intuition, but self-protection. I will teach you to build walls of light around yourself. If you liken animal suffering to a forest fire, animal communicators are firemen, who go into the fire wearing protection, not staying long enough to get burned. Your job is not to hurt yourself. Your job is to put the fire out. With practice you will learn to trust the animals and to trust that their feelings will not kill you. In trusting life, in trusting God, you will learn to open to new channels but only linger where you find beauty, harmony, and joy. You have only to experience a sea lion swimming in the sunshine or a sleeping koala bear to discover realms of ecstasy and tender sacred silence that you never experienced before as a human being. In these dimensions of sublime bliss, words utterly fail me. You, too, can experience heaven on earth in the minds of animals, and that is what makes any suffering worthwhile, but first, let's go back and explore a forgotten memory—to a time when your mind was young.

Exercise: A Meditation in Recapturing the Magic
The Child You Were

Sit comfortably, preferably outside, where you can be alone for a while. Focus on your breathing, drop down into your heart, and enter the silence. Let your adult self sleep. All thoughts, all plans, all worries of the day, completely fall away. Now you are drifting deep inside yourself. You are drifting back in time to an age you have completely forgotten. You will remember a special moment in time: a moment when you were aware. You are awakening in an age when you were very small, when you were so young that you could barely talk. Humans towered over you, but you had an inner world that they couldn't see.

What do you see here? Are there elves in the trees, tugging on your hair? Are there little people running across the grass? Do the flowers look more vivid? Do the colors look different from your point of view so close to the earth? Are there other beings around you that the adults can't see? Do they look like humans, or do they have wings? Can you talk to the flowers? Can you talk to the trees? Can you hear the angels? What do they say?

Pause for a few moments and listen.

Here in this magical moment, you can hear the thoughts of animals. What animals do you love? What do they say to you? You know they have thoughts and feelings just like your own. Here in this hologram of time, you will always be able to hear and understand the animals. Vow to never "grow up" and turn your back on the animals. No matter what the "grown-ups" say, you *know* you will never lose this magical ability.

Walls of twinkling stars rise up out of the earth and surround you in a bubble of light. Nothing dark, nothing painful, nothing frightening, can violate this wall of starlight. It shimmers and sparkles around you like a thick snowdrift, at least three feet in every direction. This liquid light is the strongest force in the universe: stronger than darkness, stronger than evil. Concentrate upon your light until it turns solid, like crystal, like marble, like glass. Here inside this armor of light, it is safe to remain innocent, because although the thoughts and feelings of animals will filter through it, nothing harmful can penetrate it. This is the armor of light that you'll wear while you practice loving and listening to the animals. By healing yourself, you can begin to help heal them.

Bring this vision of a cloak of light around you back to your adult self. Return to your waking world, feeling refreshed and new.

Exercise: Inside the Heart
Cleaning Out the Attic

Sit comfortably so you can focus on your breathing. Take a deep breath. Hold the breath for ten seconds; then, on the exhale, let any tension drain out of your body. Inhale deeply again and hold it. Count to ten. Relax on the exhale. One last time. Hold it for ten. Now let it all out. All the anxiety. Anything you've been clinging to you can let go of completely.

Now, let your focus drop down into your heart. You find yourself in an old deserted attic. The windows haven't been opened for years. You are in a chamber of your heart that has been sealed off since you were a child. The floor is thick with dust and cluttered with things you need to throw out—all the negative thoughts and beliefs that no longer serve you.

But wait. Someone's coming into the room—someone you have unfinished business with, someone who no longer belongs in your heart. This is the person who undermined your confidence and told you that you have no intuitive power. If no one appears, reach into the past and call forth your opposition. Find the person who convinced you intuition is not safe. Find the person who said you shouldn't feel for animals, that it is sentimental, crazy, unproductive, or self-destructive.

Ask this person why he or she is still in your heart. Ask this person what he or she has to teach you. Hear this person out, state your case, and ask if he or she is ready to leave. Are *you* ready to let go of all the hurt and pain this person caused? Here in the musty darkness, confront everyone who still lurks in your heart.

Now look around the room. What needs to be discarded? There's old furniture and other junk representing sorrow, fear, isolation, and inertia. It needs a good cleaning, doesn't it?

So, opening the closet, you find a broom. Run to the windows and fling them open. The morning sun streams into the dark room and the fresh summer wind blows through. Gusts of wind blow all the dust out of your heart as you sweep the floor and tear down the cobwebs. Clean out all the debris and give it to the wind. Banish all the old aches and pains. Let the wind carry the old hurts away. Now the room is sparkling clean, brightly lit, and shining.

As you turn around, you see a toy chest brimming with your childhood toys. What do you find there? What enchanting gifts have you forgotten? There is magic in this chest that will help you talk to animals, toys that bring confidence, courage, and hope. Pick out your favorites, and bring these precious gifts back with you into your waking world.

Open your eyes feeling clean and refreshed.

▪ The Afghan Hound's Itch ▪

Let me tell you about the very first reading I ever gave. Many years ago I met Jackson and Jenny, two Afghan hounds, at a holiday party in the home of Tina and Sydney. I spoke to the dogs briefly but kept it quiet, in case their mothers "didn't believe in this sort of thing." But news travels fast in Tinsel Town, and Tina and Sydney learned something about my work.

So when Sydney called to tell me that Jackson was ill, having met the dog already, I tried to make a direct connection.

I visualized Jackson, trying to picture him clearly, as Sydney described the dog's affliction to me: the gorgeous dog was literally scratching his chin off, taking the skin off the side of his mouth trying frantically to appease an itch. The vets had no suggestions except cortisone, but Tina and Sydney were looking for other solutions.

Next, I imagined I *was* the dog. I found myself *inside* Jackson's body, looking out his eyes, feeling the terrible itch on the side of my face. From this perspective, I asked him, "What is causing this irritation?"

Seeing new wall-to-wall carpeting—cream-colored carpeting—I rubbed my dog-chin against the carpet. My face itched and my eyes teared. I fought the urge to sneeze.

"Did you just get new carpets? Cream-colored wall-to-wall carpets?" I asked Sydney.

She told me she had.

"I guess he's allergic to the formaldehyde in the new carpet," I said. It was a complaint I would hear from animals for years to come. Fortunately the allergic effects of the toxins in new carpet dissipate over time.

Sydney thanked me rather stoically. No sooner had I hung up the phone than I received another transmission. In my mind's eye, I saw the other guardian, Tina, having problems with her teeth and experiencing pain in her right jaw—the same side of the jaw that was plaguing her dog. I felt that Tina was more connected to Jackson, thus Jackson was mirroring Tina's medical condition.

I called Sydney back to give her the new information. Stunned, she confirmed that Tina had just had her wisdom teeth removed; she was in the throes of a painful recuperation; and yes, Jackson was closer to Tina. There were two factors at play here: the irritation from the new carpet *and* the mirroring of Tina's pain.

This mysterious dynamic—the existence of very real osmotic pain that animals absorb from their guardians—has fascinated me ever since, and I will explore it further in later case studies in this book; but at the time, I didn't realize the extent of this widespread affliction: animals universally have sympathetic reactions to our pain and diseases.

After thanking me coolly, Sydney hung up, but my conversation with the dogs had just begun. The next night, the other stunning Afghan hound, Jenny, came to me in a dream. She told me Tina was out of work, so she and Jackson were afraid to eat because they didn't think their mommies could afford to feed them. She and Jackson were so alarmed when Tina stopped eating that they agreed to eat less and leave their bowls full so Tina could eat their food. She also explained she was scratching her left paw because Tina had hurt her left foot.

The next day I called Sydney to ask if Tina was not eating well and if she had hurt her left foot. (I had already known that Tina was looking for work.) Yes, Sydney agreed that Tina had hurt her left foot and was eating sparsely. Not only that, but the dogs had been leaving food in their bowls lately. When I told Sydney why, she stifled a laugh. Tina and Sydney were in no way hard-pressed for money—they owned a beautiful home in the Hollywood Hills. Tina was not starving to death because she was out of work. She was *dieting*. We marveled at that sensible canine reasoning: *Poverty is the only reason to starve yourself. What is a diet?*

I advised Tina to eat heartily around her dogs and tell them out loud that *her* troubles were not *their* troubles, and her teeth would heal on their own. I explained to her that if she talked to them out loud they *would* understand her.

A few days passed, and I focused on other things. Then I got the call. Tina had landed a new job working on a talk show—and would I be interested in appearing as a guest? The show was filming a special on pets and needed an animal psychic. So, I went from my first reading to my first talk show in a matter of weeks, transported by the most magical form of aerial propulsion known to man: flying by the seat of my pants.

Yesterday, in my artist's anatomy class, of all appropriate places, an intellectual was spouting off about the structural difference between the skulls of humans and gorillas. "Animals can't think!" he proclaimed to everyone in the room.

"My cat may not worry about what he's going to do tomorrow," protested another artist, "but he might have some capacity for rational thought."

"Cats can't think! They have no frontal lobe!" the intellectual proclaimed with utter certainty. This is the latest fallacy of science.

A few months ago on a hot summer night, a butterfly wandered into my kitchen. I thought to her, "If you will light on my shirt, I'll take you outside. You'll never make a living in here." When she beat her wings frantically against the window instead, I reached out for her. I must have scared her, because she shimmied up behind the blinds safely beyond my reach. I set about making dinner and in my haste, completely forgot about the little white butterfly. I had four burners all ablaze, consumed with the sizzling saucepans, when a sudden flutter of wings in my face blocked my gaze. The butterfly had flown across the kitchen to light on my shirt. There she rode on my breast pocket across the house and outside, where the second my feet hit the patio, she disappeared into the night sky.

More recently, I had an astonishing interchange with a praying mantis. I went out to my flower box to collect sunflowers, but as I reached up to clip a giant blossom, I almost dropped my shears. I was eye to eye with a tremendous praying mantis, perched in the center of an unfurled leaf, sunning himself in all his extraterrestrial brilliance. I retrieved a paper plate from the kitchen and held it next to the wide leaf.

"If you'll walk over to this plate, I'll put you in the rose garden," I said, sending the thought of his traipsing across the leaf and stepping solidly down onto the plate. Until this moment, the mantis had been planted immobile, with statuelike stillness.

As soon as I sent the communication, the mantis spun his head around and looked at me. A chill flew up my spine. Only his robotlike head moved to investigate me. Holding the trembling plate, I silently repeated the request. After a brief pause, he began his long-legged journey across the leaf. Deliberately, with surefooted grace, he stepped down off the leaf and onto the plate, the way one might step down off a dock and into a sailboat. I carried him to the rose garden, where I lowered the plate onto the grass. "Please step off," I said. Without hesitation he disembarked.

Frontal lobe, my foot. If butterflies and praying mantises can hear me, is it because they have itty-bitty teeny-tiny frontal lobes? Doubtful. If not the frontal lobe, what gives us the capacity for rational thought? Where in our brains do we think thoughts, formulate pictures, and feel emotions? Perhaps we do not think exclusively in our frontal lobes. I've had conversations with Louisiana alligators chasing marshmallows flung overboard by swamp cruise passengers. I had a conversation once with a two-hundred-pound python named Tiny and a Tagu lizard named Vivian. Supposedly these animals' brains have not evolved past the reptilian brain structure, yet they can communicate. They think and feel pain and talk to animal communicators. Could it be that we think in our reptilian brains, the oldest segment of the brain, which we share with the animals? It could be, but more probable still is that we don't know enough.

Insects don't have our brain structure, yet they can communicate. Lobsters have no central nervous system, yet they can feel fear and pain. If, as scientists estimate, only 4 to 10 percent of the human brain is in working order, how can this minuscule portion possibly fathom the functions of the other 90 to 96 percent? Does that huge majority of our brain really lie dormant? Apparently so—particularly when it comes to the comprehension of the animals around us.

I took the frontal lobe conundrum to the remarkable Dr. Francine "Penny" Patterson, president of the Gorilla Foundation, to see what she thought of it. For the last twenty years, no one has fought harder to prove scientifically that animals can not only think and feel but also *converse*. It was Penny's landmark discovery that gorillas can learn American Sign Language that made her friend Koko an international star. Penny not only debunked the frontal lobe theory, she assured me the entire compartmentalized brain theory is quickly becoming a misconception of the past. She cited the discoveries of Dr. Karl Pribram, author of *Brain and Perception: Holonomy and Structure in Figural Processing* (John MacEachran Memorial Lecture Series), whose revolutionary research indicates that the brain may not be exclusively compartmentalized at all but *holographic*. Unfortunately, Dr. Pribram has not been an animal champion, but his discoveries may help build a case for nonhuman cognitive thought.

In an interview with Dr. Jeffrey Mishlove for *Thinking Allowed*, Dr. Pribram expounds upon his claim to fame. In psychology and neuropsychology, he is known as the originator of the holographic or holonomic model of the brain:

> The holonomic brain theory is based on some insights that Dennis Gabor had. He was the inventor of the hologram, and he obtained the Nobel Prize for his many contributions. He was a mathematician, and what he was trying to do was develop a better way of making electron micrographs, improve the resolution of the micrographs. . . . Essentially, with electron microscopes we make photographs using electrons instead of photons. He thought maybe instead of main ordinary photographs, that what he would do is get the interference patterns. Now what is an interference pattern? When light strikes, or when electrons strike any object, they scatter. But the scatter is a funny kind of scatter. It's a *very well regulated scatter*. For instance, if you defocus the lens on a camera so that you don't get the image falling on the image plane and you have a blur, that blur essentially is a hologram, because all you have to do is refocus it.

. . . So one of the main principles of holonomic brain theory, which gets us into quantum mechanics also, is that there is a relationship here between what we ordinarily experience, and some other process or some other order, which David Bohm calls the *implicate,* or enfolded order, in which things are all distributed or spread—in fact the mathematical formulations are often called spread functions—that they spread out.

. . . These quantum-like phenomena, or the rules of quantum mechanics, apply all the way through to our psychological processes, to what's going on in the nervous system—then we have an explanation perhaps, certainly we have a parallel, to the kind of experiences that people have called *spiritual experiences. Because the descriptions you get with spiritual experiences seem to parallel the descriptions of quantum physics.*

At this point in the conversation, Mishlove pulls out his verbal water wings and goes wading through the interference patterns of Pribram's genius:

But what you're saying, if I can try and simplify it, is that there's a level of reality at which things are what they appear to be. I look at you and I see a body and a face. That would be the *explicate* level, where things are what they *appear* to be. Then there's an *implicate* level, which is *just as real,* but if you were to look at it, it doesn't look at all like the other.

Pribram agrees. "We experience it entirely differently—*as a spiritual aspect of our being.*"

Later in the interview, Mishlove, now far out to sea, observes:

Many neuroscientists today—it's almost axiomatic, when they talk about the mind, which they sometimes do—they say the mind is sort of located in the brain. I gather that that way of putting it is totally discordant with your own view of things.

To which Pribram replies:

Yes. There are lots of different ways of phrasing this. One is that mental phenomena are emergent properties of how the brain works, and so it's almost like the brain is secreting vision and mind and all that. But maybe a better way of talking about it would be to say that mental phe-nomena arise through *the interaction* between brain and body and environment. . . . That whole interactive thing produces an *emergent,* which we call *mind and spirit.*

Well, I hope to shout! This matches my experience! In order to communicate psychically, you must disengage yourself from your *explicate order,* let your consciousness *scatter* into the larger paradigm of *implicate order* (where you perceive yourself not as a static being but as an action in motion); then let your focus spread out to include other sentient beings within that motion, like cream cheese on a really hot bagel (if I may add my own nonscientific analogy). Honing your intuitive abilities means that the camera of your consciousness can learn to view what's beyond the blur of ordinary perception.

For our purposes, in learning telepathic communication, we will move our conscious headquarters into the *spiritual aspects of our being.* I will teach you how to "think" with your third eye, "feel" with your heart chakra, and "listen" with your throat chakra. Although these chakras, or centers of energy, are located far from the brain, in the exchange of telepathic data they are more accurate receptors. We will awaken our starlight vision, the name I've deemed to perceiving departed spirits on the Other Side, not in the third eye of even the crown chakra, but in still higher chakras, which orbit over our heads. Let's leave our frontal lobes behind for a while. From the looks of our planet, they haven't done us much good anyway.

■ Let's Monkey Around ■

I'll never forget the way Dr. Jane Goodall greeted her audience for a slide presentation and lecture she gave to L.A.'s most prestigious scientists and professors at UCLA last summer. The room was so chock-full of pomp and circumstance, I had trouble finding a chair between professors who were saving seats for their egos.

After an introduction worthy of the Queen Mother, the little blond woman strolled onto the stage. If you have never seen her, run, don't walk, to the next appearance she makes. A more radiant woman does not exist on earth. She's surprisingly small, lithe, and dainty—not what you'd expect of someone who's spent thirty years in the bush with a bunch of monkeys. She paused in front of the microphone, elegant and unassuming. A hush fell over the room, which crackled with cerebral tension. Every member of the audience had been reading about her and following her documentaries for most of her adult life. Here she stood in the flesh. We bit our tongues and held our pens ready to write, poised to not miss a single word of her wisdom.

She leaned over the mike: "Ooh, ooh, ooh," she said, quietly at first, like a locomotive in the distance. Then, "OoH, oOH, OOH," a little louder, as if the engine was coming straight at us. "OOH! OOH! OOOH!" louder still; the train was going to mow us all down.

The scientists stared straight ahead, not daring to turn their heads lest they get a glimpse of each other's eyes. As the room tittered with embarrassment, Dr. Goodall pushed her vocal capacity to its limits: "OOOH! OOOH! OOOOH!!!"

At last she took a breath. In a little voice laced with a prim English accent she said, "That means 'hello' in chimpanzee." She never cracked a smile. Needless to say, Dr. Goodall had even the most cerebrally hard-boiled professors rolling in the aisles—their egos tumbling out of their chairs. She disarmed the entire scientific community and shattered their preconceptions.

So if Dr. Goodall can "lower" herself to do it, you can do it, too. By "pretending" to be animals, you will learn about their perceptions, their feelings, their thought patterns. You will learn to stretch your consciousness. Just as you did as a child, you are about to play a game of pretending. When you reach out in consciousness, that "pretending" may eventually enable you to "tune in" for medical information and perhaps even track lost animals. (Tracking is all about asking the right questions.)

What child hasn't flapped and shimmied and loped and trumpeted around the room while some adult yelled, "You're a bird! You're a snake! You're a bear! You're an elephant!" "What does a turkey say? What does a monkey say?" To which you replied, "Gobble, gobble!" and, "Ooh, ooh, ooh, ooh!" This is where we begin to get the needed paradigm shifts, the heightened perspective that enables us to attain mobility of consciousness. Jot down the answers to these questions in your Paws and Listen notebook. Write the first thing that pops into your mind.

Exercise
Become the Animal

You Are a Dachshund

Standing in your kitchen, what do you see? (Ankles, lots of ankles!)

In the bedroom, what do you see?

What does it feel like to have the bed tower over you and not be able to climb up there by yourself?

How do you feel about the people who tower over you?

Do you like to sleep with them?

Do you understand human language?

How does it feel to be picked up?

How does it feel to eat out of your bowl?

What's your favorite food?

How does it feel to be in a crate?

How does it feel to be in a carrier?

How does it feel to ride in a backpack?

Do you know what an airplane is?

How does it feel to ride in an airplane with the cargo?

How does it feel to go to the vet?

How does it feel to be the smallest dog at the park?

How do you feel about other dogs?

Do you like to walk on a leash?

Does the asphalt hurt your paws when you walk?

How do you feel if you meet a Great Dane?

Now You Are a Huge Great Dane

Where do you like to sleep?

Do you like your bed to be heated?

Do you like to play with humans?

What's your favorite toy?

Do you like to be "trained" by humans?

How do cats make you feel?

How do human children make you feel?

What upsets you?

Do you like to swim?

Do you like to chase birds?

How much space do you need to run?

What kind of food makes your body feel best?

Do you like to listen to the radio?

Do you like to be alone?

Do you like to ride in the car?

How do you feel about other dogs?

How would you feel if you met a dachshund?

What scares you?

What does a choke chain feel like?

You Are a Pigeon

What does it feel like to sit on a telephone wire?

What does your human house look like from above?

What does it feel like to stretch your wings?

What does it feel like to soar in the wind?

How does it feel to sit in the treetops in the pouring rain?

What does the winter feel like?

Are you afraid you won't find food? Or are you confident?

What is the purpose of your life?

Do you have a mate? Do you love him/her?

Do you have children? How do you feel about them?

Do you know where your parents are?

What does it feel like to lay an egg?

Do you talk to other birds? What do you talk about?

How do you get along with other species of birds?

Where do you sleep at night?

Do you enjoy preening yourself?

What makes you happiest?

Now You're a Polar Bear in the Zoo

Sucks, doesn't it?

"But Amelia!" you may argue. "You're personifying them! You're anthropomorphizing them!" Yes, I am. That's how we learn.

"But they don't feel the kinds of human emotions we do! They don't miss their children, get angry at their mates, have abstract thoughts, and ponder the meaning of life!" If you find these types of objections bullying their way into your mind, memorize the following Corinthian Prayer, adapted from Biblical verses Philippians 4:7 and 1 John 4:18. Say it out loud three times.

Address it to whatever Higher Power you honor. I say it every morning and before every reading, honoring Sekhmet, the lion-headed Goddess of ancient Egypt.

THE CORINTHIAN PRAYER

Goddess Sekhmet,
Gently take me by the hand.
And lead me up the little path,
through the narrow gates,
through the holy of holies,
and into the Kingdom of God where all is righteousness.
For it is here that we are one with the Mother.
And we thank you, Goddess for hearing us.
Thou hearest us always.
And for leading us into the way of the truth that frees:
the perfect love that casts out all fear,
the peace that passeth all understanding,
and the way of eternal life. Amen.

This prayer will attract considerable attention from your spirit guides on the Other Side. But if you still feel resistance, try the following "Shedding the Cloak of Negativity" meditation, which I learned from Diane Mariechild's marvelous book, *Mother Wit*. Clear your mind, focus on your heart, and begin again. If you can stifle the internal critical parent point of view and let your all-knowing child play, you will make your own discoveries. Let your answers shock you. Ideas and emotions are universal—they do not belong exclusively to human animals. All animals do, indeed, think and feel the vast spectrum of ideas and emotions.

If you're convinced they can't, read this book anyway, as if it were fiction. Then see if the animals come for you when you least expect it. They might creep into the corners of your mind, gently altering the shape of your belief system. Watch your life offer up new information to support animal intelligence. Either way, wouldn't you rather err on the side of compassion?

I've practiced the following meditation from *Mother Wit* every single day for the last nine years. Nothing will get you clean as a whistle quicker than this lovely meditation. Apply it to your work with animals by visualizing your cloak composed of all the doubt you carry about your own intuitive ability.

Exercise
Shedding the Cloak of Negativity
by Diane Mariechild

Relax, deepen, and protect yourself. Here in this space out of time you are becoming conscious of the garment you are wearing, a cloak, a heavy black cloak. This dark, hooded robe is the cloak of your negativity. It symbolizes all the negative thoughts, feelings, and experiences you carry with you. Feel the heaviness of it. Become aware of the texture and the feel of the cloth. Feel the weight on your shoulders, your whole body cloaked in negativity and despair. Pause about one minute.

Now become aware that the cloak is gradually lifting up and away from your body and with it your negativity and despair. Now the cloak has vanished.

And your attention is drawn to a fountain, a fountain of light, an incredible fountain of light. And the shimmering light is bubbling up and spilling over. A shower of light, shower of stars, thousands of tiny stars, is streaming down upon you. The whole space is filled with a brilliant light.

And you realize that you are gowned in a new garment, a sheer translucent cloak of light woven from the stars. And you are wearing this robe of love, joy, and protection. It is the symbol of your soul, the loving connections you feel and sense and see. Wear it now and always. When you are ready, drift up and back to your waking reality filled with light and love.

▓ Battles Are Never Won—They Are Transcended ▓

Telepathy and Gestalt do not work from the consciousness of duality. Something remarkable happens when the two hemispheres of the brain work together in tandem. The third form of consciousness is born when neither side of the brain is hard at work. This new heightened consciousness is not found in the brain at all, but in the heart. Without this paradigm shift from head to heart, from duality to trinity, psychic ability can remain inaccessible or limited at best.

If you really want to master the art of telepathy, your commitment to finding the God/Goddess within you needs to be rigorous. Our brainwashing has been fierce. Since our earliest childhood years, our religions have imprinted us with illusions of unworthiness. The creation myths of every major world religion are suspiciously similar: the original Gods of every culture created mankind, but man immediately performed some unforgivable cosmic boo-boo (eating apples and whatnot) that caused God to fly into a rage and abandon his creation. Where God might be now, history fails to tell us. Our reconciliation with him is still projected at a later date . . . and the terms are conditional—that is, chosen people will be collected, commandment watchers will be commended, kamikazes who die in His name will get instant entry through the pearly gates, those who don't eat the forbidden foods will go to heaven and be free from the yoke of reincarnation. Whatever the pernickety terms, the initial sob story on every continent is almost identical: we were created by a deadbeat dad who dumped us here on earth and went away mad because we created some cosmic mess. Thus, we've been shamed all our lives into believing that not only is there a distinct separation between God and man, but the separation is *our fault.*

Joseph Campbell spoke of this duality in *The Power of Myth,* describing how Adam and Eve got the boot from the Garden of Eden:

> There is a basic mythological motif that originally all was one, and then there was separation—heaven and earth, male and female, and so forth. How did we lose touch with the unity? One thing you can say is that the separation was somebody's fault—they ate the wrong fruit or said the wrong words to God so that he got angry and then went away. So now the eternal is somehow away from us, and we have to find some way to get back in touch with it.
>
> There is another theme, in which man is thought of as having come not from above but from the womb of Mother Earth. Often, in these stories, there is a great ladder or rope up which people climb. The last people to want to get out are two great big fat heavy people. They grab the rope and snap!—it breaks. So we are separated from our source. In a sense, because of our minds, we actually are separated, and the problem is to reunite that broken cord.

Campbell says it is *our minds* that separate us from our God source, and I couldn't agree more. All the problems of the human race lie between our ears. That is why the most valuable channel of communication is not the mind but the heart. The dualities are present in the mind, but when you focus on the heart, the presence of inner divinity is indisputable. (My inner divinity is pistachio-flavored.)

■ Make Me a Channel of Your Peace ■

There's a saying, "The longest distance you'll ever travel is the journey from your head to your heart." The greatest paradigm shift to open your intuitive channels is triggered by moving out of a state of "trying to get" into a place of "wanting to give." Most prayer is based on trying to "get." We tend to ask the Goddess to deliver to us all sorts of goods, to answer a thick stack of questions, and we pray that we might live without pain, thus without much learning; then we might get infuriated or despondent when She doesn't clear her social schedule to immediately fulfill our requests. Neediness is a self-perpetuating state of mind. Its opposite, gratitude, elevates you into a paradigm of such loving abundance that divine grace wafts out to bless the people and animals in your life.

I'll never forget a story I heard from ex-boyfriend Benjamin, a high-powered Hollywood businessman. Every day he parlayed requests from people who, no matter how well-meaning, all wanted a chunk of him. He told me he had only one friend who was a billionaire. The friend would call just to say, "Hi, Benjamin! I don't *need* anything. I was just wondering if there's anything *I* can do for you today. Anything at all." In our society, there's an urban legend that only sharks get ahead in the business world, but I'd like to think this man's generosity of spirit was the *reason* he was a billionaire.

How often do you think the Goddess gets a phone call from an earthling just to say, "Gosh! Thanks for everything! What can I do for you today?" Could you imagine how tickled She might be to be able to take a deep breath, put Her feet up on Her desk, and not have to work late at the office?

Give it a try. Make it a practice of praying every morning to ask what more you can give, how you can help, and how you can contribute to the animals. Then sit in the silence and listen. If you don't get any imagery, hear voices, or have any bursts of inspiration, don't despair. Instead, be acutely observant of the world around you for any signs or signals of the task at hand. Trust your urges. Read billboards, listen to words of songs, if you open a newspaper to a particular page "by accident," read it, or if your friend blurts out a suggestion "out of left field," log the information. The Goddess has to use the three-dimensional holographic puzzle pieces around you to play charades. Coincidentally enough, when you find yourself in this new paradigm of giving, you may discover that your requests for goods and services got fulfilled along the way, or that perhaps you didn't really need them after all. She may dramatically change your agenda, getting you "de-hired" from employment that no longer serves you, or ejected from relationships that don't contribute to your newly assigned mission. Try to trust that in serving the Goddess to better the world, your highest good will be honored in the divine plan.

If you're suffering through an illness or trauma with one of your animals, as much as you want to pray, "Please take this pain away," the question from a higher perspective is, "What do I need to learn from this? Please let me see *the lesson* so that this situation can be resolved and not have to repeat itself." The paradigm shift of "What can I give to the animals?" will help make you a more receptive instrument for their thoughts and feelings. Start with your own in a spirit of infinite giving. Gary Larsen drew a cartoon where one dog is telling another, "My name's No! No! Bad Dog! What's yours?" If it were true that animals don't know their names, but only what we repeat to them all day, Mr. Jones would think his name is "I live to love you," and Oscar, "Can I get you anything?" This daily outpouring of love comes back to me tenfold when they allow me to see the imagery in their little furry heads.

※ God's Not Out to Lunch ※

When the savior of the Christians said things like "We are all created in the image and likeness of God" and "The Kingdom of God is within" and "These things that I do, so will you do and greater," I think he meant, "Wake up, folks! There is no separation! Take responsibility for all your magical powers!"

Theologian Meister Eckhart said that "the ultimate and highest leave-taking is leaving God for God, leaving your notion of God for *an experience* of that which transcends all notions. I and you, this and that, true and untrue—every one of them has its opposite. But mythology suggests that behind that duality there is a singularity over which this plays like a shadow game." It is in this singularity that you will find an underground channel, a network of interconnectedness like a psychic subway system just under your conscious level of awareness. Here, in this psychic mass transit system, every living being can communicate with every other living being. In this place of divine interconnectedness, God is no longer a concept, but *an experience*. You will *experience* the oneness of all living things and be able to hear the thoughts of animal friends.

In the next story you'll meet a cat who loved his mother so much, he didn't want any new additions alive and well in her mother's body.

※ Three's Company, Four's a Crowd ※

I made a house call to a beautiful young Hollywood gal, Jasmine, because her Scottish Fold Cat, Othello, was marking all over the house. Jasmine met me at the door, anxiously introducing Othello and two Siamese cats, Hamlet and Tybalt. I singled out Othello to grill, but the cats clambered around me to tell me what was wrong before I even asked the question. Tybalt spoke to me first, relaying the picture of a boy of about eight years, wearing baggy surf clothes, chic sneakers, and hip hats.

"Yes! That's my nephew!" Jasmine confirmed. "He's nine, and he's very cool."

Tybalt propelled the image of their human daddy's stomach with great urgency, so I asked the cat if their father had a medical problem. *Not anymore,* he said. The other two cats chimed in, *Daddy's all right now. Daddy's all right now.* When I unveiled this information, Jasmine's heart skipped a beat.

"My husband, Daryl, just had his appendix out!" she gasped. Hamlet showed me two children of which he was exceptionally fond, the hip boy and a girl.

"That's my niece and nephew," Jasmine said. I asked Othello if he had a medical problem that was causing him to want to mark the house.

No, he answered. The other cats chimed in, *There's nothing wrong with Othello.* I suspected that he might be marking his territory against some threat.

"Do you have a conflict with one of the other cats?" I asked.

No, said Othello. The other cats backed him up emphatically: *No! We all get along. We all love each other.*

"Are you allowed to go in a clean box as often as you need to?" Many times this is the only problem. Humans don't always keep litter boxes clean enough for fastidious cats.

No, my box is fine, Othello assured me.

The box is great! Just great! Tybalt added.

"Is there something that your parents are doing to upset you?"

Othello said he saw a baby being pushed in a stroller by their house the day before yesterday. It was a boy baby in a brightly colored hat. I shared this with Jasmine, who confirmed excitedly:

"Yes! Yes! It was day before yesterday! I let them outside yesterday and we talked to the mother of a little boy baby. Do the cats like children?" I checked in with them and told her:

"Hamlet does, Tybalt does, but Othello says, *No, I don't!*"

"He hates them!" Jasmine said. "Ask him why he hates children."

There were two children in my last home, when I was only a kitten. They dragged me upside down and pulled on my ears. They were always tugging on my fur. I hated them.

I wondered if the early trauma was still bothering Othello, provoking him to mark the house.

Finally, the cats had to get literal with me. (The animal psychic was so dense, she just wasn't getting the point.) They kept showing me Jasmine's abdomen, then her uterus. A lightbulb went on over my head. Suddenly I understood the images the cats had sent the moment I'd walked in the door. Before I'd even asked, the cats had immediately sent pictures of Jasmine's niece and nephew, the only children they knew! This was followed by Daryl's belly and a baby in a stroller.

"Jasmine! You're trying to get pregnant, aren't you?" I cried.

"Yes! We've been talking about it a lot. Daryl wants children and I don't. I'm afraid it would infringe on the lives of my cats."

"Othello thinks so, too," I said. "Othello is marking his territory against a baby who isn't even here yet. He is sensing your anxiety and acting out your resistance."

"Well, that settles it." Jasmine smiled triumphantly. She cast a wicked glance over her shoulder at her totally astonished husband, goading him:

"Oh, I would never do *anything* to make my cats feel neglected!"

Now Jasmine had some terrific ammunition to help her fight her case.

⚏ The Heart Sees Clearer Than the Third Eye ⚏

A picture may be worth a thousand words, but a feeling is worth a thousand pictures. We volley pictures back and forth with our third eye, but with the heart we exchange emotion. The heart is the oasis that remains rich and fertile because it has access to the ever-young eternal soul. This is the level where anything is possible.

Inevitably, occasions arise in the lives of our animals when we must compromise no less than in our own lives; then we have to find ways to alleviate the suffering we cause. Who hasn't heard someone say, or even said to themselves, "I know my animal isn't happy about it.

[doesn't want to be left home alone, doesn't want to be spayed, wants a bigger yard . . .]. But there's nothing I can do about it right now!"

I recently had one of my female cats spayed, and my physical connection to her is so strong, I was almost incapacitated. I had to shut down to her pain in the first week of her recovery or I wouldn't have been able to get out of bed. I will herald the day that we no longer have to give female animals hysterectomies, because the animals always complain to me about the pain. When I ask a female animal about her health, the operation is often the first thing she mentions even if the surgery took place ten years prior. Maybe someday someone will invent a form of animal birth control that is not so brutal and traumatic.

We all know when an animal is hurting—and I believe some of the more boorish human lot who protest the loudest are actually the most sensitive, because they have the most to defend. You know the phrase "He who protests the loudest . . ." Here's an example of a memorable protester and a truly unforgettable elephant.

⬛ The Elephant Trainer ⬛

My friend Rick and I spent a day at a Canadian wild animal park last summer, where we met an elephant posing for pictures before a growing line of tourists.

The elephant trainer has become a character we've mimicked over dinner ever since. He was skinny, buck-toothed, red-necked, and completely covered in tattoos. He made Mr Bean look like Cary Grant. His job was to make the elephant raise his trunk to pose for pictures.

One of our guides in the park gave me special clearance to get close to the elephant, mentioning to the elephant trainer that I could talk to animals, a fact that I would not have offered so readily. The elephant trainer decided it was his job to prove me wrong.

"Iffen yer psychic, then answer me this: Where does he sleep?" yelled the trainer. I had very little experience talking to elephants, but I did my best to center myself. I sent the picture of the elephant sleeping at night and asked to see his surroundings. He showed himself standing in a rather claustrophobic barn.

"He says he sleeps in a barn," I answered. The elephant trainer grew agitated.

"Thit's right! How many chains does he sleep in?" he demanded. I volleyed the picture of chains to the elephant and he delivered the image of chains locked around three of his mighty legs.

"Three," I said. The elephant trainer performed a little jig like a monkey who had broken free from his organ grinder.

"Thit's right! Yew stay right ther! Yew stay right ther!" the trainer commanded as he abandoned the trunk raising and picture taking for a moment to dance over to me.

"Why do you make him sleep in chains?" I asked.

"If I don't, he'll break out of the barn and run off."

"Little wonder," I said, sighing. He continued the interrogation with great verve.

"If yew kin talk to him, ask him this! What's his favorite treat?" The trainer still wasn't convinced, although a bit of excited spittle was collecting on his chin. I sent the idea of food going into the elephant's massive mouth, asking him to describe his favorite taste. The elephant was only too happy to comply. He described something small, pink, and very sweet, showing me this sugary substance sticking in his teeth. I didn't think fruit could taste so sweet, but foods taste different to various species of animals, so I inquired if it were a strawberry.

No, he said. The closest analogy I could make for the food was that it tasted like molasses. I was totally baffled. What kind of candy do elephants eat? I wondered. I told my inquisitioner:

"It's pink and very sweet. He likes to chew on something small and sweet. He says it's pink and chewy. I'm not sure what it is." The elephant trainer reached his brown fingers into his stained shirt pocket, pushing aside the can of Skoll to pull out a piece of Bakooza bubble gum. The little squares of gum were all pink.

"It's mah gum! Ah give him one after he's done with the pichers! He loves his gum!" roared the trainer. Standing this close to him, I knew that the gum *must* have been for the elephant.

At this point, I no longer cared whether the trainer doubted anything I said. I'd had more than enough.

I thanked the elephant for talking to me and apologized that people had given him such a crummy life. I assured him it was better than any circus, on par with most zoos—in the bush, he'd be dead—and at least no one was going to make a piano out of him. A few Polaroids and a good stick of gum were about as much as any elephant could hope for in today's world. I said a prayer for him; then I hightailed it out of there before the elephant trainer could continue to grill me.

Now, it was not the elephant trainer but his gum-chewing elephant that got under my skin. Ever since our encounter I have begun to get, er, *visitations*. The problem appears to be that while the human race is staying "right there," the elephants *are not*.

Every night for the last year, just as I drift off to sleep, I see elephants parading through my mind—not in tethered procession, like the circus animals of my childhood—but grave, glorious, reverent, and free. Regally kicking up clouds of dust, they disappear over the horizon, allowing me to watch them as they leave this world. They are coming to say good-bye. Why should I be privy to this bittersweet blessing? Elephants have not been a lifelong passion for me, but like the gorillas, who also visit as I tumble off to sleep, they have only recently become an obsession. My best guess is that they're visiting me, as the gorillas do, *to have their stories told* before they make their final exodus. I hear their trumpeting in the recesses of my mind, like a call to arms from a Camelot of the misty past; this time they're searching for a new world where they can live and prosper, whole and complete, unencumbered by human beings.

In researching the plight of elephants for you, I found their history to be quite fascinating. The following facts are part of an eloquent appeal to the U.S. Senate made by Ginette Hemley, vice president for Species Conservation at the World Wildlife Fund, to honor the African and Asian Elephant Conservation Acts of 1997.

> With a total wild population of only 35,000 to 50,000, the Asian elephant now numbers less than one tenth of the African elephant. The conservation needs of the Asian elephant are urgent if humans are to make a significant difference in ensuring their survival.
>
> Perhaps no other wild animal has had such a close relationship with people. In Asia, the unique relationship between people and elephants runs deep and dates back as far as 4,000 years, when elephants were

first captured and trained as draft animals and for use in religious ceremonies and warfare. Its cultural contributions are especially noteworthy. Ancient Hindu scriptures frequently refer to elephants, the elephant-headed god Ganesha is revered throughout India, and the white elephant has special religious significance for Buddhists throughout Asia.

Beyond this unique relationship with human beings, the Asian elephant is a flagship for the conservation of the tropical forest habitats in which it is found. Elephants range over long distances and across a variety of habitats that are home to numerous other wildlife species. As they need very large areas to survive, effective conservation and management of elephants can deliver widespread benefits for other endangered species such as the tiger, rhinoceros, kouprey, clouded leopard, Asiatic wild dog, gaur, Malayan sun bear, Hoolock gibbon, and countless other wildlife sharing its home.

Who will wake the sleeping Ganesha? Or has he, I wonder, already decided to evacuate his people from the planet. Is the human race really so hopeless that we cannot coexist with these sacred majestic beasts?

Poaching of Asian elephants for ivory, although far less significant than with African elephants, is still a problem in parts of South India, Cambodia, Vietnam, Burma, and Laos. Hide is turned into bags and shoes in Thailand and China, and bones, teeth and other body parts are used in traditional Chinese medicine to cure various ailments. In Vietnam, such poaching is a threat even to the remaining domestic elephants that are allowed to roam freely in forests. . . .

Ivory. Imagine it. There are still parts of this world where useless knick knacks made of ivory wield such value, elephants are heinously slaughtered in order to divorce them from their tusks. But wait. There is a glimmer of hope, and even in the absence of hope, we must persist without it. Many groups are working tirelessly to save the elephants from extinction and conserve their habitats.

The Asian Elephant Conservation Fund provides a source of support for protection of the remaining elephant populations and their habitat against further loss and degradation. The World Wildlife Fund (WWF) and other international conservation organizations such as the World

Conservation Union (IUCN) and the Wildlife Conservation Society (WCS) have been working to identify priority elephant habitat throughout the species' remaining range and to promote establishment and management of corridors and special protected areas.

I heard Jane Goodall say the only way conservation will ever work is if it is made profitable for the indigenous people. As with the plight of chimpanzees, the survival of elephants is dependent on the almighty dollar. As long as starving humans can murder animals to make a buck, they will. Paying them to *stop poaching* by teaching other means of survival seems to be the only viable solution.

If you own a computer, log on to the Web: take a look at the photos of elephant keepers and baby elephants starving on the streets of Bangkok and see if you can keep your heart from exploding into smithereens. Try to keep your heart in one piece, but don't keep your wallet in your pocket. Take that two hundred clams you were going to spend on a designer handbag *and tithe.*

Here's my challenge. If every well-fed person in America, Canada, Europe, Australia, and so on—who is not even affluent but just middle class—forfeited the purchase of one car wash, one weekly manicure, or one tube of designer lipstick and sent that fifteen bucks to a conservation organization instead, there might still be wild animals on this planet when our children grow up. Your designer handbag wouldn't last that long anyway, but maybe the elephants will.

▨ Pleased to Meetcha Before I Eatcha ▨

America has not outgrown her farm mentality. American children are taught not to connect with animals, so that they will not be inconsolable when the animals end up on the dinner table.

In her book *What the Animals Tell Me,* Sonya Fitzpatrick tells a childhood tale of her initiation into the human tribe. She communicated with the farm animals in her native England so clearly that the animals kept her informed of all the neighborhood gossip, much to the chagrin of her parents. (Sonya was clairaudient from birth.) She befriended a couple of geese who followed her everywhere she went until they ended up on a platter for Christmas dinner. Her parents had callously tried to teach her a lesson. She was so crushed by the cruelty, she shut down her starlight vision and did not recover her psychic abilities until well into adulthood.

While most children are admonished with "Now, honey, don't play with your food," the sensitives are also scolded with "Now, honey, don't talk to your food." No, it's not really funny, but the topic is so heartbreaking I have to use a little humor to keep from going insane. Laugh or cry. Take your pick.

▦ Finding Mobility of Consciousness ▦

Picture yourself as a football player on the field, where it is impossible to not take sides—you strive to win the competition for your particular team. Now picture yourself as a spectator high up in the stands, where although you may root for one particular team, from this vantage point you see the game as a whole. It is this higher perspective we are seeking. We do not fight against our humanness, our animalness, or our physical incarnations. We reach deeper and deeper into them for the divinity within. It is here we access that divinity within us.

It is through the heart that we phone home, but I can no more describe a feeling to you than I can describe a smell. "God is love" as a thought is nonsense. "God is love" as a feeling is a revelation. Clairsentience travels through a tunnel of love, but the receptors in the heart can't be activated until the tunnel is established. In the following meditation, you will find your way into a deeper part of yourself where a spirit guide resides who will help you communicate with animals.

Exercise
Contacting Your Spirit Guide

Find a quiet place where you will be undisturbed. Close your eyes, breathe deeply, and silence your mind. Now, find your way down into the earth. This may be through a hole in an old tree, a trapdoor in the ground, a cave in a mountainside or at the seaside, an antique elevator or mine shaft, or a stairway leading down into the catacombs of a Gothic castle. Climb or scramble or jump through the opening and see a winding staircase sprawling beneath your feet. If you find yourself in an elevator, watch the floors descend from twenty to zero. Count silently with me backward from twenty to zero as you descend the stairs deeper and deeper into the earth: 20, 19, 18, 17 . . .

Hear the muffled sounds of pebbles rattling down the tunnel or the far-off trickle of an underwater stream. Smell the smells of the rich brown earth, cool and familiar. See the stairs in front of you lit by a magical subterranean light. The light leads you and beckons you deeper and deeper into the warm, comforting cave. You are totally safe here. The earth holds you safely in her embrace. Feel the stairs under your feet. They may be ancient stones covered with moss, they may be wooden or carved into the rock. There may be a handrail to assist you or lanterns to guide you as you continue your journey farther and farther into the earth. Finally, as you begin to grow weary and fear you can go no farther, the light before you begins to glow like shafts of sunlight breaking through the ceiling of the cave far in front of you. As you continue to chase the light, the ground beneath your feet begins to climb. A clear, refreshing breeze sails through an opening that leads to the outer world. You breathe deeply, taking in the freshness of the air. Suddenly the darkness falls away. You find yourself outside the cave. You have ascended into an open space, a beautiful space under sunlight, or starlight, or the light of the moon.

You have entered the world between worlds, a magical place outside space, beyond time. This corner of the inner world is your own personal sanctuary. You may find yourself walking through a magical grove, the spicy sting of autumn filling the night. The fallen leaves crunch under your feet as you walk alone through the forest in the dark under the stars. Or you may be surrounded by snow, lit up like a magical kingdom by the light of the moon. The wind is cold and bracing against your reddening cheeks. Or your sanctuary may be a mountainside of flowers under the noonday sun, by a tropical waterfall on a balmy afternoon, or a sandy beach still warm under your feet, though the sun sets over the water and fills the sky with a rainbow palette of gleaming color. Do not force the environment to be something that it is not. Let the vision come to you. Allow it to be whatever it is. It will embrace you all by itself.

Now you see a path before you. Begin to walk slowly down the path that opens up before you. This is the path to your own spiritual growth. You are safe and excited as you embark on this adventure, because you know that you are equal to any challenge you may meet along this path.

Ask that a guide come forth who can help you connect with animals. Something will come down the path to greet you. It may scurry out of the bushes, fly out of a tree, or rise up out of the ocean. Whatever image appears, accept it immediately. It may be a dog or cat whom you have known in your outer life who has passed on to the Other Side. It may be a wild animal, soft and beautiful or fierce and terrible. It may be an exotic animal you cannot recognize, a giant insect or a cartoon animal in human clothes. Whatever comes to you, accept it at face value and ask of it this question: "What can I do for you that you will help me communicate with animals?"

Trust your first instinct and remember exactly what the guide tells you so that you may act upon it later. If you don't understand the answer, ask again. If the answer is nonsensical or unacceptable to you, ask for a more practical solution. Ask your guide to lead you down this path, this path to your own self-awareness. Ask your guide to help your discovery continue even after you awaken to your outer life. As you follow the guide, encourage him to speak to you about your own psychic abilities. Ask him to tell you exactly what you need to know now. Listen to his words as you walk side by side. (Pause for about two minutes.)

Now it is time to leave your guide, at least for the present, but before you go, ask him for a gift, a gift that will help you telepath with animals. This may be a crystal ball, an emerald stone, or a glowing sphere that you will carry inside your heart. It may be a necklace that will sparkle and glitter on your throat. It may be a musty old book, a vial of liquid, an enchanted cloak, or a shining crown. Whatever he gives you, accept it gladly and thank him for the magical gift. Promise him that you will use the gift and that you will come back to visit him often to learn all that he has to teach you.

But before you go, ask him for a silver cord. He will hand you one end of a rope woven of silky light. Tie the rope around your left wrist. He will hold the other end of the rope. This cord will connect you with your guide even when you return to the outer world. The silver cord will always connect you with your inner world and your own inner wisdom. Ask the guide to maintain contact with you mentally. Thank the guide for his help and prepare to come back to your waking consciousness.

Count with me silently from one to twenty: 1, 2, 3, 4, 5 . . . Feel what supports your spine underneath you: 6, 7, 8, 9, 10 . . . Start becoming aware of the room around you: 11, 12, 13, 14, 15 . . . Wiggle your hands and feet: 16, 17, 18, 19, 20. Open your eyes and awaken. Take a deep breath, feeling calm and refreshed, but be aware that there is now a gift activated within you and an invisible silver cord tied around your left wrist. You have made contact with the power within you that can talk to animals. Know that if you have difficulty receiving information from an animal today, you have only to tug on the silver cord and your guide will be there to help you.

▪ Interpreting the Information You're Given ▪

The most common complaint I hear from all students studying psychic work is not that they don't receive any information, but that sometimes they receive surprisingly clear information and don't have any idea what it means. For this reason, it is imperative that you record all the information you receive in your Paws and Listen notebook, even if you see it as nothing more than interference.

Sometimes intuitive information is not immediately recognizable. Animals are refreshingly literal. I rarely receive symbolic language that needs any in-depth interpretation, but the guided meditation is a bit different, in that you are contacting archetypes in your subconscious mind and the language of the subconscious is written in symbols. Let's look at some examples.

Remember at the beginning of the meditation, where you call out to an animal to act as your guide? In one of my workshops, two of the students were greeted by their departed human relatives on the Other Side. If human spirits come to you instead of animals, take whatever you get. Maybe some human spirits have been trying to make contact with you for a long time and because you were in an adequately receptive state of mind with this meditation, it was the first opportunity for them to appear. Let whoever wants to help, help. Don't balk if you get something ridiculous like Bugs Bunny or Daffy Duck. Cartoons have accumulated a good deal of archetypal energy. I once guided a friend through this meditation who was greeted by a cartoon dolphin standing on his hind fins, wearing a captain's hat. I've been greeted by animals I could not identify, only to have them manifest in my outer life within weeks of the meditation. Many species of exotic animals live in Africa or South America with whom we have no contact whatsoever. They still have access to our greater mind. Sometimes I see goat-like or beaver-like animals that I can't identify.

When I first began this meditation years ago, I was consistently greeted by a tailless, hoofed, piglike, goatlike, God-only-knows-what-like animal. I later found the mystery animal in the zoo. It was a baby tapir. (And cute as a button, too!) A capybara once threw me for a loop, as well. Although the same skunk usually greets me now, I seem to attract occasional visitations from a wide variety of obscure rain forest beasts.

If your guide offers you information that you don't understand, say to him or her, "Could you make that clearer?" or "Could you say it in another way?" Although the gift you ask for to help you telepath may be very beautiful and esoteric, it could also be a watermelon or a monkey wrench. One of my students received a claw from the paw of a bear. We deduced the gift might have been given to symbolize her need for more protection.

At long last, the following exercises will give you the opportunity to connect with the feelings of your own animal. Because we've already honored dachshunds and Great Danes, I will address these exercises to indoor cats, indoor/outdoor cats, and finally to horses, but please tailor these questions to your friend's species and your own needs. Sit quietly with your animal friend and put your attention on your heart. Your animal may be awake or sleeping. Your connection will be just as clear if your friend is asleep. Complete the "Contacting Your Spirit Guide" meditation first and proceed with the silver cord in your left hand. If you feel resistance to any of these questions, give the cord a tug and ask your guide to help you.

Exercise
Behavioral Gestalt with Your Own Animal

If Your Friend Is a Cat
What do you see through your eyes?

How does your food taste?

What food do you like best? What texture? What temperature?

What does it feel like to purr? To stalk? To hunt? To play? What is your favorite toy? Why?

How do you feel about the birds outside your window or in your yard?

How does your litter box feel? Smell? Is it clean enough?

(If your cat goes outside the box) Why do you do this?

How does it feel to sharpen your claws on your scratching post? On the carpet? On the couch? On a tree? On my panty hose?

Do you know I don't want you to claw the couch?

Do you understand what I say to you?

Are you deliberately careful with my fragile hairless skin?

What do you see in the backyard?

How do rodents make you feel?

How does catnip make you feel?

What does it feel like to climb a tree?

How do you feel about humans?

How would you feel if you met a dachshund?

How would you feel if you met a Great Dane?

How do you feel about television noise?

Are you afraid of cars?

What do you think cars are?

Do you know what books are?

Do you understand why humans have a written language?

How does sunshine make you feel?

What's it like to see in the dark?

How does nightfall make you feel? Moonlight? Stars?

Can you see inside your own body?

Do you understand your own medical conditions?

Do your vaccinations work?

How does a house full of human children make you feel?

What do you feel like when your parents are angry? Late? Anxious? Sick? Too loud?

What does God look like?

What is the meaning of life?

Where do you go when you leave your body?

What do you dream about?

Where do you go to get help healing your body?

What does it feel like to be outside in tall grass?

What do roses smell like? Pine trees? Sycamore trees? Rosemary?

How does it feel to have me pet you?

Where do you like to be petted the most? Your head? Your back? Your ears? How hard? Am I too rough? What touches do you not like?

What would you like changed about your household?

Am I too loud? Is my voice too high when I talk to you?

Do I scare you? Do I move too quickly?

(If there's another animal in your household) How do you feel about him?

(Check your heart. Does it speed up? Check your stomach. Does it clench or relax?) Do you love him? Are you jealous? Does he scare you? How does he look from your perspective? Is he beautiful? Is he bigger or smaller than you are? Do you feel threatened? Maternal? Protective? Do you enjoy spending time together? What do you talk about? Do you have friends that are other species? What do you talk about with other species?

Do humans look strange to you because we have only two legs?

How do you feel about me? Do I leave you alone too long?

How does it feel to sleep with me?

What's your favorite thing I do?

What's your least favorite thing I do?

What kind of music do you like?

Other Questions to Ask If Your Friend Is an Indoor/Outdoor Cat

What animal fascinates you the most?

How does it feel to make a kill?

What does a sparrow taste like? A mouse? A cricket? A lizard?

Whom do you not like? Why?

What do you think about while you sit?

What do you dream about when you sleep?

Do you have friends I don't know about?

Where do you go outside?

Do you visit other humans? Do they feed you?

Do you know other cats in the neighborhood?

Have you befriended any "night animals"? Skunks? Possums?

Do you see raccoons?

How big is your territory?

Do you understand how dangerous cars are? Coyotes?

Do you have a curfew?

Do you have a mate? Are you in love?

Can you see animal spirits on the other side? People?

Do other spirits live in your house?

When cats die, where do they go?

Have you lived before in another body? What was your life like then?

If Your Friend Is a Horse

Do you like to be ridden?

How does your rider feel on your back?

Do you like to wear a saddle?

How does the bit feel in your mouth?

How does it feel to be shoed?

How does it feel to be in a turn out with other horses?

How does the hot walker make you feel?

Do you like to gallop? How often do you need to run?

How much time do you like to spend in your stall?

How does it feel to be locked in your stall all by yourself?

Would you rather sleep where you can see other horses?

Would you like to have a pipe stall?

Do you like to be groomed?

How do cross ties make you feel?

Do you like to jump?

What is your favorite food?

Do you get enough to eat, or do you feel hungry?

How do you feel about humans?

Am I gentle enough with you?

Do you understand your commands, or do I confuse you?

Who's your best horse friend?

Have you ever been in love?

Do you have a mate?

Are you lonely?

Do you have friends that are other species?

What is your favorite activity?

How do you feel about your horse trailer?

Do you like to go to shows?

Do you enjoy competing with other horses?

Are you in any pain?

Would a chiropractor make you feel better?

Do you prefer flat surfaces or trails?

In the thousands of readings I've done over the last few years, there is one question that is the most popular. In fact, I don't recall ever doing a reading in my life where the guardian didn't ask this single question. So end your reading with: Do you know how much I love you?

◼ The Horse That Wouldn't Jump ◼

I was called to the barn of a horse who refused to jump over water. Whenever jumps with pools of water lay in front of the hurdle, the horse would stop dead in his tracks. He told me he had slipped and fallen in the rain, hurting his back ankle. Because a rain puddle precipitated the accident, he had decided all puddles of water were very dangerous. I explained to him that the incident was rare, it was only a fluke accident, and although a muddy wet trail can be dangerous, he did not need to fear the pools of water in his jumping course. His guardian called me the next week, excited to say that after two years of avoiding water, the horse had begun to jump the water hurdles again.

4

Clairaudience: Soul to Soul

What can I do? What can I do? You say you care for me. But there's no tenderness beneath your honesty.

—Paul Simon

The Difference Between Yin and Yang

Our culture is very big on yang—that's life in the bright sunlight: outer-focused, aggressive social climbing, winning over other people, winning over animals, and so on. The yin state of consciousness—that's life in the darkness: internally focused and receptive—is often thought to be passive, weak, and stagnant. But if you're afraid of the darkness, how will you ever know the moon?

When we begin to meditate, the darkness inside us looks dark. In the beginning you may see nothing in the still of the night and hear nothing but the sound of your own breath. But gradually you will become accustomed to the dark. You will quickly discover sounds in the silence and flickering forms in the shadows. Eventually your inner eyes and ears will adjust to the more subtle vibrations; the silence will become a symphony, the darkness a parade of swirling lights. Keep looking. Keep listening. Don't be afraid. You'll make friends in the darkness. There's love in there, waiting for you to find it.

The positive energy you send out is still yang energy, because it is moving outward. Even when you send love to an animal, you are not in a truly receptive state. Sending *nothing* is the only way to be receptive. Even with the best of intentions, all our chanting, visualizing, and affirming of our desires is a generator sending energy out. We are not really *listening*.

Or perhaps we are like batteries; there must be a two-way current or the battery will deplete itself; we *need* bilateral communication. So little information seems to flow in—only obvious signals can't escape our attention. Sometimes it is our animals loving us. No matter how we try to lock the door to our hearts tight, those darn animals weasel their way in. Their soft fur, their pleading eyes, their sloppy kisses. Well, some people can manage to resist them.

We must reverse the current if we are to allow anything to flow in. All force moving outward—even positive force and well-meaning force—is still force, generated in an effort to change the world around us. I am presenting the idea of nonforce. I can't call it *compassion*, because I think compassion smacks of condescension, implying we have to be patient with those we are bigger than, smarter than, or better than. The word *love* holds too many meanings for too many people. And the word *caring* can also be misconstrued into manipulative activities. We often hurt the ones we care for. In an effort to describe inner silent warmth, I will call it *tenderness*. What is missing in our interaction with animals? Tenderness.

Animals remind us that we are not just machines. We are feeling human beings with hearts as well as active minds—hearts that *break*. Aside from the few unfortunate souls in mental institutions, most humans don't have breakable brains. This must be why we try to run our world from our brain's jurisdiction. But oh, that pesky heart! Our hearts are so fragile, mysterious, unfathomable, illogical, confusing, frustrating, baffling, and infuriating. So darn yin. Our brains want to go one way and our hearts the other. It's embarrassing. And who usually wins out? The brain. In our culture, we're trained to lead with our brains. Because of our brains, we "know better," yet we hurt the animals. Who then is really the more evolved species? Humans or dolphins? Humans or gorillas? If evolved means aware, and more aware means more loving—the animals get my vote.

It's time to do some heart washing. If you've never opened your heart before, it may blow open like a bomb dropped on Hoover Dam. Sometimes the defenses go up in smoke. The bigger the dam, the bigger the mess; but after the dust settles, you may find a sweetness, simplicity, and serenity that you never thought possible.

In the next story, I met with a cat so disgruntled with an animal hater, I had to listen long and hard before he'd even begin to speak.

※ "Fred's an Asshole" ※

I was summoned to the house of a very cheerful woman to speak to her very depressed cat. The woman was concerned that Dave had become listless for no apparent reason and suddenly refused to go outside.

When I arrived at the split-level house in Malibu, I was greeted by Roxanne, a bubbly cheerleader type, and Dave, an abominably snooty white Persian cat. Refusing to speak to me, Dave eventually allowed me to sit beside him on the couch and stroke him in silence.

"What's your favorite food?" I asked. I waited for his answer and drew a huge blank.

"Where do you like to sleep?" I wheedled. He looked the other way. I tried every trick I knew to get the ball rolling, to no avail. He would not speak. He was so mad, he was not only giving his mother the silent treatment, he was giving me the cold paw. I was about to give up.

"He just won't talk to me, Roxanne. I'm terribly sorry," I said. But just as I got up to leave, I coaxed him one last time: "Isn't there *anything* you'd like me to tell your mother?"

Fred's an asshole! he said. In my mind, his voice sounded like Winston Churchill. I suppressed a guffaw, wondering how to relay this message. After all, for all I knew, Fred could be her husband, her son, or the new love of her life. I had to be more diplomatic than Dave.

Gingerly I asked Roxanne, "Do you know someone named Fred?"

"Yes!" Her eyes flew open. "It's my new tenant downstairs! I rent out the ground floor of the house." Dave chimed in:

Fred's an asshole. Tell her I said Fred is a real pain in the ass. I did. I told her just that with no equivocating, complete with British accent.

"So *that's* why Dave won't go out anymore!" Roxanne cried.

When Dave interjected: *Fred is an asshole who does not like cats.* This I put to Roxanne in not quite so many words.

"You know, I completely understand that. The tenant before Fred absolutely loved cats, so Dave used to go down there all the time and climb in his window; but since Fred moved in, he won't let Dave in through his window. So *that's* what Dave is sulking about!"

"Oh," I said, chuckling. "No wonder he thinks Fred is such an asshole. Dave isn't welcome in his house."

"He's a nice man," she said cheerfully, trying to defend him, "but kind of, you know, uptight . . . stiff. He complained about an owl outside his window keeping him up at night."

"But owls are so beautiful and magical!" I blurted out. I treasured my family of six magnificent barn owls in my backyard in Studio City.

"I know, I love them, too. The call of an owl puts me right to sleep, but Fred complained about the noise."

I laughed. "Maybe Dave's right." I spoke to Dave for quite a while about his depression and how to manage the loss of his friend, the tenant who had moved away. Dave finally agreed to start going out for a bit and maybe even try to make new friends with other people on the block.

But before I left, I felt compelled to ask Dave what his mother did for a living. I thought with her disposition, she might be an actress, an aerobics instructor, or an extra-happy therapist.

Dave conjured some pictures of what he thought his mother did for a living. He sent the sounds of her singing, making up rhymes, and jiggling around in front of crowds of people. Then he showed me bolts of beautiful fabric and multicolored scarves, emphasizing the bright rainbow colors. I was totally baffled. Could she be an interior designer who danced around, spouting poetry while she hung curtains?

I told Roxanne about the scarves and asked her, "What on earth do you do for a living?"

"I'm a clown," she said.

✳ Everybody, Do the Wave ✳

Somewhere between poetry and science, somewhere between heaven and earth, clairaudience is born. Clairaudience is the sweetest mystery any human being could ever experience. Fortunately, it is the most contagious, too. Most, if not all, of my students walk away with some level of clairaudience after spending three hours in one of my workshops. It rubs off as if by osmosis—impossible, I know, so it seems, but let's take a closer look at all this.

A tuning fork creates a frequency that cajoles everything within its circle of influence to vibrate at its own frequency, thereby coaxing every object within its sphere to participate in a harmonious chorus.

Let's dispel the big fat lie we were all forced to swallow as kids: You and I are separate. You are separate from animals, other people, and the world around you. Okay, let's dispel another whopper, this time with a new twist: Not only are we not separate from one another, our bodies are not made up of solid matter. Albert Einstein proved this in his discovery that matter is composed of particles. In 1803, a physicist named Thomas Young built on Einstein's research when he proposed the particle/wave theory after his discovery of a phenomenon called *interference*. In *The Dancing Wu Li Masters*, Gary Zukav tells us:

> . . . Young's double-slit experiment showed that light must be wave-like because only waves can create interference patterns. The situation, then, was as follows: Einstein, using photoelectric effect, "proved" that light is particle-like and Young, using the phenomenon of interference, "proved" that light is wave-like. But a wave cannot be a particle and a particle cannot be a wave. . . . The wave-particle duality was (is) one of the thorniest problems in quantum mechanics. Physicists like to have tidy theories which explain everything, and if they are not able to do that, they like to have tidy theories about why they can't. The wave-particle duality is not a tidy situation. In fact, its untidiness has forced physicists into radical new ways of perceiving physical reality. These new perceptual frames are considerably more compatible with the nature of personal experience than were the old. For most of us, life is seldom black and white. The wave-particle duality marked the end of the "Either-Or" way of looking at the world.

You might say the primary difference between a psychic, which you are now becoming, and a separatist is that psychics ride the waves; separatists are lone particles. When we think of ourselves as waves, this big ocean of human and animal energy can join at any point and flow together in harmony. Our bodies and minds are separate from one another and yet they are not. The nature of reality and the existence of matter therein is not dualistic. It is holographic. But that's just the beginning.

Young's next discovery suggests that photons themselves may be conscious. The double-slit experiment required the photons to behave differently when two slits in a screen were alternately opened or closed to allow sunlight to pass. Apparently, the photons not only appeared to be able to communicate with each other whether one or two slits were open, but they even agreed on *which* photon would go *where*. According to Zukav,

> The astounding discovery awaiting newcomers to physics is that the evidence gathered in the development of quantum mechanics indicates that subatomic "particles" constantly appear to be making decisions! More than that, the decisions they seem to make are based on decisions made elsewhere. Subatomic particles seem to know instantaneously what decisions are made elsewhere and elsewhere can be as far away as another galaxy! . . . The new physics sounds very much like old eastern mysticism.

Another indisputable example of photon communication presents itself in the selection by which radium disintegrates at a rate of one half every sixteen hundred years:

> How do we know which radium atoms are going to disintegrate and which radium atoms are not going to disintegrate? We don't. We can predict how many atoms in a piece of radium are going to disintegrate in the next hour, but we have no way of determining *which* ones are going to disintegrate. There is no physical law that we know of which governs this selection. Which atoms decay is purely a matter of chance.

Einstein never accepted quantum mechanics as the fundamental physical theory because, among other objections, he didn't buy the "pure chance" aspect. He wrote in a letter to Max Born, "Quantum mechanics is very impressive . . . but I am convinced that God does not play dice."

Further experiments caused scientists to speculate whether particles being observed under the microscope responded to the wishes and expectations of the observer, which is to say, the scientists unwittingly manipulated the matter with their minds or the particles responded in an inexplicable type of telepathic communication. Bewildered scientists are trying desperately to get a handle on how particles behave in nature when they are not "aware" of being observed, but apparently the particles dance and perform for the scientists, acting out their expectations better than any fleas in a three-ring circus.

Does this mean that all matter everywhere responds to our expectations? Does this mean *our scientists are proving* we are in fact creating the illusion of the world around us, or at least altering it by our psychic relationship with it? That our bodies and our world are just a giant hologram orchestrated by the God within us? That we are literally co-creators with God?

What does any of this have to do with animal communication? Everything. Please stay with me. There's a method to my madness. To help make sense of this in the context of clairaudience, let's replace the word *light* with the word *sound*. Let's pretend that photons, which Einstein called "drops of energy" are drops of *sound*.

Please consider that we are not static clumps of matter shaped as human beings. We are frequencies; intricate organic beings made up of suspended information, vibrating in space much like a radio station.

In order to hear someone else's music, we have only to quiet our own symphony for a moment and listen deeply to the silence. I'm going to say it again: There is information in the silence. You have only to dismiss your mental orchestra for a five-minute coffee break. Your inner orchestra leader will be stunned. She may get angry, driving the band to play on, or she may, like mine, be so relieved she falls into an exhausted heap muttering Italian in her sleep. (I *like* to turn my mind off. I get tired of trying to know everything.) If you can get the maestro to stop the music—that's silencing the ego, the id, the left brain, the critical parent—you *can* and you *will* hear the music of other living beings as it automatically flows into and through you. I know this phenomenon is as available to you as it is to me because I see it flourish in my students all the time. Think of the wave half of the particle/wave theory. Your body does not stop at your fleshy fingertips. Your thoughts wade out into the ocean of waves around you just as animals' and other people's thoughts drift into you.

※ What's Behind Curtain Number Three? ※

There's a scene in the Eddie Murphy movie *Dr. Doolittle* in which the unsuspecting doctor first finds out he can hear the thoughts of animals. The doctor accidentally hits a dog with his car. For one tense moment, the dog appears dead. Magically, he then stands up, shakes it off, and trots out of the street unharmed, but not before he yells over his shoulder, "Watch where you're going next time, BONEHEAD!" That scene was the truest account of clairaudience I've ever seen put on film.

The hallucinatory world populated with Cheshire cats and talking caterpillars doesn't pop up just when people take mind-altering drugs. The realm is an absolute, just as the realms of music and mathematics exist eternally sovereign from human thought, be they in the fourth dimension, fifth dimension, or beyond. Beethoven certainly proved this to be true when he returned with dreams of symphonies long after he had gone deaf.

Have you ever heard the music? I've dreamed Beethoven symphonies that were so beautiful they defied description. I've also heard music just as I've drifted off to sleep—a Bach minuet playing perfectly, continuously inside my head. I knew this was not a dimension I was generating, or even one that Bach had manufactured. I was hearing the same music he heard *before he heard it*. I was privy to the dimension where he *composed*. Here in the "Land of Music" lives a realm of the never-ending minuet. If only I had the skill to compose with great speed, perhaps I would have been able to attack my piano and compose a Bach minuet as he did, not from scratch, but from memory: note for note, not creating, but merely transcribing what I heard in my dreamy trance. Bach must have been so attuned to the realm of absolute music, he could hear it while he was wideawake. The talent of Beethoven, Mozart, and Chopin was nothing more than the ability to take dictation from God.

My point here is that among these realms of absolutes, there is a realm where animals talk. We can call it the realm of absolute language, and for all I know, it may be the fifth or sixth dimension. You may discover it, as I did, full-blown in your dreams, but when you train your mind to listen, you will hear snatches of it in your waking world. This is not the same realm where you practice clairvoyance; picture-talking does not demand much of a shift in consciousness; you can exchange pictures with animals, here, now, wideawake. Clairaudience, the ability to hear animals in whatever language you speak, requires a dramatic shift in consciousness and tremendous concentration.

※ The Horse and the Songwriter ※

I took a trip to a ranch in Santa Barbara to meet a horse named Apollo, and his person, Daphne. As Daphne walked me past the pens toward her stunning Palomino show horse, all the other horses walked toward me and leaned out over the fence. They called to me as I passed. *Candice! Mary!* they cried.

"Who's Candice?" I asked Daphne.

"She's a troublemaker who owns one of the horses," Daphne answered. Her horse must have loved her anyway, to have hoped I was she.

"Who's Mary?" I asked.

"She was only here for about a month, and that was quite a while ago." Evidently Mary made quite an impression on one of the horses.

When I met Apollo and rubbed his nose, I didn't open with my usual food question, because horse feed is pretty similar, although apples, carrots, and molasses are often mentioned with great excitement. I had some carrots on hand to use as bribes.

"Apollo, what do you really like?" I asked.

She sings me a song about a bird, Apollo answered. I was surprised that such a general question would merit such a specific answer. I gave Daphne the message and asked her what she did for a living.

"I write music," she replied. "Is this the song? If I sing it, will he tell you which one it is?" she asked. Apollo said, *Yes.* She began to sing a beautiful song. He didn't interrupt her but waited politely until she stopped singing.

"Is that it?" she asked.

Nope, he answered. I saw the flashing images of people flying through the air, birds, and finally, a baby. He produced the rhythm of a driving beat.

Tell her it's the one about the people in the sky, he said.

Rather reluctantly I told her, "He says it's a song about a bird, or people in the sky. Flying people. It's more up-tempo."

Daphne was perplexed. "People in the sky? What does that mean?" Suddenly, a wave of recognition swept over her face.

"Oh, my God! I know the one. There's only one line about a bird. It's about two lovers who die and meet again in heaven."

"People in the sky," I said with a sigh. I marveled at that incredible horse-logic. As Daphne sang, Apollo was absolutely elated.

Yes, that's it, he said proudly. *I helped her write it! She wrote it on my back!* She agreed that she did her best writing while riding. When I mentioned the baby, Daphne confirmed having a pregnancy scare. I asked Apollo if she was pregnant. I mean, who would know better than a horse?

No. She's only afraid she is. She will be, though, he said. There was a baby's spirit hovering around Daphne that Apollo could already see.

A dog goes along with us on our trails, Apollo said.

I asked him to describe the dog to me. He fashioned a picture with the words *short, fat, black.* When I shared the description, Daphne disagreed.

"No, my dog is light-colored and far from fat. I rescued a retired greyhound."

Apollo formulated a picture of the horse and the greyhound, talking as they walked side by side, catching up on the day's events.

She tells me all the funny things that happened in the house during the day. She chews up the brightly colored rugs. We laugh about it. She's very funny, Apollo said. When I told Daphne, she said:

"Good Lord! She does chew up all the rugs!" Even while Apollo was talking about the greyhound, he sent me the image of the fat black dog as well.

Apollo interjected, *The black dog howls along with the music Daphne plays at home.* I shared the message.

"Wait!" cried Daphne. "My old dog, Willy, was black and fat—really fat—and he used to sing along with the piano!"

"Bingo! That's him," I said. "When did he pass away?"

"About a year ago," Daphne said. Apollo conveyed the comical sight of the black dog waddling along beside them.

"He still comes along on your walks," I said.

"You know, I've been feeling him around a lot lately," Daphne said. She asked me about an injury to Apollo's front right ankle and a hoof that was diagnosed with a degenerative bone disease.

"What could make your injury feel better?" I asked him.

He sent me: *Iron. Potassium. Beta-carotene. Chlorophyll.* I dictated these words to Daphne, taking notes. (I found out later that her vet had given him these nutrients before.) Daphne complained that these injuries had ruined his brilliant jumping career. Apollo showed me his ankle and then Daphne's ankle. I got the feeling there was some connection about his inability to jump forward and her holding herself back from her dreams. We talked for a while about the mind-body connection and the way animals can mirror our psychological dramas. I told her the right side of the body is considered the aggressive side, and the foot and ankle involve moving forward in the world, balance, stepping out, standing up for oneself, "being able to stand on one's own feet."

Daphne said she worked as a secretary while she really ached to be a singer/songwriter. Her house was about to go into foreclosure, but she was scared to make "a move." She wanted to move in with Apollo. Apollo predicted a new home within the year, and he insisted that he would help her with her music. She agreed he was her inspiration— something happened to her every time she got on his back that was nothing short of magical. Music would start coming through her. It was as if her horse were a living, breathing guardian angel. I believe this is true of all our animals; they are only waiting for us to realize it.

I recommended that Daphne listen to her muse, let the house go, and start pursuing her singing career both for her own happiness and for the health of her horse.

▨ Turn Down the Noise ▨

The first step in learning clairaudience is to turn off your television set. I don't mean for an hour or two. I mean always. With the exception of an occasional documentary or an exceptional movie, I have barely watched any television in the last six years. (Although I must confess that I have personally contributed to the mayhem by appearing on television to talk about animal communication.)

Not only does most of the usual programming assault us with an inhuman level of violence, the commercials drown us in a deluge of unconscious brainwashing, tricking us into buying "stuff" we don't really need. Aside from the poor content of most television, the noise itself and the frequency of television are forms of violence unto themselves. Consider the radio. Do you blare it nonstop as background noise? Turn it off and reacquaint yourself with silence.

In the last six years of silence, my clairaudience has skyrocketed. My students who thrive on a constant diet of television and radio noise have the most difficulty tuning in to a deeper, quieter, sweeter frequency. If media noise is like cheap ice cream, jam-packed with artificial fillers, dyes, and flavors, smothered in 100 percent artificial hot fudge topping, doused with imitation spray-can whipped cream, clairaudience is like the nectar of a honeysuckle blossom. A hummingbird would never go near your hot fudge sundae, and you'll never be able to hear the tiny, quiet voices of hummingbirds if you don't forgo the artificial substitutes.

Give it a try. Oh sure, I understand if you need to indulge in an occasional *Oprah*-fix or a favorite weekly show—even I have spent more time planted in front of the tube since I discovered Martha Stewart—but create some quiet time. Plan a media embargo. When you no longer have to fight off the barrage of lower chakra drama (that's sex without love and ungodly levels of violence), your vibration will begin to rise of its own accord. The human psyche is an organic, self-healing, equilibrium-seeking being. The cream *wants* to rise to the top, which is to say that although gravity holds our feet on the planet, the nature of kundalini (your body's chi, prana, life force) is to naturally rise and create *balance*. The vibrations of greed and violence trap the chi in the lower chakras to cause illness and disease.

In the first few weeks of silence, your thoughts will rise in volume until your mental patter becomes a raucous din. This will present a beautiful opportunity to take your focus outside your thoughts, to identify with your internal witness, and to sit in the silence, apart from your mental yamma yamma. With incredible strength of will and spiritual discipline, you will be able to observe your thinking process as a detached observer. You might practice sitting in blissful silence after you explore the meditations, Contacting Your Spirit Guide or Shedding the Cloak of Negativity. Or if you prefer, skip to the final chapter of this book where you will find a meditation called An Exercise in Starlight Vision: Your Internal Rainbow. Pick the meditation that most calms and soothes your soul, then enjoy drinking in the silence of your own radiant being.

If you are a flesh-and-blood radio station, experiencing dead air-time could be unnerving at first, but if you constantly send out, and are reluctant to receive, you're going to miss a lot of good stuff. The best programming I've ever heard didn't come from me. I prefer listening to foreign broadcasts and celestial symphonies from the minds of jaguars and elephants over my own boring mental prattle.

※ The Jaguar ※

One of the most fascinating conversations I've ever had in my life was with a jaguar in the San Diego Zoo. We'd made a B-line right to the big cats, where my friend Benjamin prodded me, "Talk to the cats! Talk to the cats!"

I found that I could wake them out of a dead sleep if I sent them the right thought. We happened upon a sleeping lion, and I cast the thought of my climbing into his pen and giving him a good scratch behind the ears. Abruptly he woke up and scanned the crowd of onlookers. His eyes settled on me.

I propelled the thought again with all my might. What he did next was so remarkable, it actually scared me. He bolted upright and prowled toward me. He stopped short only at the edge of the moat that separated us. He had every intention of getting his scratching, but this zealous response only made me feel like a liar. I was promising something I couldn't deliver. I stood and sent him thoughts of love anyway. What harm was a little fantasy?

The conversation between us began to attract the attention of the crowd. People started to wonder what the lion wanted with me. No one knew exactly what was happening, but they started to sense that something fishy was going on. After all, he had pounced toward me as if he wanted to eat me. So I longingly said good-bye to the lion and moved on to the jaguar.

I found him straddling a branch in a tree, the way jaguars like to do.

He, too, was snoozing, but as soon as I approached him, his eyes were on me—and what eyes: as keen as starlight, as ancient as the moon. This pair of glowing emeralds cut right into me. Caged or not, this was a cat that didn't miss much.

I formulated the question "Happy?" He produced the feeling *Bored*. I asked him about the size of his confinement. He fashioned the image of a sprawling jungle with miles of territory to claim for his own. That was a far cry from this jail cell. I designed a picture of him eating and asked, "Food?" He said, *Dead . . . and cold*. I saw hunks of dead flesh being dropped in his cage. He was so bored from being unable to hunt, he could barely stay alive. He informed me that jaguars live to hunt. Everything else is meaningless to a jaguar.

Then the words transpired between us that I will never forget: I sent a picture of a jungle as best I could, saying, "I'm so sorry you are not in your natural habitat." His response blew my mind.

Neither are you, he said. He sent me the picture of me, barefoot in a forest, carefree and dancing like some woodland nymph. With this thought he conjured a picture of the concrete jungle I was living in, totally isolated from nature in its pristine state, a prison that was isolating me from *my* pristine state.

This was one of the first indications I had ever received that animals have opinions about other beings—strong, well-justified opinions; and that they have a sense of humans as individuals, as well as humanity and the damage humanity has done to the planet *as a whole*.

The transmission was lightning fast, as always. This I had come to expect. But the profound implications of what this cat was telling me absolutely knocked my socks off. I am a southern country girl, with aspirations of living in some mountainous, forested land someday. I have often felt that I am almost stifled to the point of extinction in the city, but I have never had another human being acknowledge that fact. Leave it to a cat to see it as plain as day.

He sent a feeling of sadness with the image of the concrete, as if I were the endangered species, not he. He knew that my body and spirit were not getting to do what they were designed to do. I sent the emotion, "You're sad."

Yes, he said, *like you*.

Humanity had built cages for us both; and even in his captivity, this jaguar had a clear conception of the damage that had been done to his natural habitat.

Go where you belong. I can't, but at least you can. Save yourself, he said.

Throughout this conversation he never broke eye contact with me. It was the longest communication I had ever received from a wild animal. Our staring match had lasted several minutes and was beginning to attract attention.

Benjamin said something like, "God, honey, he won't take his eyes off you. He must have a lot to say."

"He does," I said. They all do. Animals talk a lot about the swirl of human activity around them. Where dogs are more apt to talk about balls and hamburgers and trips to the beach, house cats are more apt to talk about religion and politics; and jaguars are more likely to talk about the destruction of the natural world. I was totally overcome with awe. For the rest of my life, I will always remember the day I received sound advice from a jaguar.

◼ Relinquish Your Agenda ◼

Only when we surrender our own thinking process can we hear anything outside our own minds. Another important point about listening is that the less judgmental you are, the more you will hear. Practice clairaudience with your animals when nothing's wrong. Remember my motto: Fix the roof while the sun still shines. The starting point is learning how to listen from a completely detached perspective without demanding changes or explanations. Then, when the time arises that you need a clear answer about an emotionally charged issue, such as your animal's health, you'll be well practiced.

Manipulation is a form of mental violence, and any living creature will retaliate. We have no right to impose our will on others. Later, after your equal partnership is established, you can work on requests like "Please go into your carrier without resistance" and "Let me give you your medicine."

When you try to troubleshoot a problem, get ready. In clairaudience, what you hear may scare and shock you. Even if you lift the veil just for a few moments to allow your animal to vent, prepare to be humbled. Your animals may articulate in ways that are more profound than you ever imagined. You will invariably find that their problems are tied in to your problems. For example, they soil the rug when you and your partner fight, their vomiting is caused by your dieting, their barking is caused by your chaos, their skin allergy is aggravated by your nervousness, their aggression is in response to your hot temper, they chew themselves raw when you chronically run late, or they destroy your carpets, shoes, or furniture because you leave them alone for too long.

When you hear their complaints for the first time, you may find their answers humiliating. The vast majority of the time, the behavior you're trying to "correct" is caused by *your own behavior*. (Tom Robbins calls it *anthropomorphic neurosis*.) This type of work with animals demands that we do lengthy soul-searching. Animals mirror our foibles. In our relationships with vulnerable creatures who are completely loving, often needy, and utterly dependent on us, we need to come to terms with the psychological mirroring that occurs in our personalities and physical bodies. Human beings are like cups. Animals are like sponges. They absorb every kind of physical and emotional problem we try to cast off.

▓ Surrender Your Superiority ▓

It doesn't matter whether you teach your dog to sit and shake a paw. What matters is that you learn from her. What can you learn from a dog?

How to really enjoy life. Spontaneity. Endless exuberance. The spirit of adventure. Affection given freely. Compassion. Forgiveness. How to free your heart. Passion. Courage. Trust. Faith. Devotion. How to abolish worry, anxiety, and fear of death. Lack of self-judgment. Lack of self-doubt.

They are here to bring our attention to the here and now. They open our hearts and teach us how to love unconditionally. You can put a Bible in your lap, a copy of the Bhagavad Gita, or a dog. You will get the same results. (Except the books won't lick your face.)

What can you learn from your cat?

Grace. Power. Fearlessness. Patience. The element of surprise. Carefreeness. Healthy boundaries. Self-protection. Dignity. Risk taking. Trusting your impulses. Aggressiveness. Acting on instinct. Impeccable timing. Speed. Balance. Recovery. How to sleep without worry. How to astral project and walk between the worlds. How to heal. How to return from death. Elegance. Sophistication. Inner peace. High comedy.

Animals are all here to teach us how to love. In our society, our thinking is backward. The cart is so far before the horse, the horse is obscured in the dust. When learning how to talk to animals, consider this: Why should they talk to you? Why should they listen to you? Your stance in communicating must be based on humility. Even so, they may need some time to warm up to the idea of talking to you. Make it a habit of explaining to animals why you are a human who can talk to them. (Because you love them.) In establishing a foundation of trust, you might try sending some reassuring ideas like this:

TRUST-BUILDING THOUGHT-FORMS

I love you.

I won't lie to you.

I won't trick you.

I'll be your confidant, your accomplice, and your friend.

I'm here for you, to help make you happy, to give you whatever you need. If you tell me what you want, I'll do whatever I can to help you get it.

Believe me when I tell you, your animals will hear you. They will understand. Your animals will comprehend every word you say, but they might not be accustomed to having you listen to them.

Here are a few lessons in listening:

Ask for their help.

Ask for their patience.

Take them seriously. Don't patronize.

Learn to embrace them with sincere participation. Your session should be two-sided; you will brainstorm together for mutual problem solving. Cooperate and negotiate to meet them halfway. Make the sacrifices to achieve mutual satisfaction. Keep your promises, and don't make promises you can't keep. When they demand a response, honor it. Here's the story of how I proved to my cat Mr. Jones that I was really there for him.

■ Mr. Jones and the Robbers ■

A perk of communicating with your animals is that they can make good house sitters. When I was living alone with Mr. Jones in my apartment at Venice Beach, I had to spend a lot of my time working in the San Fernando Valley. The Valley is approximately thirty minutes away from the beach and at least an hour and a half away in five o'clock traffic, which was exactly the time I had to go over the hill every other day.

During this time away, I kept close psychic tabs on Mr. Jones, mentally checking in on him several times a day. He had a cat-door that enabled him to explore the neighborhood, so we made an agreement that he would meet me inside every night. Even though my arrival times varied from day to day, he was never more than five minutes late getting home. Our communication was impeccable. He never let me down. So when I got this urgent communication one afternoon, I knew enough to take it seriously.

I was trapped on the northbound 405 freeway in five o'clock traffic when Mr. Jones blasted into my mind. This alone was unprecedented. I usually have to initiate communication with absent animals, even with my own cats—the animals rarely speak first—but this message interrupted my thoughts like an emergency broadcast on the radio.

Amelia, COME HOME. A wave of panic shot up my spine. "What is it? What is it?" I asked.

Something terrible is in the house! COME HOME NOW!

"What's in the house? Tell me who it is!" I begged.

INVADERS! COME HOME! JUST COME BACK HOME! Mr. Jones implored. I didn't wait to find out who was in the house. I blazed off the freeway at the next off ramp. After taking a U-turn, I sped back to the apartment.

Robbers! I fretted.

I hurled the command to Mr. Jones: "Run out your cat door! Don't let anything stop you! Run outside right now and wait for me!"

When I got there, the building wasn't on fire. The windows weren't broken, the doors weren't bashed in. Everything looked utterly copacetic. I crept up the landing with a can of pepper spray in my hand. There I found Mr. Jones waiting for me on the front doorstep, purring contentedly enough, but stiff on his feet, looking a bit disheveled.

"What is it?" I whispered. "You scared the daylights out of me!"

When I was certain I could hear no one inside the apartment, I unlocked the door and let us both in. As my vision adjusted to the dim indoor lighting, I saw the treacherous intruders.

A line of ants marched from the sliding glass door all the way into the kitchen, where they were playing King of the Hill on Mr. Jones's food bowl. His food was black with crawling ants. Pieces of dry food were being passed from one jaw to the next, assembly-line fashion, and spirited out the crack in the sliding glass door. What could be more tragic to a cat than to have his food confiscated before dinnertime? Laughing with relief, I thanked him for reaching out to me and then I gave him a fresh bowl of food.

"Gosh, Jones, why didn't you just eat them?" I asked him. (He sometimes likes to snack on ants.)

Too many, he said.

◼ Listening without Judgment ◼

Animals are not naturally subordinate to us in any way. We do not have the right to "break" them, "train" them, or "tame" them without their 100 percent cooperation. Our attitude toward them should be one of awe, gratitude, and reverence. Worshipful respect is the key that opens the first door. In your first few conversations with your own animal you might open with the following:

You don't have to tell me anything.

You can share with me as much or as little as you wish.

I will graciously receive anything you give me, no matter how small. You listen to me chatter all day; now is your turn to talk.

We'll talk only about what you want to talk about. Tell me what you want me to know.

■ "I Can Hear Anything" ■

Send love. Tell them you are willing to hear, see, and feel absolutely anything, as long as it is the truth; you will not cringe from life. This is a cumulative learning process. Take the first principle, "I can listen without judgment." Then add the second principle, "I can hear anything." Assure them, "Your truth is your truth. I do not have to agree with it or judge it in any way. My opinion of it does not matter whatsoever." Remember, you want them to open up to you, to gain your trust.

■ "I Will Not Shut Down" ■

Try telling your animals the following:

> I will not betray you. You can trust me.
>
> I will not abandon you. I'll always be here for you.
>
> I will not try to change you. I accept you as you are.
>
> I will use every method possible to try to understand you.
>
> I will put myself in your position.
>
> I will not impose my values on you. I will honor your opinion.
>
> I will not belittle or try to dominate you. You have free will.
>
> I will not threaten you with fear or punishment. I'll be fair.
>
> I will not turn my back on you even if you displease me. I'll be understanding.

■ When You Don't See Eye to Eye ■

If you're baffled by frustrating behavioral problems, think of your animals as abused kids whose lives are in your hands. They are terrified of punishment, but still they must fight to have their needs met and their feelings heard. If you couldn't speak to your parole officers, and the only way you could express your discontent would be to urinate on the rug, wouldn't it be humiliating enough in itself, without the inevitable punishment that follows? Wouldn't your need be dire to risk such punishment and humiliation? And what if you couldn't describe to the officer the nature of your problem? You could have a physical infection and be in terrible pain, yet you couldn't tell anyone, so you would be punished for misconduct. Even if you were locked in a room for hours at a time with no access to a toilet, the action and punishment would be the same. You could be trying to express some deeply felt emotion like frustration or rage at the way you are being treated, but the punishment would be identical.

Steven Covey offers a way out of this bind in his book *The 7 Habits of Highly Effective People*. The question is so simple and yet so profound: "Is the way I see you part of the problem?" If you want to manipulate, coerce, or control, the animals will become defensive. Your need to control them will interfere with effective communication. They will not reciprocate. Animals first need to be accepted just as they are. Get to know the natural traits of your animal by reading books about his breed or species. Do your homework. Read as much as you can about their native habitats, their natural desires and behavioral patterns.

■ If Animals Test You, Go the Distance ■

Accept what you get graciously and without judgment. The more you are willing to hear, the more your animals will be willing to tell you. They may test you to make sure you are "with" their experience. If you aren't shocked and you don't damn them or shame them, they may take you further. They need to know you can accept their immediate experience before they let you in on their thinking processes. You have to *earn* their trust. If you make it all the way through "what is," you may break through to "what they think about what is" and "how they feel about what is."

Exercise
Empathetic Listening with Your Cat

CAT: *You leave me alone for too long.*

YOU: Yes, I leave you alone for too long.

CAT: *I love to hunt.*

YOU: Yes, hunting is fun.

CAT: *Birds taste good.*

YOU: Yes, birds taste good.

CAT: *I like to crunch their bones in my teeth.*

YOU: Yes, crunchy bones taste good.

CAT: *I like to have warm blood in my mouth.*

YOU: Yes, warm blood feels good.

When you've won them over and they begin to trust that you won't cringe from their experience, they will give you more information. But first they'll watch to see *what you do* with the data they have offered you. When you prove you can hear anything and love them unconditionally, they'll watch to see that you further *prove* this with your *actions*. In solving any problem, always offer choices. "I understand you like catching birds. I won't stop you, but could you please leave them outside?" If there is no available substitution, create one. Find a solution, and never shirk your promises. Once you've solidified your bond of trust, you can ask your animals to do favors for you. The following story exemplifies how Rodney proved he was really there for me.

■ The Party Pooper ■

I once used Rodney as a spy, quite unintentionally, of course. My then-boyfriend and I were embarking on a weeklong vacation to Kauai, the garden island of Hawaii. It is my favorite of the Hawaiian isles, being so pristine and amply populated with feral cats. I feed the wild cats there everywhere I go. But the cats we were leaving at home, Rodney, Betty, and Mr. Jones, were being abandoned for a week and they were less than thrilled.

Fortunately my next-door neighbor had a teenage daughter, Christin, a devoted cat lover, but a teenage girl nonetheless. When Christin agreed to house-sit for our three cats, we expressly forbade her to throw any parties in our house in the hills. Christin was a nineteen-year-old girl who loved parties, so we knew the temptation to take advantage of our vacated house would be great. However, because Christin was a very responsible and considerate young lady, we were fairly confident she wouldn't turn our house into a scene from *Risky Business*. She swore on her life she wouldn't throw any parties in the house while we were gone.

The day I returned, I asked Rodney how things went while we were away.

Splendid, Rodney replied. *Christin threw a lovely party. Just lovely!*

"Oh really?" said I, quite amused. "Who came to this party?"

Two handsome brunet boys and a very nice blond girl. I liked her long blond hair, but I especially liked the redhead. He sent me a picture of a bright-eyed teenage girl with shoulder-length red hair amid several other people bustling around the house.

Tell Christin she can come back to visit me anytime, Rodney said.

"You bet I will," I replied.

I cornered Christin and said sweetly, "Rodney said your party was lovely."

Her eyes were like saucers. Her hair stood on end. "Party? What party?"

"The party with the blond girl, but Rodney said he especially liked the redhead." Christin couldn't keep up the facade. She never was a good liar, and I could read her face like a map of Pittsburgh. She choked.

"Holy crap, Amelia! I never really believed this stuff about you and the animals before."

"Rodney said the girl he liked most had shoulder-length red hair. She sounds pretty cute. Who is she?" I rubbed it in.

Totally mortified, she broke down and told me the truth.

"Jeez, one of the girls really does have red shoulder-length hair! She was the one who petted Rodney; she picked him up and petted him—but it wasn't really a *party!*"

"Oh, really? What would you call it?"

"It was only four people, and we didn't stay here. Two guys and two girls met me here before we went out, that's all." I let her weasel out of it, but not before I gave her one last jab.

"Rodney said he'd like to see the redhead again, but I'd prefer they not continue their affair under my roof, okay?"

▒ You Can't Fight Instinct ▒

A woman once called me because her cat was climbing her indoor trees. Another woman called once to complain that her chow would excitedly jump on her at their reunion after she left him alone for long periods of time. If your cat climbs trees or your dog is excited to see you, don't call an animal psychic. Cats climb, cats claw, cats spray, and cats fight. Dogs lick your face, dogs bark, dogs run, and dogs mark their territory. If you're having problems with any of these instinctual behaviors, learn to accommodate them with substitutes. Look at what the animals like and fashion a copy of it for their own possession.

> The apparent problem: Cats scratching the couch and climbing furniture, large plants, and drapes.
>
> The instinct: To sharpen claws for defense and flee to treetops for security.
>
> The actual problem: There are no trees growing in the house.
>
> The solution: Provide a proper replacement.

Fabricate your cat's native habitats as best you can. Give your cat a scratching post and build a perch or forfeit a refrigerator top where she has the best vantage point. Cats need to see all the goings-on in the house from a bird's-eye view. For long-term results, you may need to change the way you think, the way you see the world, and even the way you live.

▒ Give Your Animals Alternatives ▒

Never take away what your animal desires without offering a substitute. Be creative:

> If your cat is tearing up your indoor trees, give him his own trees.
>
> If your cat is scratching your couches, give her a vertical scratching post.
>
> If your cat is scratching your carpets, give her a horizontal scratching post.

If your cat is spraying, try to protect him from the threatening animal.

If your dog is barking, give her more attention.

If your dog is stealing your shoes, give her her own chew toys.

If your dog won't stay off your bed, give her her own heated bed, or better yet, let her sleep with you.

If your dog begs at the table, give her her own meal of fresh meat and vegetables.

If your cat won't stay off the bookshelf, clear it off and let her have it.

If your cat won't stay off the kitchen table, build her a perch or go eat somewhere else.

If your cat is asleep in your spot on the bed, go sleep on the couch.

Remember, it's her house, too.

Exercise: The Throat Chakra
A Meditation in Clairaudience

In order to hear your animal's thoughts, you will have to enter a different part of *you*. Sit with your animal and focus on your breathing. Breathe into every tight, stiff place in your body. Breathe out any resistance, any objection. Drop your attention down to your heart. When you're ready, build the — bridge of light between your heart and your animal's heart. Send your love letter to the one you want to reach. Feel the love flowing out of you. Now send out a cloud of gratitude. Say or think these thoughts to your friend:

Thanks for being alive with me right now.

Thanks for coming into my life.

Thanks for living with me.

Thanks for letting me love you.

Now pull back and sit in the silence—open and receptive in this free-floating state. And simply sit with it all: who we are as human beings, not in a dominant position, but simply as a cog in this magnificent everlasting cosmos. Nature pulses with life even without our participation; the breathtaking performance started long before we were born and will continue long after we depart. We stand on the stage of life only for an instant—hearing, acting, seeing, tasting, feeling—before we go back into the Divine Mother's arms whence we came. It is all so awe-inspiring, so humbling, so heartbreakingly tender. We are so fragile. We are so lucky to be here. Breathe in the breath of life and give thanks to Mother Earth for inviting us.

When we can acknowledge our own fragile existence, walking for only a few years on the tightrope of life, we can connect more easily and eagerly with the other animals under the Big Top.

Gently put your attention on your throat. Here it is safe to melt. The front of your neck is swirling with a luscious blue light, like liquid sky. Feel the warmth of it, the soothing comfort of this chakra as it opens like a bouquet of sky blue flowers. Tell yourself it is safe to let it open—truly safe, perhaps, for the first time in your life. Feel the petals gently unfurl. It tingles with the most heavenly blue light. This light reaches up to cup your ears like the earmuffs you wore in the snow as a child. Its caress is so long awaited and welcome. Now see a beam of this blue light reach out to touch your animal's throat. Ask your beloved friend: Will you talk to me? Will you let me hear you?

Ask your Higher Power: Please, God/Goddess, let me hear him. I'm ready.

Next, sit in the silence and listen, really listen. Conscious only of the blue light under your chin, pick up your pen and write. Go through your series of questions, this time with your awareness on your glowing blue throat. Approach all this as if you were a child. If your animal could speak English, what would her voice sound like? Pretend this is a fun game.

You may hear only consonants, snatches of sounds or words. A particular song may float into your mind. Think about the words and meaning of that song. Could your animal be using a memory to try to tell you something? When asking for names, you may hear nothing but see letters or words in your mind's eye. You may see or hear consonants in the middle of words. "Double L's" is a perfectly good description of the name "Billy." Be generous with yourself. I recently got "Margaret" for a dog named "Montgomery," and "Sharon" for a horse named "Cher." You may hear the opening letter, the prominent sounds, rhyming vowels, a particular number of syllables, or even the rhythm of the word.

You may hear nothing but feel emotions in response to your questions. Graciously take whatever you get. If you feel blocked, go back and repeat the Corinthian Prayer, do the Shedding the Cloak of Negativity meditation (page 53) or Contacting Your Spirit Guide (page 65) and begin again.

If you were dissatisfied with your results, go practice your tap dancing. Learn how to play "Misty" on the kazoo. Come back to this when your heart is light. This is no time to throw up your hands and declare, "I tried it once and I can't do it!" You would never learn how to speak Japanese in one lesson, nor would you demand that of yourself. Be fair. You couldn't learn how to read music in a single hour, either. This is a new *language* you are learning, and your intuition is a muscle, one you may have never used before. If you got anything at all, give yourself a huge round of applause and go do something that makes you laugh out loud, like reading the following idiotic story about squirrels.

✖ Nuts? ✖

I will never forget the first conversation I had with a squirrel, shortly after my initial introduction to animal communication. I was on my way to an appointment in Beverly Hills. I parked on a side street and began to blaze a path down a sidewalk that was canopied with trees. I heard a squirrel chirping in one of the trees, so I decided to try to speak to him. I stopped, relaxed my body, and took a deep breath to clear my mind. I entered the silence, but not for long. I heard the words inside my mind:

Hey, lady! Got any nuts?

Opening my eyes, I spied the little guy shimmying down the trunk of the tree. His eyes were on me, and his gaze was intent.

"No, I don't have any," I answered him.

Why not? he asked impatiently. I was speechless.

Flustered, I replied, "Well, I just don't."

"Why don't you go get some?" he asked as if I were a total fool. I blurted out, "I don't have any in my car," because, in fact, I often car-

ried nuts around to munch on in blood-sugar emergencies and to
share with any squirrels I might meet. He persisted, trying to hide his
irritation:

Why don't you go get some for me? With this, he launched an image:
it was a squirrel's concept of a grocery store, except it was a huge nut
storehouse. The other items sold there were incidental—the people-
food meant less than nothing—but this little guy knew that there
existed mighty warehouses where people stored their nuts! He conveyed the impression that people get nuts from these nut stores just
to feed the squirrels, and he knew without any shadow of a doubt that
I had access to an endless supply of nuts.

He had no concept of money, so he thought I should be able to
supply him with unlimited nuts; and he had no concept of what else I
could be doing besides feeding him, so he saw no reason why I should
not race to the store immediately and retrieve his nuts. He then sent
the picture of a plastic bag filled with shelled nuts. He showed me the
image up close so that I could see exactly what kind of nut he wanted.
The request was for almonds.

That was an awful lot of information to receive in a split second's
time, but I have since realized that that is the way it always happens.
The information is lightning fast, and there are often multiple images
to try to decipher. At the time, though, I was dazed and reeling.

"You know about grocery stores?!" I asked.

Of course! Why don't you go get me some nuts? I'll wait right here, he
answered.

His reasoning was impeccable. I found it difficult to debate. "I
can't. I have something else to do." He began to lose patience
with me.

Hurry and finish, then get my nuts. I'll wait right here. He clung
upside down on the tree trunk at eye level and stared me down.

"But . . . but . . . my appointment will take over an hour. Will you
still be here when I get back?" I blubbered.

I can't wait all day, you know, he barked. I guess he couldn't take it
anymore, because I heard him scoff, *Idiot!* as he scurried back up the
tree.

On the way out of my meeting, I checked the tree to see if he was
still there, but he was gone. He'd given up on me. He must have
decided that even though I was a telepath, I wasn't a very bright

telepath. The intelligent thing to do would have been for me to drop everything and go get him some nuts. Anything else was a ridiculous waste of time.

Since that humiliating conversation, I have spoken to hundreds of squirrels, even squirrels in Manhattan's Central Park, who solicit themselves with voices like New York cabbies; but I have rarely had a different conversation. I ask them about their families, homes, and health, but all they want to talk about is nuts. Squirrels don't give a damn about animal communicators. They find no need to speak to the human race.

Most cats and dogs divide people into two categories: people who can talk to animals, and people who cannot talk to animals. Squirrels couldn't care less whether or not you can speak their language. They divide people into only these categories: people who have nuts, and people who do not have nuts.

Reader beware! I know what you're thinking! And no, people who *are* nuts is not one of the options.

5

Troubleshooting: Film Clips—Sending Sequences and Complex Messages

I disappoint some people when I discuss intuition because I firmly believe that intuitive or symbolic sight is not a gift but a skill—a skill based in self-esteem.

—Caroline Myss, *Anatomy of the Spirit*

⬛ How Do I Say It? Sending Complex Messages ⬛

Give animals information! Animals understand every word you say! You may not believe this because your animals do not readily respond to commands. There are two reasons animals ignore commands. Either you're sending mixed messages, or they simply don't want to do what you want them to. Perhaps they give you a response that you don't hear and therefore don't understand.

Remember, your thoughts must always match your words. Think only in affirmatives. Send only thoughts of what you *do* want, not thoughts of what you *don't* want. This takes a lot of concentration and mindfulness, as well as years of practice. If you send the thought, "Don't bark!" your dog will hear, "Bark!" He won't register the "don't." To make matters worse, you are probably sending pictures of what you don't want. This is just our natural tendency as human beings. We project our fears into the world so our animals and human friends act them out. When this happens, you might think you had a premonition that something bad was going to happen, as in, "I just *knew* that dog would try to bite me," but, in actuality, the thought you sent was received by that dog and *encouraged* him to do exactly what you did not want. Thinking only in the affirmative takes an enormous amount of mental retraining. Be patient and honest with yourself. It's not fair to your animals if you send a mental command of what you *don't* want and then punish them when they act on it. This is where the notion that dogs respond to fear originates. Remember that whatever you send, be it positive or negative, will be exactly what the animal acts upon. Always give them alternatives and possessions of their own so that they can be directed to their own belongings.

Some Positive Commands About Negative Behavior

"Don't claw the couch!" becomes "Only claw your scratching post!" (Make sure your cats have one.)

"Don't bite!" becomes "Keep your teeth in your mouth!" or "Keep your jaw shut!"

"Don't pee on the rug!" becomes "Only use your box!" (Or only go outside.)

"Don't jump!" becomes "Keep all four paws on the floor!" (Send with this the feeling of having all four feet connected to the floor.)

"Don't bark!" becomes "Keep silent."

"Don't chew up my slippers!" becomes "Only chew your own toys!" (Make sure they have toys of their own.)

"Don't lie on the counter!" becomes "Only sleep in your
own bed!"

You get the idea. Use your imagination to reverse negative commands and send the opposite imagery of the negative action.
Although most animals do understand the word *no* when it is isolated
as a command, they do not understand it in a sentence. "No biting!"
means "Biting."

Imagine that you give your cat a command like "Don't scratch the
couch!" With this, you send the picture of the cat scratching the
couch. The cat receives the command "Scratch the couch!" There's
anger in your voice, so he knows you really mean it. He waits until he
has your full attention, then he attacks the couch and scratches with
vigor, just to accommodate you, all the while wondering why the hell
it's so important to you that he scratch the couch.

When he proudly does it in front of you to prove he understood
your command and is willing to comply, you yell at him and chase him
around the house, clapping and screaming, *"No!"* Then you corner
him and toss him outside. He lands with a thud. *Well, that's a fine
how-do-you-do!* he thinks, baffled.

Of course, the cat thinks you're nuts. He deduces that humans are
a bunch of knuckleheads. He needs to scratch and you just told him
to scratch the couch! When you send these mixed messages every day
for a number of issues, the cat resigns himself to the fact that you
can't be trusted. He vows to tune you out completely and ignore
everything you say. Why shouldn't he? When he does what you *want,*
you explode, yell at him, and chase him around the house.

Recently, I had my neighbor's cat Gidget spayed, and that is how I
worded her command. "Ignore your stitches!" I also sent her a psychic
sandwich, which is an extremely effective three-step process. Send
the negative sandwiched between two positives.

※ Sending Sequences: The Psychic Sandwich ※

First, I sent the image of the behavior I wanted: the cat sleeping
peacefully and walking around with her mouth as far from her tummy
as possible.

Next, I sent an image of the behavior I didn't want: her ripping out the stitches with her teeth and having to take another grueling trip to the vet to get sewn up again. With this I sent the word *no*.

Finally, I sent a reinforcement of the behavior I wanted: the cat happily ignoring the stitches with the incision healing without interference.

Gidget took the suggestions and healed beautifully, without nipping at the stitches.

I was on my way to visit a ferocious German shepherd attack dog. Before I even arrived, I sent the request of the dog curling up at my feet, docile, with his teeth in his mouth and his mouth shut. When we met, he obliged me by keeping his jaws shut and rolling on his back to show me his tummy. This is not usually the case with barking dogs; some have a job to do and won't stop barking at a stranger no matter how hard you try to pacify them, so please don't judge your progress by your communications with unknown dogs. Silencing dogs is perhaps the hardest feat you could attempt.

Begin to watch your fears. If you think you will have a terrible time getting your cat into his carrier, you probably will. If you're sure your dog will bite the groomer when he gets a bath, he probably will. If you're sure your horse will shy on a particular trail, he probably will.

If you are facing a dreaded situation with your animal, mentally run through the entire scenario of what you *do* want to happen—and *only* what you do want to happen. Your positive imagery will bring around the desired result. And I reiterate: be patient! This training takes time. Our animals are so accustomed to receiving mixed messages from us that when we reorient our thinking in this positive way, they will need some time to get acclimated to it.

※ More Advanced Communications ※

We've talked about how it works and why it works. Now let's talk about making it work for you.

I met a beautiful animal lover named Grace at a party thrown just so I could see the photographs from her safari in Africa. She questioned me about methods of rescuing insects. I told her that many insects are receptive to telepathic communication. I have had great success with most varieties, with the exception of fleas, ants, and hornets. (Fleas say, "I'm hungry. Buzz off"; ants say, "I've got my orders, lady"; and hornets don't give you the time of day before they sting the hell out of you.) She complained that she was having sorry luck with ants inside her house, and I sympathized. I have been able to connect with ants only one at a time, when the scouts are out alone. A single ant may turn around at your mental suggestion, but once the army is marching, I have found it impossible to deter the whole platoon. I suggested cream of tartar in the doorways and entrance cracks.

Grace wanted to know how to catch hard-to-reach spiders to put them outside. I honor all spider savers everywhere, but even some of my best friends are not spider savers. There's something about having too many legs that gives most people the willies. I wonder where we get this prejudice. Most people are fine with four-legged animals, but more than four is considered just *too many legs.* I remind my friends that spiders are magical and intricate beings and that most are completely harmless. What on earth is more dazzling and awe-inspiring than a dew-laden spiderweb spun in a single night? I can't carry around enough building material in my *arms* to build my own house, much less in my *abdomen,* nor do I have the smarts to perform such a feat. Spiders are represented in mythology by the powerful Greek goddess Arachne, and I give special credence to any animals that have gods created in their image. I also remind my friends that every creature, no matter how small or leggy, is just a little animal trying to make a living in the world.

Imagine that you are a spider. You just built the most magnificent home of your life. (If you were a human, you'd be an architect to rival Frank Lloyd Wright.) You've picked a prime piece of real estate, out of any drafts but in an open corner where you spied a few gnats moving into the neighborhood. You worked like a mad fiend all night, crafting your dream home. The next morning, you're waiting quietly for breakfast in your glorious new house, thinking your spider-thoughts, maybe humming to yourself, minding your own business, when a shadow descends upon you—a really *big* shadow. The monster proceeds to spray some toxic chemicals in your direction and destroy your perfect new home with a really big bristly stick. Fortunately you are still young and spry, so you manage to outrun the monster and hide yourself—albeit trembling and terrified—in the molding of the ceiling. Later, when you dare to emerge and make sense of the tragedy, you find the wasteland that was once your home, much like Scarlett returning to Tara after the Yanks have pillaged the mansion and burned it to the ground. You wonder at the hideous beast that tried to kill you and—is your mind playing tricks on you?—when you backed up far enough to get a decent look at it, did it really have *just two legs?* Two legs! Eeuuwh! How disgusting!

I told Grace I rescued a spider from inside my house almost every day, and I find spiders to be incredibly receptive. If I can reach them, I put a bowl or water glass over them, slip a magazine under the bowl, then turn it over gently to carry them outside. But if they are on the ceiling or wall over my head, I hold a pitcher under them and say, "Drop!" They usually drop into the pitcher and allow me to put them outside. She was amazed that this could work so easily, but she promised to give it a try.

The next time I ran into her, she breathlessly told me she had tried telepathy on a spider. She held a pitcher under him and begged him to drop. She sent the thought of the spider inside the plastic pitcher and the thought of the spider outside in the green grass. Nothing happened.

She waited until she ran out of patience; but just as she had given up and walked away, she happened to turn around and get a glimpse of the spider. It was dangling in midair by a thread! It had dropped! Elated, she captured it and swept it off to safety.

I assured her this is a very common occurrence with me as well, that when I give up on a communication and walk away, the creature responds after the fact (not unlike most men). Sometimes they need a bit of time to figure things out. I mentioned to Grace that the thought of the grass might have confused the spider. It may have looked at the plastic pitcher and wondered why a human was sending a command to drop into the grass when there was no grass. Here comes the tricky part: sending sequences to explain what you want and why you want it.

Your command is actually a two-step process. First, you see the creature from the outside doing what you want it to do. Visualize the spider dropping into the container. Then, get inside the creature and try to imagine what it sees. *Be* the spider and see yourself inside the plastic pitcher. Feel the cool container under your feet.

The "why you want it" command is a three-step process: use the psychic sandwich.

THE SPIDER-SAVING SANDWICH

1. Visualize the spider dropping into the container. Send that thought first.
2. Visualize the spider living safely and happily outside in the grass.
3. Reinforce the thought of it dropping into the receptacle as a means of transportation to freedom.

It sounds complicated, I know, but believe me when I tell you, all living creatures are intelligent enough to follow these chains of thought.

Fifteen minutes ago, before I sat down to write this, I captured a cricket in my kitchen sink. I explained the situation to him: that I needed him to stand still while I scooped him up in a water glass to transport him outside. I admit I am somewhat afraid of insects, even harmless ones like crickets, so I asked him not to jump, but to stand still. He didn't do what I requested. He had a better plan. As soon as I lowered the glass into the sink, he hopped right into it, even though I held it several inches away from him. Animals are amazing. You may never realize *how* amazing until you start practicing these skills on a daily basis.

Most houseflies will fly right out the door if you open it and say, "Go!" They respond better if you see them as friendly and curious, not obnoxious and dense. I give them a few moments to buzz around me and investigate what they came in to see before I ask them to leave. They don't always listen, but the number of times that they do respond is really remarkable.

Remember to send only what you *do* want. See the insect, send the feeling of the patio under his feet and the sun on his back. Don't threaten to kill him. If you send the image of a can of insect repellent, the threat won't work anyway, and if you send him both the patio *and* the spray can, you'll just confuse him, so he'll go about his business while telling all his friends how stupid humans are.

I recently heard a story about termites that gave me a good laugh. I met Phineus, a delightful storyteller, up in the mountains of Topanga where he volunteers at Wildworks, an animal rehabilitation facility for mountain lions and other wild animals. On hearing that I was an animal communicator, Phineus asked if I talked to insects; he inquired if I had read the *Findhorn Garden,* an amazing collection of secrets about spiritual gardening, where the "king" of each tribe of insects was contacted for negotiations. These United Nations treaties in Lilliput garnered remarkably effective results. The human equation always offered alternatives and tithed sacrifices for the little ones. For instance, one cabbage at the end of each row would be tithed to the caterpillar king, who, of course, psychically appears with an eeny-weeny crown on his head. (Far be it from me to poke fun. I once met in meditation Alice's caterpillar, complete with attitude and opium pipe.) The Findhorn gardeners claim that the promises *are kept.* The "pests" adhere to only the established territory! I haven't tried it yet, but that doesn't mean it doesn't work. I certainly have stated repeatedly throughout this book that all the successes I've had in negotiating behavioral changes in animals were brought about by offering *desirable alternatives.* Were you to lure the little ones away with something they liked *even more* than your cabbages, you might not even have to bother their busy and probably testy king.

But here's the story that made me squat on the floor and laugh until I was red as a rutabaga. Phineus told me he had a sensitive friend, a reader of the *Findhorn Garden,* who once discovered her house was riddled with termites. She didn't want to poison them and her house. In sacred meditation, she invoked the king of the termites, who appeared complete with tiny golden crown, and she begged him to remove his people from her house. Just to cover her bases, she proffered up a delicious rotting log outside her window. Two years have since passed with no more signs of termites. They apparently packed their bags and left her in peace. A psychic visited her house recently, and on a whim, the termite exorcist asked the psychic if she could "tune in" to see if any more termites lived and lunched in the house. In trance, the psychic said, "They've all moved out except for two. Yes, only two remain. They're an elderly couple who say they were too tired to make the move, but they promise not to eat anything *structural.*"

Less funny, but just as important, I got a call from a friend whose two indoor cats tested positive for a variant of Feline Infectious Peritonitis. Even though where Erin lives is coyote free, she can't let the cats go out for fear that they may infect other cats. At their request, she has started taking them for walks in the backyard in cat harnesses. She called in a panic because her boy cat had broken out of his harness and made a mad dash away from her. She did not catch him again easily. When she got the cats back in the house, she told them they had to stay in the backyard. Both cats stopped and listened to her. Erin said they both froze in place, wide-eyed, as if they had heard her, but she didn't know what they said back. I told her their question was Why? Erin had successfully sent the pictures of the cats in the backyard, but that wasn't enough. She admitted that when she takes her cats out, she is afraid they will bolt, so she sends the wrong message, the pictures of what *not* to do. I told her to send the words and images of only what *to do*, in other words, the cat walking contentedly beside her on his lead.

To give a command or request is not enough. You must explain *why;* and as with human children, "Because I said so!" is a lame excuse. If you don't give sufficient information, you may only succeed in tempting your animal to do what you don't want. Again, human children are an excellent example. If you give an animal the command to "Stay out of the street," your dog may wonder, *What's in the street?* and want to investigate for herself. Here we get into more advanced communication sequences.

There are times when you absolutely must send the pictures of what your animal's dangers are. I send to my cats exactly what will happen to them if they stay out after dark and get caught by a coyote. It is gruesome, but it works. Erin needed to send pictures of her cats getting hit by a car or killed by a big dog, because those are the dangers in her neighborhood. Animals can hear and see what *not* to do in this way without thinking that you want them to go out into the street and get hit by a car. Sandwich the negative information between two affirmatives. For instance, since I have four kittens living in my backyard, the love of my life, Mr. Jones, has moved out into the front yard. If the message I want to send is, "If you venture out into the street, you will get hit by a car," I use the following technique.

THE CAR-AVOIDING SANDWICH

1. Send what you *do* want. I see my cat from my point of view, sitting peacefully close to the house, away from the street. Within this same command, I see the street from his point of view. As I *am* he, I watch the cars whiz by and feel the soft grass under my body, where I watch from a distance.
2. Send what you *don't* want. I send him the imagery of his getting hit and killed by a car, both from my point of view and from his own. As I said before, it's gruesome but it works. It's necessary.
3. Send the outcome of what you *do* want. I see him again resting safely in the grass to reinforce the thought "This is what I want you to do. I've shown you what will happen if you do what I don't want you to do. Please stay near the house."

Afterward I ask if he understood or if he has any questions. Remember that what animals need more than anything in the world is information. They need explanations because they need to be included in your reasoning.

▓ Translation ▓

The easiest part of communication is receiving the images from animals. The hardest part is interpreting the information correctly. Please remember that psychic communication is like playing a game of charades. The animals will try to get their point across any way they can using their own experience, which may be very different from yours. For instance, a small pile of earth in the yard might be called a *mountain* if you are speaking to a hamster. A puddle may be called a *lake* if you are speaking to a snake. Keep in mind, you are seeing things through their perspective, not yours.

But more often than not, problems in interpretation arise because the information is so amazingly literal. As soon as the right side of the brain receives an image, the left, critical side will try to interpret it, for better or for worse. This is why it is imperative that you blurt out exactly what you receive immediately without trying to interpret it, or at least write it down no matter how impossible the transmission seems. Ambiguous imagery tends to make sense later. The goal is to risk being wrong and feeling foolish. Without taking the risk of being wrong, you will never open the possibility of being right. Receiving information without deciphering it is very challenging. Consider the following examples of how my students learned to interpret their information.

✖ Mr. Jones's Nemesis and Rodney's Cat-Sitters: ✖ The Workshops

"Silver!" one woman cried out. She had no idea what she was talking about. Her courage was astounding.

"Silver! Oh, my God! That's what I got, too!" cried another brave student.

We were sitting around a blanket on a balmy horse ranch in Coronado last April, the week after Easter. Seventeen people were learning to telepath with animals for the first time in their lives. The subject was Patricia, a dappled floppy-eared poodle, who luxuriated in a wicker basket in the middle of our circle. I had suggested that the students ask the dog, "What's your favorite food?" Although most of us agreed on beef or liver, when the two students cried out, "Silver!" Patricia's human mother got a smile on her face she could barely contain.

"It must be a fish, because it looks like silver scales," one of the women rationalized. Her left brain kicked in to try to analyze what her right brain was doing.

"No, no! Silver is right!" Patricia's mother broke her vow of silence. She explained, "Patricia stole a chocolate bunny out of my daughter's Easter basket and ate the entire thing! It was wrapped in silver tinfoil!" We all gasped. The information was right on target.

At one point in my lecture, I told a story about a client who had recently passed away. I wanted to keep her anonymous, so I made up a name. Instinctively, I chose the name Loretta. While talking to another participating dog, Amber, I told her father that she excitedly showed me pictures of a party that had taken place last Christmas but was *not* a Christmas party. Amber sent me images of crowds of people milling around in the house, lots of food, flowers, and many paper plates. Amber said to me, *Tell Daddy I said the party was beautiful.* When I conveyed the message to Amber's father, his eyes misted over. "Yes, there were a lot of flowers and paper plates. It was a funeral for my wife. She died last Christmas. Her name was Loretta." Evidently his wife was with us in spirit that day and had *loaned* me her name.

The group went on to receive thoughts and emotions, access buried histories, investigate injuries, and discover the nutritional needs of fifteen horses. The success rate of the students that day was seventeen out of seventeen. Every single student tapped his or her God-given abilities to communicate with animals. One woman, Felice, correctly identified a red-and-pink-floral chair as Patricia's favorite sitting place. She went on to view an entire scene in her mind's eye of the dog chasing a squirrel in the park the week before. Patricia's mother confirmed the accuracy of the information. Felice told me breathlessly after the workshop, "I don't just see pictures, like static snapshots! I see *motion pictures,* like clips from a movie! It's so amazing, isn't it?" Yes, it is.

In a prior workshop, held in a vet's home, nine people made contact with several dogs, an iguana, and my own cat Rodney. I had the answers to Rodney's questions on flash cards, facedown in my lap. I asked the group to ask Rodney the names of his cat-sitters. (Their names were Suzanne and Suki. Suki was a tricky one. I didn't presume that anyone would get it perfectly right.) When we checked the answers, five of the students had written down Sue or Suzie. The other four had written Susan or Sue Ann, and one even got it on the nose: Suki!

I asked them to ask Rodney who was the nemesis at home of my other cat, Mr. Jones. Rodney knew the nemesis because they visited each other in the courtyard. I had the cat's name and color written on flash cards in my lap. The color was solid black, and everyone got it right, or they at least said "dark."

His name was a difficult one: "Mishka." One of the women said, "Whiskers," while another said, "Scratchy." Almost everyone got some variation on the "ska" sound, which I thought was fascinating, because when you say the name Mishka, it is not the "m" sound that gets the most emphasis. It is the "ska" sound that is so prominent, so that's what the students picked up right away.

※ The Canine Snorkeling Gear ※

In one of the workshops I taught on a horse ranch, a woman named Yolanda brought her two German shepherds. I always ask some of the students to bring their animals from home and write down the answers to a few test questions on flash cards. This way, when the group questions the animals, their human parents will be able to confirm the correct answers without any shadow of a doubt. (This particular story is one of the cases quoted in my chapter in *100 Top Psychics in America*.)

Yolanda dressed the dogs in different costumes every year to pose for the photo on the family Christmas cards. So she had even better confirmation than flash cards: she had Christmas cards from years gone by. We asked the dogs to tell the class about their favorite costumes.

The students' answers were astonishingly accurate, and we had the cards from Christmases past to confirm them. When one student saw floral fabric, there was a postcard of the dogs in Hawaiian shirts to match. Another student saw red bandannas. Sure enough, Yolanda pulled out a postcard of the dogs dressed as bikers with red bandannas around their necks.

It was the teacher who let her left brain foul everything up. I kept seeing the dogs with some sort of hollow tubing strapped on their heads, the straps wrapped under their chins. I couldn't imagine what these stiff tubes were supposed to be.

"I see plastic tubes strapped to their heads. What was it? Snorkeling gear?" I asked.

Yolanda laughed as she showed me the picture of what I thought was canine snorkeling gear. The dogs had toy reindeer antlers tied on their heads.

※ Barney and the Beer Cans ※

My favorite incident with a skeptic took place in one of my lectures at a horse ranch. In fact, Barney, the skeptic, was the *manager* of the horse ranch. Many of the women who kept their horses at his ranch had bamboozled him into allowing me to teach there. He made it very clear to these silly women that they were wasting their time, and even though he'd allow them to have my seminar there, he was not going to participate in any of this absurd nonsense.

Oddly enough, when the group reached the point in the workshop where we walked from horse to horse to practice our telepathy, a little red-faced man appeared in the barn, lurking just within earshot of wherever we were standing. He pretended to be busy with chores, but nonetheless he lurked in the periphery. When I Gestalted one of the horses to diagnose its injuries, and Barney overheard the horse's owner confirming, "Yes! That's right! That's right!" he couldn't stand it anymore. Emerging from the shadows, he quickly introduced himself before he blurted out, "Will you talk to my horse?"

I opened with a few preliminary questions before I asked his horse, Jupiter, "Will you tell me a secret?" (When you ask an animal to tell you a secret, that's when all the fun begins, but you must always ask the animal's permission to share the secret with his person. I never reveal the secret hiding places of cats.) Asked for his secret, Jupiter laughed as he shared with me this story:

Barney had been riding him at sunset the prior spring, following a blond woman on a light-colored horse. Jupiter thought it was about the month of April. Returning from a long ride, they approached a stone bridge, just outside the gates of the barn. Jupiter was upset because Barney had been drinking, so right before they reached the bridge, he threw him. The fall didn't hurt Barney; it just gave him a good scare. I saw the glimmer of a frozen margarita in a glass and heard the horse having a hearty laugh. Suddenly a very distinct three-dimensional picture of a beer can blasted in my mind's eye.

When I told the story to Barney in front of the entire class, I thought he was going to soil himself. Thank goodness he had a great sense of humor. Though embarrassed, he excitedly confirmed everything his horse had said.

He blushed red as a beet, admitting, "Yeah, I guess I did drink a few too many beers. The blond woman, Cheryl, was drinking margaritas, but I was drinking beer." He turned to his horse, chuckling. "So you did that on purpose, did you?"

"Jupiter wanted to teach you a lesson!" I teased him. Barney may not have understood the lesson his horse was trying to teach him the day he threw him, but he sure understood the lesson he was taught the day I was there. I didn't need to try to make a fool of the skeptic. His horse did it for me!

⚫ When Animals Refuse Your Request ⚫

Oftentimes when I feed my Maine Coon cat, he eats only a few bites before he walks away from the bowl. I can see why cats have the reputation of being finicky eaters. If I couldn't talk to him, I would get quite frustrated. There are several reasons cats won't eat that most people do not acknowledge. The first complaint is temperature. Cats cannot eat refrigerated food. Remember that when they make a kill, the food is warm. To a cat, warm means fresh. Cold means old. I warm water over the stove and pour a few teaspoons of it over Mr. Jones's food, to serve it slightly warm.

The second complaint is monotony. Animals need their diet varied as much as it would be in the wild. The idea that juggling food flavors makes an animal more finicky is rubbish. Giving an animal the same food every day of his life is very cruel. It's like making a human being live off of nothing but cold oatmeal.

When you communicate with them, you will be able to ask them what they want on a particular day and plan their meals so that they have something to look forward to just as if they were human. I always ask Mr. Jones, "Beef or salmon today? Tuna or chicken tomorrow?" This helps him be less finicky.

People assume that because a cat doesn't eat his food the moment he is presented with it, he doesn't like the food. That is not usually the case. When Mr. Jones walks away from his food bowl, he usually says, *I'll finish it later.* When I ask, "Do you like the flavor?" he says, *It's okay, but I'll eat it later.* Having been a starving alley cat for most of his life, he just likes to know the food is there. Invariably he comes in after a walk or nap in the yard and wants to finish his breakfast. If I take it away, he'll be very upset.

Cats often want to come back and finish their meal later in the day. If their meal is fresh meat or fish, dole it out in small amounts and refrigerate what they don't eat so salmonella isn't a danger. Warm it up before you give them more and make good quality dry food available for snacking. I also don't agree with the notion that you should feed them only once or twice a day and if they don't eat at that instant, you should take the food away. They have as much right to eat whenever they want as we do.

■ Don't Make Your Animals Diet ■

Food rationing rarely works, and you will only succeed in making your friend hate you. There's no better way to destroy communication than to put your animal on a diet. "But my dog is overweight!" I am often told.

"There's a reason your dog is overweight," I often reply. "Your dog is locked in an apartment for eight hours a day."

There's a reason animals overeat. Either there's no nutrition in their pet food—the cheap food sold at the market—so no matter how much of the junk food they gobble down, they never feel satisfied—or your animal is bored. Don't put your dogs on diets. Feed them fresh meat and vegetables and run them. Run them every day. Run them until they can't run anymore. Run them until *you* can't run anymore. It'll keep you from having to diet, too. This also applies to horses. Don't be so quick to ration their alfalfa. Run them.

Feed your dogs and cats fresh meat and vegetables every day and the best quality animal food available. Remember, what you spend on food now, you'll save in vet bills later.

■ Who's Eating Whom? ■

Aside from complaints about vaccinations, cats and dogs tell me the biggest culprit in destroying their health and happiness is commercial pet food. There is so little nutritional value in some types of canned and dry pet food, animals can scarf down huge amounts of it and grow fat while actually suffering from malnutrition. These commercial foods can contribute to a plethora of diseases and emotional problems, the least of which is aggressive, insubordinate, and/or lethargic behavior. Most medical and psychological problems with dogs and cats can be solved by feeding them fresh meat and vegetables instead of canned or dried food. Don't read this page after a big meal, because what I'm about to tell you will make you sick.

Guess what's really in your pet's food! Other cats and dogs. In her marvelous book *Beyond Obedience: Training with Awareness for You and Your Dog,* April Frost sites several cases of sick dogs with serious illnesses (thyroid disease among them) enjoying full recoveries after their switch to a diet of fresh homemade food. April gives us the straight scoop on what some commercial pet food really is. She quotes Helen L. McKinnon, author of *It's for the Animals!* McKinnon reports:

> My more thorough investigation of commercial pet food was initiated after reading the shocking article "Does Your Dog Food Bark? A study of the Pet Food Fallacy" by Ann Martin, which appeared in the March 1995 issue of *Natural Pet* magazine. I read with horror of diseased cats and dogs euthanized, and the barbiturate found unaltered in the end product—my dogs' food. (One small pet-food plant renders 11 tons a week of euthanized dogs and cats which were sold to a pet food company!) . . . Commercial pet food is allowed to have additives, chemicals, excess sugar, and sodium (salt).

Other animals, even road kill, can end up in commercial pet food. (Many vets remain suspicious that even more unsavory products, such as poultry feathers and fecal matter, can end up in the mix in some of the cheaper brands of pet food.) The proteins from these animals are then denatured with charcoal and dye. *Denatured.* For me, that's the perfect description of what commercial pet food does to our animals. It "denatures" them.

Of course, rendered animal products are used in many ways: for ceramics, cellophane, candy, cosmetics, crayons, detergents, insecticides, floor wax, livestock feed, soap, textiles, and more. The gelatin that comes from hooves, horns, hides, and bones can end up in everything from vitamins and gelatin to marshmallows and ice cream. The collagen is used for bandages, glue, and more. I violently object to many uses of animal products. (I've listed cruelty-free companies in the Resources.) My greatest objection comes down to feeding animals their own species.

If we're feeding our cats and dogs other cats and dogs, isn't it a bit unrealistic to expect them to behave perfectly and maintain radiant health? How can excess sodium and sugar be good for animals? These aren't nutritional sources animals would consume naturally.

Although I personally suspect the worst of commercial pet food, there is no veritable direct link between those rendered materials and their effects on the animals that consume them. But let's consider it from a processing point of view. The whole food movement for humans recommends that we eat food as close in form to the way nature provided it. We may never know exactly how much nutrition is lost from the way we process our food, whether during rendering or any other treatment. Most nutritionists tell us that merely cooking fruits, vegetables, and meats depletes some of the vitamins. Shouldn't our animal companions eat a diet closest to the one nature intended?

There's an easy alternative to commercial pet food: Feed your animals what you eat. If you own dogs, feed them healthful, whole foods right off your dinner table (mashed potatoes and green beans included), or better yet, make their food from scratch. There are a number of cookbooks on the shelves for canine and feline diets that will teach you how to balance the protein/carbohydrate ratio. I recommend Helen McKinnon's *It's for the Animals Natural Care and Resources,* which is filled with helpful information including "Helen's Big Batch Recipe" to make homemade pet food in bulk. This topic is also covered in a spectacular book called *Love, Miracles, and Animal Healing,* by Allen M. Schoen, D.V.M., and Pam Proctor (Fireside Books). The brilliant and eloquent Dr. Schoen not only explains how to balance nutritional needs but offers a treasure chest of information about herbs and alternative health care. If you have cats, give them fresh raw meat (seared only on the outside to kill bacteria), fish, and vegetables whenever possible. I'll say it again: What you spend on food now, you'll save on vet bills later. If you simply must feed your animals dry or canned food, read the labels. Go to a health food or specialty store where you can find foods with no "by-products" (beaks, talons, feathers, hooves, and chicken shit) and that are preserved with vitamin E. It's almost impossible to find such food in any grocery store or even most pet food stores. The only dry foods my cats nibble are listed in the resource section of this book: Nature's Recipe, Flint River Ranch, and Katzenflocken (yeah, from Germany).

▓ When No Means No ▓

The best way to gain your animal's trust and open channels of communication is to respect his right to say *no.* Of course, I don't mean letting him run out into a busy street, but often we must put our pride aside and let our animals have their way out of mutual respect.

I often give commands to my own animals that they do not immediately act upon. When asked, "Will you come sleep with me?" Mr. Jones sometimes replies, *I'm comfortable where I am. I'll come visit you later.* In this case, *no* does not mean no. Don't go shanghai your animal and make him do what he doesn't want to do, thinking he didn't receive your request. He probably heard you. Respect his wishes and let him do what he wants. It will encourage him to do what you want later.

Never have I seen more issues of control than with horses and their riders. The horse world is finally making strides toward more compassionate training through the work of horse whisperers like Monty Roberts, author of *The Man Who Listens to Horses,* who invented a revolutionary cruelty-free system of training wild horses based on body language. His method of "gentling" is incredibly compassionate and so effective that it should soon make the old sadistic forms of horse breaking obsolete. Unfortunately, though, most riders don't know when their animals are in pain, so they mistake pain for laziness or disobedience and further break the trust of their horses.

Blue Monday, a gorgeous Irish draft, is my best horse-friend, and our history together is truly extraordinary. Her rider, Denise, met me for a tarot reading one December many years ago. She told me her story through a flurry of tears: although she had leased Monday for three years, Monday's owner had decided to terminate the lease and take the horse back unless Denise was able buy her for the outlandish sum of $25,000 and three of Monday's babies. Denise did not have that kind of money and was utterly heartbroken about the loss of her horse. Evidently the feeling was mutual, because in the other woman's ownership, Monday had begun to starve herself. She had lost 250 pounds.

When I tuned in to Monday, she told me she would not live without Denise. She also said the owner would come down in her price, Denise would magically come up with the money, and by the end of March she would belong to Denise. Three months later the original owner decided she had no use for an emaciated horse, so she offered to sell Monday for $6,000. At the beginning of April, Denise bought

Monday back. It was the happiest reunion I've ever seen. Immediately Monday gained her weight back, and the two have been ecstatically inseparable ever since. How could this horse predict her future? We'll never know, but we're mighty glad she did.

I received my first English riding lesson last summer on Monday's back, in a ring in Palos Verdes. When Denise suggested I take Monday to the farthest corner of the ring, Monday stopped dead in her tracks. When I asked Monday why she simply wouldn't budge, she said, *Bees. There are bees over there.* With this, she sent the image of a flowering ice plant and bees buzzing above bright fuschia blossoms.

I couldn't see any flowers in the distance, but I did see a hillside of ice plants. When I told Denise that Monday was afraid of the bees, Denise was floored. Yes, there were bees down there and Monday was indeed terrified of bees. They tormented her in the wash racks, too, but Denise had never made the connection. Monday had always shied away from the far end of the ring, and Denise had never understood why.

Rather than give the horse a swift kick and tell her she was lazy or stubborn, I sat still on her back and mentally talked to her about her fear. "They bother you, huh? If you'll take me to the edge of the ring, we'll steer clear of the ice plants. We'll make a broad circle around the flowers. That way, the bees won't come near you." Without my giving any physical command whatsoever, Monday began to move again toward the ice plants and the dreaded bees. She just needed to be heard. True to my word, we gave the bees a wide berth.

Problems with horses can often be solved easily by observing and respecting their fears, which so many riders are unwilling to do. I have yet to work with a horse who didn't complain, *If they'd only show me what they want, I could do it. I don't always understand what they want.* Most horses even request that I teach their riders to picture talk so that they will understand their commands. If you send the picture of where you want the horse to go and what you want her to do, she will almost always see the picture in your mind and respond instantly. Henry Blake, author of the trilogy *Horse Sense*, wrote that he became so telepathic with one particular horse, he was able to stop giving physical commands altogether. I also hear horses lament, *She never lets me do what I want to do.* I recommend that riders spend some time letting the horses have the reins. Have some sessions where you let them do what *they* want to do for a change. Let them carry you wherever they want to go. Trust their decisions. They're often better than yours.

Unfortunately, there are times when you must do something against your animal's will. When the issue is of great necessity, and you simply must have an animal's cooperation, there are ways to get around *no*. Let's look at some difficult situations and explore ways to give a series of commands.

Exercise
How to Send the Message "Come Home"

Take a moment to relax and center yourself. If your animal is missing, you probably need to calm down. Say a quiet prayer to affirm that your Higher Power will guide your animal back home. The Corinthian Prayer (page 52) works well in this situation. Pretend you are your animal. Mentally locate your animal and see out his eyes. We will explore this technique extensively in the chapter on tracking through Gestalt, but for now, ponder this: If you were your animal, where would you be? See your house from the outside from your animal's point of view. *Become* the animal, and race toward the house with all your might.

If night has fallen, flicker your porch lights off and on. Visualize your house glowing like a beacon, guiding your animal home. Use the two-step process I call point-of-view Ping-Pong: First, from your perspective inside your human body, see your animal coming into view. Then, from the perspective of your animal, see the house, the balcony, the porch, the door, and your human come into view. Run toward the flickering lights. As the animal, jump into your human's arms.

This exercise takes tremendous concentration, especially the practice of moving your consciousness into theirs, but the technique works. When my kittens are out after curfew, I've found that seeing them from the outside is not enough. I must go inside them, leave the wild cats I'm flirting with, leap the cold stone wall, and run toward the light at breakneck speed. I see them saying to their wild cat friends, "I've got to go home! I've got to get home right now! My mother's calling me!"

I've also found that I sometimes have to make a commitment of patience. I'll stand at my sliding glass door and send the thought to the curfew offender, "I'll stay up all night if I have to. I'll wait here *forever* until you come into view." Usually the cat shows up immediately. Sometimes it does feel as though I'm waiting forever, but the cat invariably comes home. And on rare occasions I go to bed and read, only to get up later and find the straggler on the patio, nose pressed to the glass. Never punish your animals when they come to your psychic call, even if they should not have stayed out late. Punishment will destroy their incentive to respond to your telepathic requests. Reward them instead. God only knows what they were up against out there.

Exercise
How to Send the Message "A Trip to the Vet"

See the animal walking into her carrier peacefully and willingly, or at least without resistance. Do not imagine your animal fighting tooth and nail to stay out of the carrier even if that's what she did last time. Talk to her all the while, and explain everything that she's about to experience. You wouldn't want to get dragged into a doctor's office when you had no idea what to expect, what kind of procedure you were going in for, or how long you would be there—when you didn't even know you had a doctor's appointment that day!

Explain in mental pictures: the animal sitting contentedly in the carrier, having a peaceful ride in the car, sitting in the waiting room without incident, being docile and cooperative with the doctor, patiently undergoing her examination or treatment, joyously riding home in the car, having a happy homecoming with the other people or animals in the house, and getting some wonderful reward when it's all over. Talk to the animal the entire time you are in the car, not in high screechy baby talk, but in low, quiet, calming tones. Be gentle. Speak softly. Classical music or soft jazz on the radio is very soothing to animals. If you are nervous and frightened yourself, take a few deep breaths, say your prayers, and *get calm*. Don't let your animals see you sweat! They will pick up on your fear, and you will make them nervous. Comfort them continuously while they are in the vet's office.

During your consultation, remember: *You are in command*. Your vet does not have carte blanche to perform expensive tests or administer medication without your permission. You have a right to know *every move* your vet plans to make, both in your presence and behind closed doors—*in advance!* Without advance warning, you cannot prep your animal with information. You also have the right to take time to consider an option without getting pressured into a snap decision. Even if this means taking five minutes in the washroom or the parking lot to contact your internal divine guidance, stay in control. Don't allow yourself to get intimidated by white coats and fancy plaques on the wall. Yes, your vet's knowledge and experience are valuable, but so is your intuition.

If your vet and you agree on procedures you weren't planning, explain to your animal exactly what is about to take place. For instance, if your animal is getting an injection in his back: "You are about to feel a sting between your shoulder blades. It is a medicine called ___ to help cure your problem. Relax your body. Be patient and still, and the pain will only last a few seconds." If your vet isn't communicating what he is about to do next (and they usually don't), ask, so that you can relay the information to your animal. Don't hesitate to make a pest of yourself and riddle your vet with questions. When vets try to pretend I'm not in the room, I shamelessly interrogate them with, "What-are-you-doing? What-are-you-doing? What-are-you-doing?" Believe me when I tell you, if I can transfer information to my animals in time to mentally prepare and comfort them—it's worth it.

Praise your animals constantly throughout the ordeal, telling them how brave they are, how generous it was of them to be so tolerant, how proud you are of them, and what a big treat they can look forward to when they get home. If you must leave them overnight, wheedle as many plans out of your vet as you possibly can, so you can tell your animals what they're up against. Coax a departure time out of your vet, even if it's an estimate, and relay this to the best of your ability. Your animals will be less likely to panic if they know what to expect.

You will be astounded at the change in their behavior when animals are included in the human agenda around them. Giving them information will make the ordeal ten times easier for all of you.

※ Time Out! ※

One of the biggest erroneous beliefs I've ever encountered about animals is that they can't tell time. This single myth causes more pain and heartache for the animals than anything I've ever encountered. It's right up there with "They can't feel," "They can't think," and "They don't understand what we're saying." The fact that other animal communicators even perpetuate this balderdash really chaps my hide. There's a popular myth in America today that your dog doesn't know the difference between five minutes and five hours. Yeah, right. Isn't that suspiciously convenient for people who leave their dogs alone for long stretches of time and pretend the dogs *won't notice?* Just because your dog is happy to see you when you've been gone for *twenty minutes* or when you've been gone for *two days* does not prove that your dog doesn't know the difference between twenty minutes and two days!

The current misconception is that humans live in "linear time" and animals do not. Albert Einstein already cleared this up for us when he proved there is no such thing as linear time *for anybody.* Case in point: Go to your dentist for a root canal, then spend a week on the beach in Kauai, and see which one goes by quicker. *There is no linear time!*

Remember my words. You're not going to see them anywhere else: *Animals can tell time!* I've seen the phenomenon confirmed consistently for the last ten years. My dear horse-friend Blue Monday helps me illustrate this point. After our lesson and the revelation about the bees, Denise put Monday back in her stall. Denise kissed her and said, "See you tomorrow." I interpreted for Monday, who answered, *See you at ten.* I almost had to pick Denise up out of the dirt. She had, indeed, been thinking that she would visit Monday the next morning at nine or nine-thirty, which was not their usual time together. Denise always came in the afternoon, but the next day she was going to make an exception. Why did Monday not say, *See you at nine-thirty?* Denise ran late. Monday knew Denise ran late. Denise admitted she probably wouldn't really get to the barn until ten. Monday is an exceptionally smart horse.

Always, always, always tell your animals exactly when you're coming back! Keeping them in the dark about your comings and goings will make animals neurotic, fearful, phobic, willful, depressed, angry, withdrawn, and even prone to sickness and injury.

I have asked my cats to be in by five o'clock sharp only to come home and find their noses pressed against the sliding glass door at 4:57. Mr. Jones even gave me "the business." *You're late!* Don't ask me how they know. They just do.

I used to have a neighbor with a dog named Max. Max told me that he was going to the vet later in the week. When I asked if he knew what day his appointment was on, he said, *Wednesday.* His mother nearly fainted when she confirmed it was true. I've also heard animals say things like *There's a baby coming in March, We're moving at the beginning of next year,* and *Daddy's going on vacation in July.* It is a very common occurrence. I rarely give a reading where some issue of time does not come up.

Last September I spoke with a dog who told me to tell his mother, Charity, she was not to go *back east* without him or *across the big water,* either. (I felt the big water was a flight to Europe.) I asked him when she had taken these trips and he said, *April* and *August.* Charity confirmed she had flown "back east" in April and to Italy in August.

Every time you're leaving your house, tell your animals where you're going and when you're coming back. I don't care if you're going to the grocery store for fifteen minutes. *Tell your animals when to expect you back.* If you take your dog and leave him in the car while you're in the store, give him an estimated amount of time he'll have to wait for you. Better yet, don't leave him in the car. Never is this more important than with chained-up dogs and horses in stalls. They have a right to know when they're going to be set free. If you care for horses, *always* tell them when you're coming next to let them out. Better yet, put them in a pipe stall where they can see other horses at all times. This single change in your actions can cure a plethora of behavioral problems.

Exercise

How to Send the Message "I'm Going Out of Town"

People frequently ask me how to send the images of being apart from their animals. It's quite common for animals to act listless or fall ill while their guardians are away because the animals don't know where you are, why you've left them, or if you're ever coming back. They often assume they're being punished or that you have abandoned them completely. Animals with abandonment issues are especially prone to skin allergies, digestive disorders, and obsessions over grooming. I recently worked with the horse of a Los Angeles–based actress, Katerina, who spends many months a year shooting on the other coast. Her horse had developed chronic skin lesions. Katerina had no idea her horse's allergies were emotionally based until he told us he never knew why she left him, how long she'd be away, or who'd be caring for him in her absence.

How would you feel if your spouse disappeared off the face of the earth without offering you any explanation of where she was, if she'd ever return, or what you did to deserve such harsh punishment? To make matters worse, when we obliviously stroll back home to our animal friends, we expect them to forgive us instantly without acting out.

How do you explain you're going out of town without them? Give them information! Put most of your energy on a *happy homecoming*. Keep sending images of yourself coming home to your animal so he knows that no matter how long you're gone, *you will definitely come home*. Give him *a job* to do while you're away. Follow this with an image of how many dark nights you're going to be gone. Last year I vacationed in Paris (where I was snubbed by many haughty poodles), and this is how I explained my disappearance to Mr. Jones:

First I told him, "At the end of May (that's in six weeks) I'm going to be gone for ten dark nights. I'm giving you a vacation away from me so that you can take care of your cat-sitters, Suzanne and Suki. They need you. They will feed you at eight A.M. and five P.M. every day. The other neighbors, Brandt and Tammy, will visit you every night. I will be flying in an airplane across the ocean so I can see new territory. I will be receiving phone messages every day from Suzanne to make sure you are okay. If you need any assistance, Suzanne will tell me and you will be taken care of instantly. It will be your job to stay home and guard the house while I'm gone."

I also added precautions like "If you smell smoke, run out your cat door, not under the bed!" and I allotted other jobs like "Please keep Suzanne entertained. I promised her you would show her what a consummate soccer player you are." Tell your animals *where* you're going and *why*. (Believe it or not, they do have some concept of what an airplane is. I've even had airplane flights described to me in great detail by animals who have actually flown.)

When you return, *bring your animal a wonderful gift.* The only way animals can reconcile your long trips is for them to think that you've been *out hunting.* Proudly show them you made a "kill." (I brought Mr. Jones some French butter from Paris in my coat pocket. He didn't really buy the fact that I needed to fly to Paris for ten days to retrieve a pat of butter, but he thought it was hilarious. I recently had to spend three nights in the gorgeous mountain town of Idyllwild just to purchase a fine catnip cigar for him. Now, *that* was more like it.)

The entire time I was away, I mentally checked in on Mr. Jones several times a day, and *counted down with him the number of nights until my return.* You will be at your most receptive right before you fall asleep at night. Continually check in with your animal and see what you perceive and feel. Fire off images of yourself petting or sleeping with your friend. Propel waves of peace, comfort, and *joyous images of a happy homecoming.* Flood your friend with thoughts of love. I find that I often dream of my animals after I commune with them right before I doze off to sleep. You may dream that you are at home with them or that they are on the trip with you. You may even feel the warmth or weight of their presence in your bed while you are still awake.

I can't emphasize this enough: Count down the days and keep your focus on the homecoming. Perpetually launch images of yourself walking through the front door (or the door of their stall) to give them a big hug and shower them with gifts. The difference in their behavior will be astonishing.

▦ Interpreting Double Imagery ▦

When you receive double or echo images from your animal, and you often will, the translation can become rather tricky. If you have a backache while you are Gestalting an animal and the animal returns the feeling of a backache, does that mean he has a backache, too? Yes. Trust the double imagery, no matter how close the simultaneous information appears. It is astonishing how often our feelings and illnesses coincide, but this is exactly why I believe many "cures" should be given to both parties, the animal and the person. Would Rodney have suffered from stomach problems if I didn't have them myself? Could I have physically or psychically passed them on to him? Yes.

You will get information that is reinforced by the world around you. As I was preparing for a recent reading, I walked through my kitchen thinking of Jo, my agent, and a friend I needed to call named Joan. I also flashed on the name Clara. When I went to my couch and opened the envelope of pictures for my reading, I found that I was reading a cat named Cleo (Clara). Her parents asked me how Cleo liked her cat-sitter, John (Jo or Joan). Later in the reading, Cleo told me, *Carolyn is a very smart woman.* I noticed that Caroline Myss was the author of the book on the coffee table next to me. Since I had been reading *Anatomy of the Spirit*, I wasn't sure if the cat's message was for me—yes, Carolyn Myss is a very smart woman—or if the message was for Cleo's parents. I took the risk and told Cleo's father, Bob, who assured me he had been working with a Carolyn—a very smart woman!

Cleo showed me an image of her under the white couch in my living room. I knew she couldn't mean she liked to sit under *my* white couch, but I wrote it down anyway. Her parent's *white couch* turned out to be a bed with a white bedspread and dust ruffle. Her feline friend, Butch, told me his favorite tree had five-pointed leaves. He showed me the mulberry tree in my backyard. Well, since I knew he didn't sleep shaded by my mulberry tree, I knew he must have a tree with five-pointed leaves in his backyard. You get the idea? Your animals may show you *your* bathtub when they mean their bathtub, *your* pink bathrobe to indicate their pink bed, maybe even *your* human grandmother to indicate their human grandmother. After your initial meditation, always open your eyes and let your attention float around the room. Your animals may be using your personal collection of mental graphics to wire in their imagery.

> *The really valuable method of thought to arrive at a logical coherent system is intuition.*

> —Albert Einstein

Exercise
Practice: Build the Bridge

Practice with the animals in your neighborhood. A cat may come up to you as you walk past her house. Instead of seeing the cat as an inanimate object, build the bridge.

1. Drop down into your heart. Unplug your mind. Breathe. Achieve inner focus.
2. Reach out with love. See a beam of light radiating from your heart to connect with the heart of the cat.
3. Retreat. Deepen the awakening. Wait in the silence.

You might hear the cat say, *Hi. My name is Bernice. I recently lost my mate to cancer.* (I don't know how animals know the names of some of their illnesses; they do.)

Or you may not receive anything clairaudiently. In this case, all the incoming data will work like a Web search or a pinball machine knocking your questions through different mazes (chakras), challenging you to receive answers in different subtle modes.

For instance, you might ask, "What's your name?" and hear the "b" sound or the "r" sound (Barry, Bernard, Barney). Or perhaps you won't hear the name at all. You might receive a sudden flash of a black cat, larger than the one you're talking to. A stab of pain in your stomach or an ache of loneliness in your heart might follow this image (loss, separation). Remember, it happens instantaneously.

The normal, rational thing to do at this point would be to disassociate, to tell yourself you're imagining all this, and to give yourself a good swift kick in the head. But if you don't, and you listen carefully while assembling the different images and sensations with lightning speed, you will find this cat has given you a nonverbal story line: The black-and-white cat (heavy and big-boned, so he must be male), a warm feeling of affection connected to him (he lived nearby and she loved him), the depth of the attachment (they spent years together), the feeling of loss (his death; she feels bewildered without him). Cancer could come as a word—the "c" sound, the "s" sound, as a stab of pain somewhere in your body, as a vision of the cancer tumor itself, or as a sudden flash of memory of a human you knew who lost her battle with cancer.

You could follow up questioning by asking, "Live together?" Send a thought of the two cats sleeping together on a couch or bed. An immediate image will follow. For instance, a *Yes* answer might be the image of the two cats sleeping yin-yang, superimposed over the imagery you sent and thereby confirmed. The cat might correct it slightly and send back the image or feeling of two cats sleeping together on, say, a bookshelf, but not touching. A *No* answer could be an image of the two cats meeting outside on the wall. If you are more clairsentient than clairvoyant, you may feel the cold wall under your paws and the wind in your face, meaning the cats didn't share a house; they were neighbors.

You may get this much information, but it's perfectly all right if you don't. You may get nothing but a feeling of intense sorrow radiating out of this cat. You may just get a "hunch" that something happened to her mate.

If you have the courage to trust yourself and your own perceptions, you will find yourself in a wonderful position. Rather than ignoring the cat as all the humans around him inevitably do, you may actually be able to *comfort* her in her time of grief. This is an honor that few humans around you will step forward and accept. You may be the only living being in this cat's world who can offer her any comfort. (That's what makes all this worth it, when your friends call you "crazy.")

The cat may ask you questions, too, like *Where do you live? Do you have any food? Can I follow you home? Can I see the inside of your house?*

This is a tough one. It wouldn't be easy to justify to a primary guardian why you wanted to borrow her cat. And God forbid the cat says *I'd rather live with you,* as they often do, obviously preferring humans who not only speak their language but actually stop to take the time to practice. I keep spare cans of cat food in my car for hungry cats I meet out on the town. Give your friend some water. If it's a stray or appears to be undernourished or unkempt, take it home. God/Goddess will reward your kindness.

There's nothing new about this exercise. A montage of information is already being catapulted at you by every animal you meet. Always! We are so busy being preoccupied and self-centered and sending out mental signals that we cannot receive incoming data. Watch what you're *already* feeling, sensing, and seeing when you meet a new animal. What impressions come to mind about how this animal might feel? What would his voice sound like if he were human? What memories stream in? What other human or animal does this animal remind you of? Why?

Remember, if you don't get anything, retract your energy. Focus on your breathing. Quiet your mind and try again. Toss the mental ball (the question), then wait in the silence for an answer. When I can't get anything, I tell the animal, "I can wait forever. I'm going to wait right here *forever* until you answer me." This usually opens something up. Maybe it's the vibration of patience itself that makes the animals respond. Maybe they simply need some time. Maybe they need as much time remembering how to talk to us as we need remembering how to talk to them!

▓ The Hollywood Heavy ▓

One of my favorite cat clients was a character named Ralph, a twenty-two-pound black-and-white fluff ball. His person, Myra, called me in a panic, because Ralph had stopped eating. He was the love of her life, and rightly so. She was quick to admit (rather loudly) that she loved Ralph more than she loved her own husband. She was a woman after my own heart. She was a high-powered Hollywood casting director, and Ralph was a high-powered Hollywood casting director's cat. The two jobs were equally prestigious. Myra mailed me a photo of Ralph so I could tune into him.

Ralph was one of my most baffling cases. When Myra first called me, Ralph was terribly sick, refused to eat, barely moved, but insisted that he did *not* want to go to the vet. He couldn't tell me what had made him sick, aside from thinking it was something he ate. I spoke to Ralph, via photograph, for three days while we tried to narrow down what was wrong with Ralph's stomach. Because he wasn't vomiting, we ruled out food poisoning, but Ralph kept using the word *poison*. I questioned if he had eaten some spoiled food. Nope. I probed him about eating poisonous insects like spiders, wasps, or anything unusual he could have caught and ingested. Zero. Zip. Nada. Finally, he gave me the clue we'd been waiting for. While body-scanning him, I felt a piercing pain between my shoulder blades.

Something poked me in the back, he said. I saw a stinger going in, but I couldn't make out what kind of body the insect had. Ralph couldn't tell me because he hadn't seen it coming. When I gave Myra this mysterious information, she cried:

"Oh! Jesus! Why didn't he say that in the first place? I just got him vaccinated! The vet stuck the needle between his shoulder blades!" We deduced very quickly that Ralph's sickness started as soon as he got home from the vet. The poor cat literally didn't know what hit him. The vet had given him one of those multiform booster shots, and even with his great stamina and girth (to say nothing of his outrageous personality), Ralph's system couldn't handle it. We talked about the toxicity of some vaccines. Yes! They *can* cause serious health problems for your animals!

Well, after I spoke to Ralph about his needs—he said that if he were left alone he could sleep it off—Myra took him back to the vet just to give him a piece of her mind, and what a mind.

Confronted with, "Damn, you idiots almost killed my cat!" her expensive traditional vet tried to appease her with a sheepish story about how the vaccine could not have caused the problem. Most vets claim that vaccines are totally safe, and recommend a lifetime of them.

Many holistic vets disagree and believe that some vaccinations are no longer necessary on an annual basis but can be distributed every three years or less frequently depending on the animal's personal needs and exposure to disease. I asked my Dr. Craige if he could give my kittens doses of the vaccines according to their weight. He told me most vets don't—they give the same amount to a one-pound dog that they give to a sixty-pound dog, and yes, your animal could get sick or even die from being overvaccinated. Some holistic vets agree that much lower dosages of vaccines are equally effective. Others recommend the initial series of shots for young animals, and occasional follow-up shots, but they think that annual vaccinations for older cats do more harm than good. Some vets feel vaccines are less likely to cause complications if the vaccines are split up unbundled, and I have always insisted that animals do not get vaccinations while undergoing any type of surgery, which would only add more stress to their healing processes. Vaccines can save lives, but they can also undeniably wield nasty side effects and may even contribute to severe health problems. Unfortunately, holistic alternatives, like nosodes, are not yet mainstream because they haven't been adequately tested. The vaccine controversy is a prickly pear.

In conclusion, Ralph kept his own word, and when his mother stopped meddling with him, he made a complete recovery. I think her telling off the vet in front of him was the best medicine she could have given him.

▓ "I Tot I Heard a Puddy Tat" ▓

You will know you are gaining a fluent knowledge of telepathy when you not only generate commands but also instinctively respond to the requests of animals. There will be instances when you respond, but you aren't conscious of what you're responding to. Maybe you're already doing this. At this point, you've become not only a sender but also a receiver, thus achieving what I call *telepathic bilateral communication*. In her book *Spoken in Whispers: The Autobiography of a Horse Whisperer*, the British animal communicator and damn good writer Nicci MacKay described her initiation into clairsentience. It did not sound like loads of fun. She woke in the middle of the night feeling the pain of a sinus infection. The searing pain was accompanied by a burning desire to see her horse. Rather than put aside the illogical whim, she ran outside to find her horse suffering from painfully impacted sinuses. By acting on instinct, she was simply responding to the needs of her horse. Perhaps your animals may be such strong senders that they can actually interrupt your thought processes to get their messages through, like Mr. Jones and his ants. Oftentimes, though, you might not be able to discern who started the conversation.

Such transmissions happen with my cats on a daily basis. I often blindly walk to the door in a Stepford wives stupor and open it to find Mr. Jones or Cyrus Chestnut on the doorstep gazing up at me. (Mr. Jones and Cyrus Chestnut don't like to use the cat door.) I tot I heard a puddy tat.

It'll happen to you, too, and when it does, don't dismiss it as coincidence. Give yourself credit for the miracle of being able to hear animals, and make sure you document it in your Paws and Listen notebook. (Then send your best stories to me so I can compile them, take all the credit, and have myself a new bestseller.)

▨ Working with Photographs ▨

Photographs are my preferred way of working, because I do not have the challenge of contacting an animal in person while he's active or distracted, nor am I subject to the owner's cross-talk and fears. Whenever I've scheduled to meet an animal in person, I request the photographs in advance, so I can sit with them for at least two sessions before I meet the animal. The information starts trickling in for me before I open the envelope and look at the pictures, sometimes before the morning mail has even arrived.

A photograph is a blueprint of information. I have no idea why it works. It just does. I once tracked a dog from a fax sent from across the country. The reproduction was terrible. The dog told me he had run north to the main thoroughfare above his small town. When I asked the dog's guardian if she could identify a street called Appalachian Highway, she confirmed the name Blue Ridge Parkway. (So the fax was not sent in superfine mode.) This was one of the only times I've received the *meaning* of a word instead of the *phonetics*. I would usually have blurted out a sound-alike or rhyming phrase. In the following passage, I will walk you through the exact process I experience every time I do a reading.

Recently, I met with a horse named Winchester. As soon as the mail arrived the week before the reading, I sat with his unopened envelope of photos. I jotted down the word *April,* then the names *Tammy, Yvonne,* and *Cherise.* I wrote *I'm afraid to go on the trails because I fell on a snake once and threw my previous rider. I knocked my right hip out of alignment.*

When I opened the envelope and saw this gorgeous horse, I wrote *I love the little boy with the red hair. Blue striped overalls. Montana with snow. Three cold winters. Devon.*

Then I saw the owner's name, Tamara, and read her letter. "Thank you for reading my horse, Winchester. I got him in April." I breathed a sigh of relief. With the verification of the words *Tammy* and *April,* I knew I had the right horse on the line. Tamara's questions read: Who are his human friends? Why is he so afraid to go on the trails? Has he ever been injured? How old is he?"

The next day in the shower I got the name Skyler and Dexter. When I met Winchester and Tamara and read Winchester's answers to her questions, she beamed like a 100-watt bulb.

"My best friend's name is Yvonne. He loves her. Cherise owns a horse over there! The woman I bought him from said he came from Montana. I wanted to make sure she was telling the truth. Skyler and Devon are my two nephews who just visited Winchester. Devon is the redheaded toddler."

So *why* does this work? I don't know. I also couldn't explain gravity to you, but I do know that if you trip, you'll fall down. And I also know that if you meditate on a photograph you can contact that animal. If I can do it, everyone can do it. *How* does this work? Let's investigate this process together.

Exercise
Reading Photographs

Make an agreement with one of your friends to do trial readings for each other. Again, I must emphasize, reading your own animals may not be the best starting point. Your first attempt should not be with a member of your own animal family. Too many preconceived notions or too much emotional debris could block your antennae. You will learn to communicate fluently with your own animals after you have mastered this technique with a detached volunteer.

Ask questions that are easily confirmed. If you try to determine the past of a rescued animal, there may be no way to verify the intuitive data. The only means of obtaining concrete validation on an animal with a mysterious past is if a few people read the animal simultaneously and get the same answer. If not-yet-validated data explain the origin of a present phobia, you know you're on the right track. Say you picked up on Winchester's fear of snakes on the trail *before* you read the question written by his owner. Any question you answer *before* you are asked indicates you have made a successful connection with the animal. You can bank on it. For this exercise, pick a friend with an open mind and a good sense of humor.

1. Select a few pictures of one of your animals that capture his personality. Make sure you can see clearly into the animal's eyes. Photos of animals who are looking directly at the camera seem to work best. Seal the photos in an envelope with a list of questions. If you are reading more than one animal, more than one animal could cause an unexpected party line. Swap envelopes. Make a date to get together with your friend to review the information at least three days after the initial swap.

2. Sit quietly with the unopened envelope. Find a time and a place where you'll have no interruptions for at least thirty minutes: no kids, no phone, no TV, no radio, no spouse running power tools. If you live in a town or city, you might benefit from earplugs to block the noise. Cities are roaring with frequencies outside the level of your awareness. Have your new animal communication notebook and a good pen handy. Don't use your computer because machinery can alter your signals.

3. Put the envelope in your lap or, if you're lying down, rest it on your chest. Start with the Shedding the Cloak of Negativity meditation (page 53). Focus on your breathing. Relax and center. Clear your mind. Enter the silence. Drop your attention down into your heart. Take three deep breaths, releasing any tension in your body or mind on the exhale. Pick up your pen.

4. Before you open the envelope, take a moment to free-associate and jot down whatever comes to your mind. Don't hold back. Don't criticize yourself. (During my second horse reading last week for a horse named Mama, I jotted down the words *Bozo* and *Bonzai* on the unopened envelope. I chided myself for being ridiculous. Do as I say, not as I do. When I reached the ranch, the owner, Kim, had no idea what I was talking about and knew no one named Bozo. She left the stall and later came back with tears in her eyes. "The new groom's name is Horatio Bonocelli, but everyone calls him *Bonzo!*")

In this case, if you were reading Mama the horse, you might have heard no words at all, but seen an image of a clown in your mind or maybe just the bright red hair, or perhaps an acquaintance would flit into your mind who reminds you of Bozo. Let your imagination roam.

What do you taste? What do you smell? What memories float into consciousness? Memories of snow might have led you to Winchester's Montana. Memories of someone named Sherry or Cheryl might have led you to Winchester's Cherise. Don't inhibit yourself. Let it be whatever it is. Winchester showed me a pumpkin, sitting on my third eye, as plain as day. I wondered if he ate pumpkin or if Pumpkin was his nickname. After this, I saw him running on the beach with great white birds. He sent the phrase, *Tell Tam I'm not afraid to go in the trailer on the freeway*. His guardian, Tamara, confirmed that the images she kept sending him were a trip to the beach in Santa Barbara she was planning for the following October. The pumpkin image came from her anticipation, thus his anticipation, of galloping through pumpkin patches.

When I wrote "Bozo," I felt stupid. I felt wrong. When I wrote "pumpkin," I thought, This woman's going to think I'm a lunatic. It's okay. Feel stupid. Feel wrong. Just write it down. A definition of courage: Feel the fear, do it anyway.

This is not the time to judge yourself. We want this process to be *fun*. Close your eyes for a moment, then open them and let your hand write whatever it wants. Let God use you for a little while. Your imagination will take the driver's seat. Colors, tastes, words, snatches of songs, memories, unusual sensations, unusual fantasies, bursts of emotion. These are what you're looking for.

When you've "tuned in," you'll feel ever so slightly different. Your eyes may not roll back in your head. No speaking in tongues. This change is subtle. You may get slightly dizzy. I prefer to work lying down, covered in a thick layer of cats.

If you feel stuck, take a moment to think about the funniest thing that's ever happened to you in your life. Can you remember something, anything, that makes you laugh out loud? A passage from a book? A scene from a movie? This will raise your vibration instantly. (Boy, that was easy.)

You'll know you've reached the desired altered state of consciousness when you can't stop smiling. Your body feels light. The top of your head may tingle. You might experience a new clarity in your thinking process. Your thoughts may be brighter, crisper, or they may appear more suddenly. I can tell when I've "tuned in," when the new thoughts surprise me and seem foreign, as if they're coming from left field. If you simply can't write fast enough, you know you've struck gold. There's a peacefulness here, a lack of self-awareness, but an excitement, too. A current of energy, of joy, of momentum. If you feel a sudden mental acceleration, you know you've shifted from AM to FM.

If you don't get there this time, reread the meditation Contacting Your

Spirit Guide (page 65) and try again. If you still don't get anything, that's all right. Continue the exercise.

5. Open the envelope and look at the pictures. Pick the one that "speaks" to you the loudest. Don't read the questions yet! Fight the temptation to read the letter. Let's do some sleuthing on our own first. You can start with the usual opening questions:

> What's your favorite food?
>
> What color is your best toy?
>
> What does your bed look like?

If your pen is moving, you're doing it right. You might not get answers to all of these questions. I don't always, either. If you don't get an answer, skip the question and go on to the next. Don't let your momentum be broken. Let's keep going:

> Who are your favorite human friends?
>
> What are their names? What do they look like?
>
> Who are your favorite animal friends?
>
> What are their names? What do they look like?
>
> What do you do for fun?
>
> What's your favorite activity?
>
> Where's your favorite place to be?
>
> Is there something special you want me to tell your person? (For this one, pretend you *are* the animal. Feel the emotions in your stomach aching to get out. Feel a tickle in your throat longing to speak. Jot down whatever you need to say.)
>
> Have you ever had an injury? (If you don't get an answer, go on to the next question.)
>
> Have you ever had a surgery?
>
> How is your health?
>
> Are you in any pain?
>
> What food supplements would make you feel better?
>
> What foods do you crave? (Gestalt. Go inside. Feel your tongue salivating. What do you taste? What do you see? What is it called?)

You may get one word or image, a sentence, or the question may just prime the pump for a whole page of conversation. Use the question as a launching pad. The questions are just a point of departure for allowing the animal to reveal whatever he needs to vent. Remember, if you draw a blank, skip the question and come back to it later. Sensitive subjects may not be easy to approach. When you've finished the questions, ask if there's anything else the animal would like to tell you. Let your mind go silent. Picture your body as an empty glass. Let the animal's words fill you up. Go blank again. Let God's words fill you up. Do this with all your photos, then stash the pictures and the photos and go do something else.

There are four places where you can check back in later with your animal friend:

1.   In meditation and prayer.
2.   In the shower.
3.   Driving in the car.
4.   Right before you fall asleep at night.

The conditions of communication put us in a slight trance. The shower is especially effective. I can't count the number of people who say they get their most inspired ideas in the shower. I've heard that Steven Spielberg gets his most inspired ideas while driving. (That must be how he designs his alien characters because the L.A. freeways look like the bar in *Star Wars*—wall-to-wall freaks.)

Anyway, take your notebook to bed with you. Right before you nod off, think about your animal friend. Jot down anything new that comes to mind. Ask your animal friend to come to you in a dream. Prepare yourself. (A few nights ago I dreamed about a constipated hamster with a Brooklyn accent screaming his head off—and I don't even *know* any hamsters.) You will be inviting your subconscious to open to a whole new dimension. Keep your notebook handy in case you remember anything interesting upon awakening.

The next morning, "tune in" in the shower. Take your notebook to work. "Tune in" on your way to work.

In these interims between sitting with the pictures, snatches of new data will fly your way, like the bits and pieces of a foreign broadcast getting picked up on your internal radio. Mark my words! Write everything down that appears foreign to your usual thinking process, no matter how obscure. If you find a name floating around in your head but you fail to write it down, when the guardian brings it up, you will kick yourself. Write down everything you suspect might be coming from your animal friend.

The next day, do a clean reading from scratch. You may get a lot of new data, or you may get some of your old data reinforced.

The night before I saw these two horses, I came back fresh and asked Winchester, "What did you do today?" *I ran!* he said. *I ran so fast! It was wonderful! I walked with Polly!* When I told Tamara, her eyes almost popped out of her head. She confirmed that Winchester had run the day before and walked next to a horse named Polly. When I came back to Mama the second day, she said: *The little girl's name is Angel. Tell Mother to sing me the night songs.*

Tamara confirmed Skyler and Devon, but couldn't confirm Dexter, so I hoped that Dexter would be for Kim and Mama. When I arrived at Mama's barn, Kim pointed out the horse named Dexter. She also confirmed she called her baby girl an angel, but she couldn't decipher the meaning of *the night songs*. At the end of our reading, after Kim found the man called Bonzo, her husband walked into the barn and put her baby girl in her arms. Without thinking, Kim blurted out, "My angel!" and she started singing "Twinkle twinkle, little star . . ." She caught herself mid-"twink" and clapped her hand to her mouth. "Oh, my God!" she wailed. "It's the night song!" Then she burst into tears.

AMELIA'S GOLDEN RULE. Trust. Trust yourself. Trust the information no matter how insane it sounds. People with clowns' names. *April.* The month? *Montana.* The state? *Dexter! Skyler! Pumpkin! Night songs!* Goofy stuff. It means nothing to me. You will get goofy stuff that means nothing to you. Great. Write it down.

AMELIA'S SILVER RULE. Let it be nonsensical. Don't analyze anything. With all your might, resist the urge to make sense of the material. Your analysis will slay you.

A month before I read Winchester and Mama, I read a horse named Dandy who told me, *I like to drink the green water best. Amy, bring the horse candy! The little boy plays a musical instrument.* (She showed me a metal box and sent the word *horn.*) Numbskull that I am, I thought it might be a harmonica, so I wrote down *harmonica.*

When I arrived at Dandy's stall, the first thing I saw was a big green plastic water bucket alongside a few other colored buckets. Dandy's owner, Suzie, confirmed that Dandy favored the green bucket. The horse candy? It is exactly what Dandy said it was. It's a special product wrapped in cellophane called "Horse Candy." Suzie had brought it to Dandy only weeks before. The instrument? Suzie's twelve-year-old boy, Aaron, often brought a miniature Walkman to the barn strapped around his neck. The *little metal box* did indeed resemble a harmonica and sounded to a horse like a *horn*.

On the other hand, I got these same phrases, *green water* and *horse candy*, from two other horses and they meant two other things entirely. For an Appaloosa named Maverick, *I like to drink the green slushy water* meant just that. It was not the color of the bucket. The water itself was green because his owner, Gwendolyn, had been giving him buckets of water mixed with Chinese herbs. This was a good indication that the herbs were working. For another horse, Dazzler, who told me, *I like the red horse candies, the little round red horse candies!* the candies turned out to be red grapes.

AMELIA'S PLATINUM RULE. Write what you get verbatim. Don't let your left brain "help you along" by adding conjunctions or smoothing out your grammar. Your notes may sound like baby talk or caveman grunts. As well they should! The best example of this lesson also came from a horse named Maverick, who told me, *I want to go back to the house by river. I want to run by river.* (His guardian, Gwen, had asked me if Maverick was happier back in his new barn or if he'd like to be moved back home to his house in Malibu.) Of course, I assumed he meant "the river" and that the river was a body of water. Who wouldn't? But after years of trial and error, I had learned not to act smarter than the horses, so I read the notes to Maverick's mom: "I want to go back to the house by river. I want to run by river." Thank God I didn't add any determiners. The house was not by a river. *River* was the name of Gwendolyn's dog! River, the dog, no longer ran with Maverick as he always had because he was left back in the house in Malibu!

※ Remember, This Is a Game of Charades ※

Maverick also taught me a memorable lesson when Gwendolyn asked me what Maverick was allergic to. At first he showed me long sharp nettles on bushes, with the word *No!* When I asked again, he showed me pine needles with the words *Allergy! No!* I wondered how on earth a horse could be allergic to pine needles. After a process of elimination, Gwendolyn and I deduced that Maverick wasn't allergic to pine needles. It finally occurred to her that she had been giving Maverick allergy shots. The needle he'd been referring to was a hypodermic syringe. The message was not *I'm allergic to pine needles.* The message was *No more allergy shots!* Maverick felt the shots were doing him no good.

So you see, you don't need to know what you're doing while you do this. Chances are, you *won't* know what you're talking about. If you can get past the discomfort of feeling completely out of control, you may come to find that uncertainty is the beauty of this process. Not knowing is what makes it fun!

After you've completed your reading, swap your photos back with your friend at a designated time and agree to listen to each other's notes without judgment. Be generous with each other and creative with your interpretation. In one of my workshops, I had Rodney as my assistant. I asked the group what Rodney stole out of my grocery bag earlier that week. The only clue I gave was that the item was wrapped in plastic. The answer was a piece of blue cheese. The vet in the group got it on the nose and cried "Cheese!" But another student in the group had written down "Artichoke." Blue cheese does indeed have the gooey texture, strong flavor, and grayish color of an artichoke. The student shook her head with disappointment, but I insisted she should give herself some credit.

Don't yell, "No! No! You're wrong!" Just because you can't confirm the information doesn't make it wrong. Jot down the information you can't identify because it will probably make sense later. You might not know what your animal is up to behind closed doors. Betsy, my book editor, can personally attest to this. The morning I met her, she put two photos of her cats under my nose and said, "Do it." Even though I was in Betsy's office looking at her photos for the first time in front of an audience and I was jetlagged, I managed to squeeze some information out of her new cat, Rebecca. When Rebecca told me, *I like to sleep on a red pillow,* Betsy said, "No! I don't have a red pillow!" That night Betsy came home and remembered she had a rust-colored pillow. Indeed, she found Rebecca sleeping on a rust-colored pillow on her living room couch. It was matted with gray fur. The next morning she woke up to find Rebecca sleeping on it again. Try to support your friend's intuitions and back it up with conclusive evidence later. The validation will come.

A few precautions: Some embarrassing situations might be revealed. For instance, animals act out when couples fight. They despise screaming and yelling. They can even become physically ill because of turbulence in their households. If you find loud arguments in your friend's home and your friend is a hothead, look out. The animal is bound to reveal the secret. Also, most animals feel bored and neglected, and for good reason. Most animals *are* bored and neglected! But if you say so to your friend, tempers may flare. If you have to drop a bomb on your friend, proceed with caution; a comment like *Daddy loves his new blond secretary* may get you in a lot of hot water.

But more often than not, there will be tears. Tears of relief, tears of awe, tears of joy. You will hear your friend say, "I *thought* that's what was going on! I just *knew* that's how he felt!" And you will say the same. You will amaze each other with a few choice titbits, maybe more, that prove beyond the shadow of a doubt that *Yes, you can do this!* Your friend can do this! We *all* can do this! Animals can talk!!! All we need to do is learn how to *listen*.

6

X-ray Vision: The Body Scan

We have come full circle. Our earliest ancestors passed on a rich psychic heritage: prophets, oracles, shamans, healers make up a vital portion of our history. Yet, as the Age of Exploration took off and science became revered, what had been considered natural for so many thousands of years was then labeled superstitious nonsense or condemned as the work of the Devil. Seers were deemed to be witches and burned at the stake for their so-called crimes. Later, industry and technology—focused always on rational explanation—drove more nails in the coffin of the psychic. But now, there is an increasing movement of people who realize how much of our soul we've sacrificed. That split just isn't necessary. Envision a future where all of our analytical accomplishments and the psychic work hand in hand— realizing the best of both worlds. That's where I believe we're headed.

—Dr. Judith Orloff, *Second Sight*

▓ The Loaded Question ▓

"Is he ready to die?" The vast majority of the calls I receive come from animal lovers asking such a question. The crux of animal communication is to improve the lives of our animal friends, to make them more comfortable, and to alleviate suffering. Our agenda should not be just to prolong life—it is not the *duration,* but the *quality* of life that matters most—but to honor death with grace and dignity. I will concentrate on the passage into the spirit world in the next chapter, but first, I'm going to share with you some techniques to transfer your consciousness into the bodies of other living beings and feel their feelings.

"Are you in any pain?" is the most important question your animals could ever answer, and I assure you that by the time you finish this book, if you practice the exercises regularly, you *will* be able to obtain that answer.

If you are a person who suffers from headaches, stomachaches, backaches, mild arthritis, achy joints, melancholy, anxiety attacks, or nightmares, you know that these are not life-threatening illnesses, but simply persistent annoyances. You may have afflictions your doctor can't diagnose or treat, beyond suggesting that you take an aspirin. You would have even less luck obtaining help for these irritations if you couldn't tell your doctor what you were feeling. If you were an animal, there would be no hope of getting help from a vet for these persistent aches and pains, either physical or emotional. You—as that animal's owner—are his *only hope.*

Many animals have to be almost incapacitated before their owners realize there is something wrong. Every day I check in with Mr. Jones to see how he's feeling. Because he can explain his feelings to me directly—he gets occasional headaches and upset stomachs and complains of his itchy skin—he does not need to "misbehave" to get my attention. Sometimes when animals are not feeling well, they display behavior that owners see as insubordinate. This is especially true of horses. Before you scold your animals for bucking, shying, kicking, biting, ruining your bedspread or carpets, stealing your belongings, destroying any of your property, barking, chewing on your furniture, or even just being unsociable, check in with them first to see how they're feeling. Any sort of "misbehavior" is likely a cry for help and understanding. Animals tell us in these indirect ways unless you develop your clairsentience and learn how to body scan through the use of Gestalt.

Webster's dictionary defines Gestalt psychology as "the study of perception and behavior from the standpoint of an organism's response to configurational wholes with stress on the identity of psychological and physiological events and rejections of atomistic or elemental analysis of stimulus, precept, and response." In plain English, that means Gestalt is the ability to see the world from someone else's point of view. Let's edit that definition down to "perception and behavior from the standpoint of another organism."

I use it as a verb in this book, because there is no better description of the action except to say, "I Gestalted him." It means I performed a body scan, aligning my consciousness in the animal's body, briefly, and with her permission cohabiting the same physical form. It's easier than it sounds. You will see the world through your animal's eyes, which will also be essential later when we explore the possibilities of tracking lost animals. Gestalt is the only way to give effective commands (from the inside out) and search for painful problems in an animal's body.

Gestalt is nothing more than a concentrated form of creative visualization—a game, really—that we all engaged in as children when we pretended we were something else. If you pretend you *are* the animal, you can identify a myriad of physical complaints. It is so simple, we've forgotten how to do it, and many of us who remember how to do it have forgotten how to *trust* it.

The challenge is this: you must know and accept everything that is going on in your *own* body *first*, before you can enter the body of another being. You must have an acute awareness of what is happening in your own body, so that you will be able to differentiate between your physical sensations and those of your animal friends. Your first challenge may simply be to learn how to *get in your own body.* The emotional challenge is the same. When you know and accept your *own* emotions, you can sort out what *you are generating,* as opposed to what emotions are emanating from your animal. Therefore we will concentrate first on cleaning our slates and getting in touch with our own bodies.

Exercise
Getting to Know You:
A Meditation in Body Clearing

Let's take a few moments to sense and feel what's going on in your own body. This is just an opportunity to notice, to sense, and to feel without trying to change or judge any pain or condition.

Take a deep cleansing breath. Hold it for the count of three, and on the exhale envision all the fear, anxiety, worry, doubt, and stress flood out of your body: 1, 2, 3. Now take a normal breath and exhale. Once again, take a deep cleansing breath and hold it for the count of three: 1, 2, 3. Release any last bit of tension and let it melt out on the exhale. Now take a normal breath. But on this, the final cleansing breath, see a golden glowing light filling your lungs and permeating out into your body like the sun coming out from behind a cloud. Hold it for a count of three and feel it warming every inch of you: 1, 2, 3. And finally let it out.

Put your focus on the top of your head. Let it drift down your neck. How does your neck feel? Tight? Stiff, or supple and relaxed? Open your eyes and become aware of what you see. Now, close your eyes and note anything you might see behind your eyelids. Any colors? Any lights?

What do you hear right now? What do you smell right now? What kind of taste is inside your mouth?

Float down into your shoulders. How are your shoulders today? Are your arms relaxed and comfortable? How does your left hand feel? What is the temperature?

How does your right arm feel? Your right hand? Is it cool and dry, or moist?

Let your attention slide down your spinal column. How does energy flow?

How does the alignment feel? Again, we are not trying to change anything, just locate and identify sensation, without judgment.

How does your heart feel right now? With your eyes closed, is it difficult to locate it? Without touching your heart, can you feel your heartbeat? Can you identify the rhythm of your own body? Put your hand over your heart. Are you familiar with your heartbeat? Let yourself be soothed for a moment by your best friend, your heart. Feel its devotion.

Put your focus on your stomach. How is your digestion today? Are you hungry? Is there something you could eat that would make your body function more smoothly? Pause here a moment and see if you receive any intuitive impressions. Any tastes, smells, images.

How do you feel emotionally today? Are you frustrated? Pressured? Sad? Relieved? Angry? Antsy? Lonely? Joyous? Buoyant? Energetic?

Lower your focus into your hips. How is your weight distributed at this moment? What is your relationship like with gravity?

Let your focus slide down your left leg. Is it tense, sore, or relaxed? Warm or cold? Does it feel constricted or expansive? How does your left knee feel? How's your left foot? Feet take a lot of abuse. When was the last time you checked in with your feet? Send them a postcard sometime.

Now, slide down your right leg. How do the muscles feel? The bones? Envision the leg in motion. Imagine it under pressure, holding the weight of your body. How does your knee feel? Your right foot?

Now bring your focus back up into your heart and focus on your breathing. How do your lungs feel? Is your breathing shallow or deep? Labored or easy? This comforting breath was here from the moment you were born and will be with you until the moment you ascend. Here, inside you are two loyal friends you can always count on: your breath and your heartbeat.

Back here in your heart, take a moment to expand your awareness and feel your entire body. Has anything changed? Now feel your *relationship* to your body. Has your relationship changed? What are your feelings at this moment toward your body? Are you less resentful? Less impatient? More accepting? Relaxed? Confident? Happy? Has your body communicated any needs you weren't aware of before? Take the cues that you might need more exercise, more sleep, more quiet time to yourself, better nutrition, and so on.

Note the passage of time. How much time has passed since you started this exercise?

Don't be surprised if you cry a lot when you first start practicing these techniques. That's repressed emotion being released. Old feelings of sadness or anger may surface when you take the time to get in touch with your feelings. You may need to allot yourself a considerable amount of time for venting before you try to contact another being. Unless you release your own emotional debris, it will interfere with and be *projected onto* your communications with your animal. Only an empty glass can be filled.

I am about to guide you on a trip inside another living body. You could just as easily explore another human animal, but for now, practice on an animal friend. You're going to go in and have a look around. You will take your consciousness with you in a very small form, so small and mutable in size, you can travel through an animal's bloodstream. Legend has it, the ancient Egyptians trained their temple initiates to travel in their *Ka* (astral body) to see inside the bodies of their patients. After the initiate was "winged," having successfully completed his temple training, he could become a medical seer. His job would be to accompany the doctors in surgery, drive the patient's spirit from his body for the duration of the surgery, and psychically help guide the surgeon's knife. You, too, can travel in your own *Ka* in order to investigate the physical body of your animal friend.

Within your animal's body you may find what I refer to as the Speaker or Higher Self, the part of the animal's soul that can answer your questions in whatever language you speak. You'll ask your questions mentally and hear the voice inside your own head. You will not hear as you hear with your ears; the voice comes from a deeper place. This is subtle energy work that requires ardent concentration and unshakable trust. This ability may not manifest for everyone. You may be limited to the search for pictures and sensations, both physical and emotional, but these, too, are sacred gifts no less important than language.

"But it's only my imagination!" your mental demons will argue. Yes, it is. Your imagination is creating the entire 3-D holographic world you experience every day. Remember Einstein's statement, "Imagination is more important than knowledge." Imagination *leads us* to knowledge. Imagination is the initial creative impulse, the divine predecessor to anything we encounter in the outer world. Imagination is the spark of God within us—God's vision, God's voice, and God's feelings—and because we are created in the image and likeness of God, imagination is *all there is.*

However, you may need to sort out your own fears and projections in order to get accurate information. Objectivity is crucial, so when you're learning, choose an animal with whom you can stay *completely detached.* This first volunteer could be the animal of a friend or neighbor or one of your own who is in good health and brings up none of your emotional issues. Hone your skills when you're not afraid for your animal's health. The more you practice in a relaxed environment when there is no threat of injury or disease, the more likely you will be able to stay objective under pressure in a real emergency. An artist's anatomy book for animals may be of help to you if you are unfamiliar with the skeletal structure and internal organs of animals. You might investigate that first before you explore the following exercise.

Exercise
The Body Scan

The body scan is not a replacement for veterinary care, but a useful complementary tool. Using the body scan *in addition* to traditional Western medicine can help you make more informed choices, and you can use it as a guide when your vet presents several methods of treatment. It may help you discover what forms of herbs or traditional medicine work best for your animal. For the sake of consistency, I am going to write this exercise as it would pertain to a dog or cat, but feel free to substitute "hoof," "wing," or "arm" whenever "paw" is not appropriate.

Sit comfortably near your animal and focus on your breathing. Let your attention slip down into your heart. Relax there and breathe for a few moments, just being grateful for this gift of breath, this one constant in our lives. As long as we are alive, our lungs are at work, peacefully, powerfully inviting more life force into our bodies.

Before you look inside your animal, let's take a quick inventory of your own aches and pains. Where are you tight and stiff? Let your focus glide down your body, down each arm, into your neck, back, pelvis, legs, and feet. Breathe into the tight spots and let the tension go. Make a mental note of what hurts inside your own body so you won't confuse your own issues with those of your friend.

Gently bringing your focus back into your heart, retreat into the sanctuary of the light, and say the Corinthian Prayer (page 52) silently to yourself. Repeat the exercise Contacting Your Spirit Guide (page 65), or any of the other meditations that help you center and ground yourself.

Next, ask your animal for permission to mentally "see" inside his body. You will be entering his physical form with your own spirit, so your animal might not be comfortable with that level of intimacy. If he gets up and leaves the room, go practice your tap dancing, then try this technique again later. Most animals enjoy this communion and welcome the attention. The feeling of merging consciousness is usually very pleasurable. If your friend seems to relax at your suggestion, go ahead and make contact. Picture yourself as a very small being: an elf, a fairy, or a tiny point of light.

Hop out the top of your head and fly over to your friend. Slip into his crown chakra and slide down into his left forepaw.

Feel the shoulder. Feel the knee. Feel the paw, the bottom of the pad. Is it tired? Is it sore? How is the circulation? Is there any obstruction in the leg? How is the alignment? Does the leg function properly?

Now, climb back up the front leg and glide down the other forepaw. Again, you are looking for stiffness, problems with bones, skin, muscles, and circulation. Envision applying pressure to the paw. Envision yourself walking. Envision the rotation of the ankle. Is there pain present, or does the joint move smoothly?

If you feel sensations in your *own* arms and hands, this is *exactly* what you are looking for. Remember that you are two places at once, projecting your attention inside the animal in your very small astral form while simultaneously recording sensation in your own body. If you are investigating known problems, ask for the answers you seek. For instance: "Did this bone not mend correctly?" You might get flashes of pain in your own body or see pictures in your mind when your friend offers up information of his own volition. Your animal may send a message like "The hot concrete burns my feet," showing you a glimpse of the sidewalk with the sensation of stinging in your hands. These messages may or may not be accompanied by language.

Sensations are valid information as well. If you don't get clear images, just keep going. This work takes practice.

If your patient is a cat, see how it would feel to flex your claws. Fabulous, isn't it?

Rise up into the animal's throat. Check his larynx. How does it feel to meow or bark? How does it feel emotionally to speak and not be understood? If your friend is a dog, how does it feel to be silenced? Do you ache to speak? If your friend is a cat, how does it feel to purr?

Descend into his heart. Look around. Is it strong? Is it clear? Does it function properly? Does it feel good? How does it feel emotionally? Are you lonely? Do you, as your animal, need more love? Are you left alone too long? Would you like the company of another animal? If you get hit with a wave of sadness or joy in *your own* body, you know you have successfully made contact.

Slide over into the left lung. How does it look? Is it pink? Is it clear? How does it feel to take a breath? Is it loose or constricted? Move to the right lung. Is it healthy? Is it strong? Do you feel any irritation, burning, or constriction in *your own* chest as you explore your animal's lungs?

Focus your attention on the animal's stomach. Is it upset or at peace? Is he hungry? Ask questions like "What kind of foods are difficult to digest?" Picture the food going into the animal's mouth and wait for a response in *your own* stomach.

"Do you have any allergies?" Envision the animal ingesting or in contact with the suspected culprit, then wait to see if the irritant has any effect on your own body.

"What would help your digestion improve?" Envision the animal eating any herbs or supplements, and wait for a response from your own body. If you have no suggestions of your own, simply focus on the animal's stomach while conjuring the sensation of nausea or pain. After you've sent this message—your animal will understand it as a question—sit in silence until your animal offers something up. You may see a color, feel a texture, smell an aroma, hear a word, or taste something.

If your animal is balking at taking some medication, ask: "Does your medication upset your stomach?" Envision the animal receiving his medication, then wait for a response in your own body. The response to medications may surprise you. Animals often experience the same nausea, thirst, dizziness, anxiety, headaches, lethargy, or other side effects that plague us when we take medications.

If you're trying alternative treatments with your animal, you may also ask, "Do your herbs, vitamins, or acupuncture work?" Visualize yourself as the animal before he started the herbal or physical therapy. How do you feel? Next, visualize yourself as the animal after you've eaten the pills or had acupuncture treatments. Now how do you feel?

Look in the bowel. Does it feel uncomfortable, or is it functioning smoothly?

Use your *own* feelings while you're in here. The thought of a "bad" food or drug may make you cramped, queasy, panicky, or even tearful. The presence of disease may be perceived as a darkness, heaviness, pain, or sadness.

Ask the animal to pull your attention into any organ that is in pain or is not working properly. Feel free to ask general questions like the following:

"Do you think acupuncture or a chiropractic adjustment would help?" With this, envision the procedures performed by a qualified holistic vet.

"Do these help make you feel better or do you want to get better on your own?" Check your body to see what it feels like "before" and "after" the therapy or adjustment.

You may not hear *Yes* or *No* answers, but a feeling of discomfort or a rush of relief is enough information to let you know you're on the right track. If you feel *anything at all,* consider it encouraging feedback.

Rise up into the spinal column and slide along it vertebra by vertebra. How is the alignment? The cartilage? Is it supple and flexible? Is there any pain? You may see inflammation as flashes of red light. If you have a good connection with the animal's inner voice, you may ask: "How did this happen?" Be aware of any emotions such as fear or rushes of adrenaline and any accompanying imagery.

Put your focus on the animal's right hip. Is there any pain or stiffness, or does it function like a well-oiled machine? Envision it in motion. Is it creaky? Glide down the animal's right hind leg. Put your focus in the ankle, the foot, the pads under the foot. How does it feel? Envision it supporting the body's weight. Now how does it feel?

Glide over to the left leg and feel the muscles, the strength of the bones, and the structure. If the animal is in good health, you will feel a burst of vitality in your own left leg. It feels especially thrilling to be in the body of a strong, sinewy horse or a happy, muscular dog. Psychically exploring a healthy animal may feel better than being in your own body.

Concentrate on the animal's tail. (I love this part.) Feel how it connects to the body through the coccyx. Travel down to the tip and see how it feels to have a tail. Check every link. Imagine that you could wag your tail. Does every inch feel good?

Check the skin. Does it feel comfortable, or dry and itchy? The skin is a particularly good gauge of your connection. If your animal suffers from skin allergies, you will find yourself itching and wanting to scratch the spot.

Next, let your attention float up into the animal's head. Go into the sinuses. Ask if he gets headaches. Go into his eyes and check his vision. Investigate his ears. How is his hearing? Is he prone to mites or infections? Go into his mouth and check his teeth. Are they fairly clean? Look for pain and inflammation. Check the alignment of his neck and jaw. If you salivate slightly and want to smile, all is well; but if you feel pressure or pain, or see red or black flashes, you have hit a hot spot.

Go wherever you need to go in the body. Ask. Look. Listen.

When you've finished your psychic spelunking, hop out of the top of the animal's head. Return to your own head and thank your friend for letting you explore his body. Awesome, wasn't it? Now is the time to build a wall of protection. Visualize a cocoon of light around your animal friend and a separate wall of white light encasing you, safely dividing your physical and emotional issues. You need to make a clean departure for the health and happiness of your animal. In order to avoid leaving any of your unconscious negative patterns or residue in your friend's energy field, see him safely protected in a bubble of light. Meanwhile, if *you* pick up *his* aches and pains, aspirin won't help you. If you do feel any unusual sensations or emotions, construct the cocoon of light around yourself and go about your business. With time, the sensations will fade away.

In the course of this exercise, you may have received nothing more than a wordless command. You may simply have had a gut feeling. Watch your urges closely for the next few days. If need be, call your vet and have your friend checked out. Better safe than sorry.

You may also find that the drugs or diet your friend is on is not working. I highly recommend seeking out a veterinarian with knowledge of holistic, alternative, and Eastern medicine. Keep an emergency surgeon nearby, but find a holistic vet even if you have to visit the next state. I don't care if you have to drive a hundred miles. It'll be worth it.

When you feel comfortable with the body-scan technique, feel free to practice on human beings. Make it a game you play with your spouse and children. Teach your children how to perform the body scan on you, and record their findings, as most children have *not yet forgotten* how to use their X-ray vision. The beauty of working on humans is that they can actually *answer you in English.*

※ "Find the Cancer" ※

Chris called to schedule a house call with me to talk to two of his three dogs because he was so excited by the stories his vet had told him about my work. Chris told me that his dalmatian, Savannah, had a cancer called hemangiosarcoma, and that his Australian shepherd, Riley, had immune-related thrombocytopenia. Asked if I would mind having the vet sit in on the reading, I said, "Not at all." Positive energy is always welcome. Expecting the trust and support of both men, I wondered why I had a gnawing feeling in my stomach on the drive over.

From my car on the way to Chris's house, I reached out mentally to make contact. I asked for the spokesanimal to come forth, the one animal who volunteers to speak for the group. I found that Savannah was only too happy to oblige me. I saw in my mind's eye a cheerful dalmatian. I said: "Savannah, right? How are you?"

I've been eating Milk-Bones. Lots of Milk-Bones! Daddy gave me lots of delicious Milk-Bones! she said.

"When?" I asked.

Last night.

"Why are you so excited?" I asked.

Daddy's having a party. Lots of people are coming! We're waiting for a very special woman! A woman that can talk to animals! The party is for me, so that the magic woman can talk to me!

"I'm your woman. Are all the guests waiting for me?"

Yes. The surprise guests answered the question of why I had that nagging feeling in my stomach.

"What can I tell your daddy you need?" I asked.

Yellow! Yellow! she replied. I saw a flash of bright yellow light emanating from her spleen. With this, I heard the word *spleen* distinctly. This esoteric stuff from such a rowdy little pooch really surprised me.

When I arrived at Chris's house, I was disappointed to find a roomful of beer-drinking skeptics. I wasn't sure how I'd manage in a room full of tipsy people, some of them hostile. I decided to persist, and

was thankful to find that the dogs' enthusiasm more than counter-
acted the humans' negativity. When the gorgeous Australian shepherd
bounded into the room, I forgot all the people.

"Hi, Riley! How are you?" I asked.

I'm very lonely! My girlfriend moved away.

"Were you in love?" I asked.

Yes, I'm still in love. My mate is the only dog for me.

"These two dogs don't keep you company?"

Oh yes, I'm fond of them, but I love her, her, her!

"What does she look like?" I wanted to know.

Smaller than me. Elegant. Beautiful.

"Where did she move?" I asked.

*Up north. She says there are lots of pine trees in her neighborhood.
There are hills. The air is cool, very fresh and clean.*

When I repeated this description to Chris, he confirmed that Riley
had a dog friend who moved up north to Oregon. The dog and her
person still come down to Los Angeles periodically to visit. Riley and
I were off to a good start, so Chris and the half-dozen beer drinkers
were flabbergasted. Body scanning Riley to investigate his health, I
found pain in the small intestines and a very upset stomach.

"Is this stomach problem chronic?" I asked.

No, it's just today.

Chris confirmed that Riley didn't have his Pepcid that morning,
although he's supposed to take it every day to counteract the effects of
his nauseating medication. I questioned him:

"Riley, how are you doing on this medicine?"

*I hate it. It's hard on my kidneys. It makes my head feel funny. My
mind races like it's going to explode. It gives me headaches.*

He sent a rushing, speedy sensation, making me feel panicked and
out of control. Fortunately, his vet was sitting right next to me. When
I vented his complaint, he said some dogs react positively on this
medication and instantly feel better, but Riley had bottomed out on it.
Dr. Edwards was thankful to get the confirmation. Riley curled up in
a big snoozy heap at my feet—a big luscious old polka-dotted heap.

*I have painful diarrhea. I think it's from the medication I'm on. I feel
a burning sensation. Tell Daddy that for me.*

"I will," I said. Chris had noticed the diarrhoea.

"What do you need to make you feel better?" I asked.

Iron. I'm very iron-deficient. He relayed the information that this was somehow linked to the platelet problem caused by his illness. (Animals often pick up on the medical lingo their vets use in their presence.)

And tell Father I'm sorry I'm such a burden. When I did, Chris's eyes filled with tears.

"Tell him he's not a burden. Tell him it's my pleasure to take care of him. Tell him I'll do anything to make him feel better." He choked back the sobs.

"He feels so guilty," I said.

So much money. So much time. So much care. Tell him I'm sorry, Riley said.

As I translated for him, Chris urged me, "Tell him that it's not his fault. He was born with it."

Just then Savannah came in to join the conversation. What a character! I was instantly in love with her. I told Chris about the Milk-Bones Savannah had shown me in the car on the way over. Absolutely amazed, he said he had never given the dogs Milk-Bones until last night, when Savannah had eaten several. He admitted he had been bribing the dogs so they wouldn't gossip about him to the animal psychic.

I decided to lighten the mood by using one of my favorite gambits. "Hey, tell me a secret," I asked Savannah.

Last week I stole fried chicken off the table.

I asked her, "Is it okay with you if I tell?"

All right. She chuckled. I told her dad her little secret.

Chris cried, "That was her? She did? That was you? And we blamed Riley!" Chris laughed.

I focused my attention on the adorable dalmatian.

"Hey, Savannah. What's going on?" I asked.

Daddy doesn't love me. I tried not to laugh, because I knew it wasn't true.

"Why do you think that?" I asked.

He got all these other dogs. I was here first. Reeling, Chris confirmed. Now came the moment that the room full of skeptics had been waiting for.

Chris suddenly challenged me. "Savannah just had a cancerous tumor removed. *Find it!* Where will the cancer grow next?" The entire room stopped talking and gave me their undivided attention. I admit I was shaking when I Gestalted Savannah for a body scan. This goading was as nerveracking as a talk show. No matter where I tried to investigate, the little dog navigated my focus back to her upper gums.

"Is the cancer in your upper gums?" I asked her silently.

Not yet, Savannah answered, still holding my consciousness firmly in her mouth, not allowing my focus to budge. Finally I took a deep breath and a big risk. I broke the silence in the room.

"Was the cancer in her gums?" I asked. "She says she's afraid the cancer will reappear in her upper gums." Chris and Dr. Edwards locked eyes. After a moment of stunned silence, he said quietly:

"The cancer was in her gums. We had it removed from her lower gum, and we're afraid it will spread to the top." Instantly Savannah displayed for me her spleen chakra, glowing with a bright yellow light. I couldn't make heads or tails of it, but after all my years of doing this work, I had learned not to ignore even the most baffling details. Reluctantly I told Chris and his vet about the light in Savannah's spleen. Dr. Edwards solved our mystery.

"This cancer was an unprecedented case," he said. "It was one of seven cases in America where this particular type of cancer was not centered *in the spleen.*" My heart skipped a beat. Suddenly Savannah's imagery all made sense. The accuracy of her communication was astonishing! The vet asked if the cancer had spread to her spleen.

Not yet, she answered, blasting me with a brilliant charge of yellow light. I suggested Chris give her all the yellow things he could find, to surround her in yellow.

The vet offered, "We'll put an amber spleen chakra stone on her collar. Ask her if the cancer will spread to her upper gums."

"Savannah, has the cancer spread to your upper gums?"

No, but I'm afraid it will, she answered.

I tried to word my question more carefully:

"Will the cancer spread to your upper gums?"

No, but I'm afraid it will. I got the distinct impression that this was not Savannah's fear, but her father's. She showed me her father checking inside her mouth, obsessed. Sharing her concerns, I explained she didn't feel pain, only fear, and I asked Chris how often he was checking her mouth.

Caught and embarrassed, Chris admitted he was compulsively checking her mouth five times a day, *expecting* the cancer to manifest.

Begging him to just give her a week off, I urged him to praise her every day. "I'm so *proud* that you healed yourself! The cancer is *never* coming back! You are perfectly healthy, and you will *never* get sick again!" I tried to convey to him the concept that the message he was sending was one of *looking for cancer*, not *supporting her recovery*. Finally making the connection between the two dogs with rare blood diseases and their human father, I asked Chris what on earth was wrong with his blood. He confided he was deathly anemic. We talked for a few minutes about "osmosis illness," and the repercussions of letting your emotional debris spill over onto your animals.

I wanted to cheer up Chris and Savannah and get their minds off her illness. "Savannah, tell me a secret. I want to tell your dad something funny," I said to her.

Tell him I stole a pillow, a pouch filled with tobacco. When I translated, Chris roared with laughter.

"Oh, my God! My tobacco! My pipe! So that's what happened to my pipe!" Chris dried his eyes, and Savannah let me end the evening with laughter, not tears.

A year later Savannah succumbed to the cancer, but she was my champion. The roudy dog had given me a crash course in Gestalt, and never before or since have I been blessed by such a master teacher.

⬚ Janet Jackson and the BBs ⬚

The biggest blunder I ever made was by asking a cat if she *wanted* to go to the vet. My friend Tony called me early in the morning, hysterical about his cat, Janet Jackson. She was suddenly listless and seemed very sick. Now, Tony could talk the balls off a bull and was a mother hen to his brood of eight cats. Seeing how it was first thing in the morning—my brain was still soft-serve as I nursed my first cup of chicory coffee—I thought Tony was overreacting. Dismissively, I asked the cat, "Do you want to go to the vet?" Big mistake.

Janet said *No!* and informed me that she hated her vet, the man couldn't help her, and she would heal on her own.

"What's wrong with you?" I asked.

I don't know, she said.

"What happened?" I asked.

I'm not sure, she said. Janet didn't seem overly concerned about her condition, so I didn't feel the need to Gestalt her. I only *spoke* to her about what had happened. She said she took a fall from a high wall by a rooftop, but she was going to be fine. She showed me big swarthy workmen carrying things in and out of a vacant apartment. I saw her fleeing from the men and landing on the asphalt below.

"Fall?" I asked.

Yes, she said. When I shared this information with Tony, he confirmed he knew the apartment filled with painters (on the third story of his building), and he identified the wall. Janet assured me she had no broken bones, so we left it at that.

That night, when Janet was worse, not better, I mentally checked in with her to ask if she wanted to go to the vet.

That man can't help me. I'll heal on my own. I only need to sleep, she said. After this, I didn't hear from Tony for a few days, so I hoped for the best, even though I kept receiving a sick, plummeting feeling from his cat. When she sent me the word *poisoning,* I called Tony to check in. Even by this time, I had neglected to give the cat a really thorough Gestalt.

Tony repeated the horror story of what he and his brave little cat had endured. The day after we spoke, he had taken Janet to the vet. Several hundred dollars later, Tony took home a dying cat. After many expensive tests and X-rays, the vet found a BB pellet half-buried in the skin near the cat's stomach. The vet removed this single BB but, having found nothing else, the vet just assumed the cat was recovering from the fall. (He deduced that Janet had taken a fall after the pellet hit her.)

This was the first piece of information Janet had been accurate about—that vet couldn't help her very much. Panicked, Tony took her to a different vet who X-rayed her again to find another BB the first vet had missed. This second BB was lodged in the cat's kidney, causing toxins to leak out into her body. The vet performed emergency surgery to remove the BB. This was the other piece of information Janet pinpointed: the word *poisoning* was an accurate description of her ailment as the puncture in the kidney was literally poisoning her.

A few weeks later, Tony located the teenage boy with a BB gun, who was shooting cats for fun. (The little idiot was the son of one of the workmen.)

This case was the most unforgettable mistake I ever made. The information the cat gave me was accurate, but my line of questioning was all wrong. If I had Gestalted her first, would I have found those tiny BBs? I'll never know for sure. Could I have saved Janet days of needless suffering? What if Tony had taken my advice and not taken the cat to the vet? Janet surely would have died and I would have been responsible.

Did I ask the wrong questions? What cats *want* to go to the vet? On the other hand, animals *can* tell you if a doctor is necessary or if a particular vet can help. Tony's cat was right about that male vet.

Asked the initial question "What's wrong with you?" Janet did not mention her kidney. If she had known the piece of metal was there, she probably would have told me about it. Her shock was so great, she didn't know how to explain her experience to me. Janet taught me one of the most crucial lessons I have ever learned: Gestalt! Gestalt! Gestalt! Don't just *ask. Look!*

▦ Dream a Little Dream of Me ▦

People often ask me if their animals can describe their dreams to me. Of course they can. They can describe their dreams to you, too, if you practice your Gestalt while your animal is asleep. Nothing throws off a bad mood quicker than entering an animal's dream. If you sneak up to your animal while he's sound asleep and gently rest your head on his back or stomach, you may catch a snatch of filmstrip, just before he wakes. Most cats dream of hunting. You can tell by the way their paws and mouths twitch ferociously while they dream. I'm sure their most brag-worthy feline safaris take place in their sleep. When Mr. Jones is out like a light and I creep up to rest my forehead on his luxurious back, oddly enough, I usually see the same scene: he lies at the water's edge, peeking through tall rushes and exotic grasses, spying on great white birds—too big to eat, the size of ducks or swans. They are to him blissfully beautiful. Sometimes he prowls among the birds on this overgrown shore. Sometimes he's soaring in the air, flying with the great white birds—seagulls, perhaps. Now, what makes this funny is the fact that Mr. Jones is part Maine Coon, the only breed known as "fisher cats." They were once seafaring cats, considered good luck to have aboard ships back in New England when America was founded. Maine Coons are known to like the water. If it's genetic, I don't know, but Mr. Jones, like J.R.R. Tolkien's elves, dreams of the sea.

▪ My Day at the Zoo ▪

If you have a decent local zoo that doesn't break your heart, you might want to pay your respects and try the following exercise. If you're one of those people who is too sympathetic to tolerate the zoo, just skip this exercise and go on to the next chapter. I admit, I have to turn down my clairsentience and rely more on clairvoyance so the animals I visit don't drown me in a deluge of boredom and frustration. No matter how we feel about them, zoos are not going to go away. They are becoming the last refuge for many animals threatened by extinction. Rather than boycott the zoos, as almost all my friends do, why don't we give them financial support instead and build the animals the kinds of sanctuaries they deserve?

I began drawing last summer at the Los Angeles Zoo. Animals love to be drawn. They find the exchange of energy to be invigorating, but like most human models, they sometimes find it difficult to hold still for long periods of time. Speaking to the animals as I drew them, asking them to take different poses for me, I was quite surprised by which animals were the most responsive to my communication. I assumed that the apes and monkeys would be the easiest to communicate with, as well as the large cats because of my rapport with felines, but this was not the case. With no competition, the most receptive of the animals was the rhinoceros. Not only did he march out directly in front of me, taking a long pose, he grilled me as I drew him, asking, *Did you draw my feet yet? My feet are extraordinary.* He even turned around at my request and modeled his other profile.

The second biggest hams on my assignment list were the elephants. The tender and sensitive giants respond remarkably well to psychic requests. This may be the reason they have often ended up in circuses. If you ask them to do something, they are usually only too happy to comply. Two elephants walked over and posed for me, in joyous regal poses. They recognized my mission immediately. Classes of artists are a regular appearance at the Los Angeles Zoo, although I didn't realize this at the time.

I was surprised to find the coyote to be a wonderful communicator, and I admit I am absolutely smitten with the polar bear, but my favorite conversation took place with a tiny Capuchin monkey, who flew to the front of his cage when I sent him a thought. His wife was anxiously pacing back and forth on a branch behind him. You may not believe me, dear reader, when I tell you how clear our communication was. When I sent the thought "Will you come down here and talk to me?" he asked, *Are you an animal communicator?*

"Yes!" I replied. I'd never had an animal ask me flat out like that before. Evidently I was not the first animal communicator he had ever met. He grabbed the bars with both hands and poked his head between them to get a closer look at me.

You mean you can really hear me? he asked. He wanted to make sure. It was almost too good to be true.

"Yes!" I answered. He hopped up and down, pointed at me, turned around, and yelled at his mate, *Hey, honey, you've got to see this! There's an* animal communicator *down here!*

I heard her haughty answer, *I'm busy! I've got better things to do! Tell her to go away.*

I'm sure you've seen cartoons of the monkeys at the zoo watching us as if *we* were the sideshow attraction. That's exactly how I felt when one monkey was gawking at me while another wouldn't give me the time of day. But I had a wonderful conversation with the little guy, and I will share my questions with you as a practice for when you go to the zoo. Take your Paws and Listen notebook with you to document your answers, and try to locate an animalkeeper to validate your information. If you cannot get direct confirmation from a zoo attendant, ask the following questions about the animal's lifestyle and habitat. At the end of the day, look for the answers in an encyclopedia, library book, or Web search.

Exercise Communication
Your Day at the Zoo

Have your Paws and Listen notebook handy. Take a deep breath. Relax on the exhale. Steady yourself. If you're standing, become aware of your feet and how your weight connects you to the earth. Lower your awareness into your chest. Quiet your mind and, for a few minutes, focus only on your breath. Give your mind permission to let go. Feel your chest rise and fall, peacefully, quietly. When you're ready, gently move your attention into your heart. Feel a light in your heart begin to spark and awaken. Your heart begins to glow and expand, glowing brighter and brighter until a tendril of light reaches out of your heart toward your chosen animal. The beam of soft light forms a bridge between your heart and the heart of the animal. Reach out with love. Think the thought "I love you. I love you so much. I'm so grateful that you exist." Let your awareness slip out of your body and cross the bridge.

You'll know you've made contact when you feel a lightness that almost sweeps you off your feet. You might feel warm or dizzy, or feel your stomach drop. You may experience a profound peacefulness and lack of worry. You may see a wash of white light or feel your eyes mist over with tears. When the gratitude and love engulf you, you'll know you've successfully built the bridge. When you're ready, send these images and words:

1. Would you like to talk to me?
2. What's your favorite food?
3. What's the name (or names) of the human(s) who feeds you?
4. What does this human look like?
5. What is your scheduled dinnertime?
6. What would you change about your food?
7. Do you have a mate?
8. Do you have children?
9. Were you born in the zoo?
10. If not, tell me about your arrival at the zoo.
11. Can you tell me about your native habitat?
12. Do you have any questions about human beings?
13. Can I help you understand your living situation?
14. Is there anything you'd like to ask me?

Remember the twofold process: point-of-view Ping-Pong:

First see the animal giving you an answer from the outside through your perspective.

Then, see the animal giving you an answer through his perspective. If your chosen animal is hiding inside, sending the thought of him walking into view might bring him out of his hiding place. To coax an animal nearer, send the thought of him approaching you. If he's sleeping, your thought might even wake him up. Remember, though, that the animal does not have to be awake to converse with you. It is not the waking mind that you are contacting.

Stay inside your body, and in your moments of silence, quietly notice any changes in your own body: buzzing, tingling, heat, strength, melancholy, aches, pleasant sensations. Even if you don't hear words or see concrete images, you know you've made contact if your attempted body scan evokes sensations or emotions you've never felt before. If you feel appendages that are not your own, you've made a successful contact.

Gestalt the elephants. If you feel an almost orgasmic sensitivity in your nose, you know you've achieved mobility of consciousness.

Gestalt the kangaroos. Do you feel a delicate dexterity in your hands but a powerful burst of strength in your legs? What does it feel like to sit back on a pedestal tail?

Gestalt the sea lions. How much fun is it to swim? If you feel the heavenly caress of water slipping past your fins, and it feels *more divine* than any water you've ever felt, you're in a sea lion's body.

Gestalt the monkeys. How does it feel to hang from your magnificent tail?

Gestalt the flamingos. What do your legs feel like?

Gestalt the alligators. What do your teeth feel like?

Gestalt the tigers. Have you ever felt so resplendent? Have you ever experienced such *deep states of grace*?

Gestalt the gorillas. Are they really so different from us after all? Jot down your answers so you don't dismiss these transmissions later.

▓ How Did You Do? ▓

First of all, don't be disappointed if the images you get about the animals' food come back a bit muddled. They may be eating compressed vegetable sticks or bowls of grain or mush that you can't identify. Take the color and the texture of the food as a viable answer. You may even Gestalt them and get the taste.

Second, don't be surprised if someone asks you, *Can you get me out of here?* They may even follow this up with the heart-wrenching reasoning *If you can hear me, why can't you get me out of here?* Answer with pictures of their native habitats being encroached upon. Tell them that by keeping them in the zoo, we are saving them from extinction. Tell them that you're sorry their living quarters are so small (you will hear an onslaught of complaints), but that humans love them and treasure them and zoos are the only places where we can ensure their survival.

I know these communications are advanced. To envision a desert or a rain forest on the other side of the world where you've never been might take a vivid imagination on your part. Send them a psychic sandwich.

⚫ The Why-You're-in-the-Zoo Sandwich ⚫

1. Send the imagery of the animal getting fed, being safe and well cared for, albeit a bit cramped.
2. Send images of poaching, trees disappearing, and animals starving, or whatever is at stake for that animal's survival. (I know it's grim, but the animals have a right to know the truth.)
3. Return to the images of the animal flourishing in captivity.

As always, give information. Give, give, give information! Answer their questions as well as you possibly can. They are as curious about us as we are about them, if not more so!

When you've finished your conversation, thank the animal profusely for taking the time to talk to you. They so appreciate being appreciated. They may ask you to come back and visit again, and if they do, make sure to keep your promise. There is no greater honor than to be befriended by a wild animal.

7

Radar:
Tracking Through Gestalt

*For a person has not only perceptions but a will
to perceive, not only a capacity to observe the
world but a capacity to alter his or her observa-
tion of it—which, in the end, is the capacity to
alter the world itself. Those people who recognize
that imagination is reality's master, we call* sages,
and those who act upon it, we call artists.

—Tom Robbins, *Skinny Legs and All*

⊠ Flight School ⊠

In mentally tracking an animal, you will use both Gestalt and
remote viewing, which I'll explain shortly. These are skills, not
gifts. They are not talents but activities we *engage in*. I dare-

say, both Gestalt and remote viewing are not only *learnable skills* but *arts*. To learn to travel out of body at will may take a lifetime of diligent practice. Allot at least the amount of time equivalent to completing aeronautical flight school at your local airport. How many hours of flight school do you need to attain your pilot's license for a jet airplane?

On the other hand, you may surprise yourself. These techniques have been taught for thousands of years in the priesthoods of Egypt, China, Tibet, Brazil, Ireland, and Greece, to name a few. The American Indians, the Africans, the Aborigines, the Inuit, and the indigenous people of Mexico and Central America are no strangers to remote viewing. In *Jambalaya* (HarperSanFrancisco), Luisah Teish shares a colorful account of alchemical skills passed down to her through her African Yoruba ancestry. In *Women Who Run with the Wolves* (Ballantine), Dr. Clarissa Pinkola Estes weaves a rich tapestry of myths and practical magic in her Hispanic heritage as well as many other cultures around the world. If you are aching to investigate out-of-body techniques taught by the ancient Egyptians, pick up Joan Grant's *Winged Pharaoh* (Berkley Medallion). We've inherited legends of tracking and medical Gestalt from every culture on earth, in every recorded era of time, and rumors of those unrecorded, including the Neanderthal cavemen. The Bible is filled with Christian and Jewish seers who saw visions of people and events occurring outside the range of their five senses. Most of the Christian saints were known to have taken a walk on the psychic wild side. Let's demystify this out-of-body business.

Tracking is nothing more than an exercise in concentration. When we track, we enter the body of the lost animal *and* travel in our own astral bodies simultaneously. We'll use point-of-view (POV) Ping-Pong for the most accurate details. (That is, we alternately look out the eyes of the animal *and* visualize them from the outside.)

I discovered remote viewing by accident. Until I tracked a runaway cat after the devastating Los Angeles earthquake, I thought the only method of tracking was through Gestalt, seeing the world from an animal's perspective. This illusion was shattered when I found myself watching a particular yellow-striped cat from the outside, my awareness hovering across the street from where he crouched under a semi-collapsed apartment building. Afterward the cat's person told me the cat was *blind!* Clearly, whatever I was doing was *not seeing out of his eyes.* That was my wake-up call. I realized I had been doing what I now call remote viewing all along.

If I can do it, you can do it, too. Start right now with your own animal and practice before there is any need. If you don't know where your animal is right now, you may not be able to get confirmation on all your questions, but you will get at least partial validation. Sitting with your Paws and Listen notebook handy but far from your animal, ask your animal what he sees from his own point of view and what he feels under his feet. Allow yourself to "guess." Allow yourself to "be wrong." Just let your imagination wander. Jot down the answers to your questions, then go find your animal. Was he where he indicated?

Exercise
Tracking

If you have a dog, let one of your friends take her out for a ride. Tell your friend to make the excursion special so you will have unique things to identify: a visit with human friends, unusual landmarks, special food, and unfamiliar terrain. After or during the excursion, jot down the answers to these questions:

> What do you see?
>
> What do you smell?
>
> What humans do you see?
>
> Whom are you with? What color is her hair?
>
> Where are you going?
>
> Are you having fun?
>
> Is the window down?
>
> Did you drive far from home?
>
> What did the ground look like outside?

Did you have anything special to eat?

Did you play any special games? With what toys?

What kind of trees did you smell outside?

When your friend returns with your dog, let her prompt some questions based on what she did with your dog. Show her your notes and confer.

If you have a cat: At a designated time, have a friend come over while you're not home to visit your cat. Ask your friend to bring unusual treats, special toys, and specific music. At the appointed time, check in with your cat and jot down the answers to these questions.

Who is visiting you right now?

Do you like him?

What do you see?

Did he bring you something special to eat?

Did he bring you something special to play with?

What kinds of sounds do you hear?

☰ Tracking a Missing Animal ☰

The first question you ask a missing animal is "Are you injured?" Before you track for whereabouts, body scan for physical injury. The most common form of death for a dog or cat is to be hit by a car. If you ask "Did you get hit?" or, if it's nighttime, "Headlights?" you might be able to determine if they're on the Other Side. Even if they are, you may still succeed in hearing their story. The divine essence never dies. You may progress with questions like these:

What do you see?

What was the last thing you saw when you left the house?

Which door did you exit? Backyard or front?

Did you turn left or right?

At this point, do a POV Ping-Pong. Pull up into aerial remote viewing by focusing your attention on the chakra floating about a foot above your body. I call it the moon chakra because it orbits just above our heads. A complete meditation on the activation of this chakra will follow in the next chapter. For now, use the moon chakra to exit your body and pull up into a bird's-eye view.

Can you detect north? South? East or west? You are floating midair above your neighborhood. From this point of view, ask the animal to retrace his steps. You may see a trail unfold beneath you (out the door, over a red brick fence, one block north, turn right, cross a big street, and so forth). Use your own knowledge of your neighborhood, such as landmarks, to structure your questions.

Now do another POV Ping-Pong: Reenter the body of the animal. Ask him to retrace his steps, using sense memory to show you his path. Ask:

> What did you see? (Ivy, a swimming pool . . .)
>
> What did you feel? (Cold brick under his paws as he climbed the fence, fear as he crossed the street . . .)
>
> What did you smell? (Gasoline, exhaust . . .)
>
> What's on the ground? (Pine needles, sycamore balls, children's toys, cold sidewalk . . .) Is it concrete or grass?
>
> Did you see other animals? (Ducks, dogs, birds, insects . . .)

As we track, the questions we ask are imperative. Again, if you don't get anything, don't despair. Start sending images out *to be corrected*. If the animal accepts the image, the picture in your mind will get fortified and the image will seem to grow in size, weight, or clarity. If you're asking for a smell, a *Yes* answer will give you a strong waft of the aroma. If the image is rejected, it will evaporate into space, fading into nothingness. A *Yes* answer may also generate an excited flutter in your stomach or a peaceful feeling of certainty. *Yes* answers provoke in me a feeling of acceleration, of excitement and extreme speed. The *Yes* answers speed along faster and faster like an avalanche. If you feel like you're riding a very fast roller coaster, you know you're cookin' with fire and you have successfully "tuned in."

Let's continue:

> Do you see flowers? What color are they?
>
> What shapes are the leaves on the ground?

How many dark nights have passed since you left home?

Are you hungry? Thirsty? Have you found food?

Are you alone?

Are there other humans around you?

Are you sheltered at night?

What are you hiding under?

What can you see right now?

Can you show me anything unusual? (Look for landmarks: street signs, house numbers, flagpoles, schools, child-crossing signs, yard ornaments, boats parked at the curb, bridges, drainage ditches, and so on.)

Are you trapped in someone else's territory?

Do you know how to get home?

Why haven't you returned home?

Why did you leave?

Are you not happy in your home?

I rarely track professionally anymore because it is too taxing on my emotional energy and I often can't justify returning an animal to a place where he doesn't want to be. House cats may get cornered in another cat's territory or trapped in a garage or attic; happy animals rarely run away (except for earthquakes or on the Fourth of July, which causes pandemonium all over America). The vast majority of people who've called me over the years to track their dogs did not have happy dogs. The problems are pretty common: leaving dogs cooped up for eight hours a day, then failing to walk them often enough or far enough, will make them want to run for their lives. Dogs were designed to run. Nothing is more imperative to the health and well-being of a dog than exercise.

The other primary reason dogs take off is that they're lonely. Dogs are pack animals and prefer to be kept in groups of two or more. A single dog is usually a lonely dog. You know how all the dogs in the neighborhood bark at each other incessantly? They get to know each other by their voices alone. They want to finally meet those dogs face-to-face whom they've been talking to through the fence for so many months or years. When they get the opportunity, they either run away to find other dogs or are spirited away by other lonely dogs.

Cats who are locked in usually want out. Cats who are locked in at night (don't misunderstand; mine are, too) might jump at the chance to escape the house and spend a few nights out under the moonlight and stars, flirting with the night animals. I've even had to do a bit of bargaining with Mr. Jones to give him a later curfew once a month when the moon is full. A cat needs moonlight like a fish needs water. Cats are nocturnal. Despite the threat of coyotes, nothing I say or do is ever going to change that.

Wandering cats usually return home once the fight is over, construction workers have left, the deliveryman is gone, or whatever caused the disturbance has dissipated. My rule of thumb is "Don't panic for three days." If you're well versed in these tracking techniques, go ahead and track for your own peace of mind. Sometimes cats show up three weeks later, unscathed, mysteriously smug, and suspiciously fat. On the other hand, they have a right to move out if they want to. (Years ago I lost my best cat, Tucker, to the two teenage girls across the street. The smart-aleck simply left me for two younger women. I was heartbroken, but I respected his decision. I had adopted a new cat off the street whom I thought was Tucker's girlfriend, only to find it was a boy, and oh, what a mess. . . .) Most urban cats' lives are pretty dull, so I think they're entitled to an occasional excursion. "But the cars! The cars!" you may object. I know. A bird in a cage is no bird. Birds were meant to fly, dogs to run, cats to see the world if they so choose.

Practice tracking all the time, every day, when there is no threat or fear present. Shut your eyes right now and ask yourself, "Where is my animal?" Locate her through remote viewing. See her from the outside. Now, do a POV Ping-Pong. Let yourself see out her eyes. Is she standing up or lying down? Is she awake or asleep? Is there grass under her body or dirt? Wooden floor or tile? Carpet or bedspread? What color is it? What room is she in? Now, go find her and see if she's where you thought she was. If you practice this technique every day, in time you will master tracking.

※ Affirmations for Clearing Negativity ※

In order to travel outside your body, you must be able to let go of your belief in space and time. You need to be acutely in the moment. Here are some affirmations to help clear your mind.

My job is to let go of the past.

All doubts, all failures, all disappointments, are in the past.

The present moment is crystal clear.

The present moment is teeming with infinite possibilities.

Anything could happen right now. The present is not predetermined.

The future is free to change. I am completely free in the present moment.

I am free of all limitation. All limiting thought patterns are in the past.

I gladly release any negative patterns that repeat themselves and cause me pain.

There is nothing in the present moment except silence and light.

There is nothing inside me but the gentle, tender hum of life.

I acknowledge that within me is the answer to my every question.

I delight in awakening to my infinite potential.

I can go over and beyond any success I've ever achieved before.

I move from glory to glory as my third eye opens and I am filled with insight.

※ Remote Viewing: The Big Picture ※

We tune in to the divine whole first, then direct our attention to one of the other parts of the whole. This process is not "from you to an animal." The process is "from you to God/Goddess to an animal." We ricochet off God/Goddess. Divine intelligence is your go-between.

Without the awareness of the macrocosmic whole, of being only a small piece of a larger divine entity, we cannot surrender our identities long enough to leave them behind even for an instant, which is exactly what we must do in order to connect with the mind of another being.

In this state of grace, there is a sensation of motion, of flight. We are only cells in the body of the divine, just as the cells in your body have their own identities. Those cells can send an SOS to your brain. A cut finger tells the brain of its pain, which immediately sends assistance to heal the break in the skin. We get this kind of help, too, when we pray. Our thoughts reach out to the divine and because we are connected through a cosmic nervous system, our prayers hit their mark. Without the awareness of the divine body around us, we can't maneuver our consciousness within that body. In order to navigate our consciousness out of our own body and ego, we need to develop our awareness of the earth around us.

Exercise
Meditation: Connecting with the Earth to Discover Implicate Order

You see, the beauty of science is that it's basically based on sharing. Now, the more carefully and clearly I can define something—and the reason we want to quantify is not because we're interested in quantities, but because then you can communicate and share much more clearly than if you can't have quantities. So all of science is based on the notion of sharing, and we need to define things. If some Buddhist tells me, "I've just had a high experience," or "I've just seen the light," and I don't know what the hell he's talking about, then I can't share that. But if he gets me to have the same experience, that begins to be science.

—Dr. Karl Pribram

Sit outside directly on the ground. If you don't have a yard, go to a park. The earth must be directly under you, supporting you. The earth reaches up into you. You reach down into her, feeling like a green, growing plant. The smells of the earth, the sounds of wind in the trees, fill you. Your mind goes green. Your thoughts are swept away by the openness of the sky, the headiness of oxygen. Surrender to gravity. Think of the magnitude of the earth—the vastness of the planet. Give in to the awe, the terror, of being so small, like an ant or one fragile blade of grass barely poking up from the earth. This is a milestone—to accept our vulnerability, to feel for a few moments our own seeming insignificance. You are only a tiny animal on a huge spinning ball in space, outnumbered by billions of other tiny animals. *Give in* to the fear. This is not your *destination*. It is *the beginning*. The awareness of our minuscule size is a necessary discomfort. It helps us appreciate the size of the living, breathing planet. Humility is the doorway. As in *Alice in Wonderland,* where Alice gets small before she can get big, we learn to get small. It's the first step.

You will shrink your ego and identity to duck under the door to the cosmos. Your body is like a tiny blade of grass glued to the massive earth's surface by gravity, but you are not your body. When you feel so small that your body disintegrates into the earth, disappearing completely, your ego will surrender and something inside you will pop.

Suddenly you've crossed the threshold. You can travel out of body. You've left the confines of your own mind, free to travel at will in the mind of God, of the world, of the universe. Now you can commune with the whole and ask questions directly. Some answers may be bypassed or filtered out. There are events in our future we are not allowed to know, but the amount of information available here will astonish you. Here you can dialogue directly with God/Goddess. The *you* that you know will become a lucid, bodiless interrogator. Once we cross the threshold, we can retrieve enough of our conscious minds to keep it with us as we seek out other living beings.

▩ So Much Talk of Trance ▩

I do my Connecting with the Earth meditation outside every morning to center myself. This exercise trains the mind until this process becomes ingrained in you. Without practice, few people can silence their minds even for an instant, and fewer still have a consciousness of being a cell in the body of God. Not until you've incorporated these paradigm shifts will you be able to travel freely in your Higher Self, out of body.

My office is my couch, where I put up my feet, lounging in flannel pajamas, surrounded with half-empty take-out containers and dirty teacups. Piled high with gray tabby cats, I silently go to work. With a notebook and a good pen on my knees, juggling photos of show horses and gorillas above the sleeping cats, I let myself slip into my Higher Self. It takes no more effort than reaching out to flip the dial on a radio. With lists of questions sent by the animals' owners dangling above the photos and cats, I ask the questions with my conscious mind, but I listen with my Higher Self. It's all in a day's work.

Of course, not all my attempts at tracking have been glowing successes. Most of the animals I've tracked have been killed and are on the Other Side, but I'd like to share with you two of my favorite stories. The cat in the woodpile gave me the most immediate gratification because all three of us involved—the cat, her owner, and I—were telepathing successfully in unison.

▓ The Cat in the Woodpile ▓

Evelyn, a beautiful Irish woman, came to me disheveled and tearstained. She worked long hours as a nurse, but in her off-hours her greatest joy was spending time with her house cat, Tabitha. Tabitha was a house cat by choice and never ventured outside. However, spooked by workmen bringing in a new couch, she'd run out the door and had been missing for three days. Because Tabitha had never been outside before, Evelyn was desperate.

The first piece of advice I gave her was a logical one, not a psychic one, and it is the first suggestion I offer to everyone who is missing a cat. The best time to hunt for a lost cat is in the wee hours of the morning around two or three A.M. If the cat is scared and disoriented, he will find a place to hide during the waking hours, and he will be very reluctant to come out until he thinks the coast is clear. Often, cats get cornered in another cat's territory, and coming out into the open would precipitate a fight. This is especially true of house cats, who have no territory of their own. When they escape, they always find themselves in someone else's territory, because one cat or another sanctions off every block. Think gangs.

Studying the photograph of the sweet calico cat, I was able to contact Tabitha instantly, to ask her favorite food. She said, *Tuna.* Her voice was weak and tentative. I knew she was alive and in trouble.

"Are you hurt?" I asked as I scanned her body for injuries.

No, just sore, she said. Tabitha showed me her back and hips.

"Fight?" I asked.

Yes, she said. I saw two flashes of fur as a big dark cat chased her down the street. My chest constricted with fear.

"Can you show me what you see?" I asked. Suddenly my perspective changed. I saw what was in her line of sight: a blue-and-white house across the alley.

She said she had passed big yellow children's toys over the fence when she ran to find a hiding place. She couldn't tell me what they were. She didn't know for sure. Asked to send the pictures, she conjured a huge confusing construct of green metal poles and a yellow vehicle that resembled a miniature car. She didn't know what to call them. I deduced the toys were a swing set and a yellow "Big Wheel" toddler bicycle.

"Reveal yourself from the outside," I requested. Immediately my perspective changed: I saw an iron grate she had climbed through. Tabitha was now crouching down under a house. Above the grate was a staircase and beneath that, a big pile of firewood. She was using the firewood for cover.

"Can you come home?" I asked her.

No, I can't come out. He won't let me. She was terrified of *him.*

"What does he look like?" She sent me the image of a big black tomcat.

Can Mother come get me? I'm hungry and I want to go home.

"I will try to bring Mother to you, but you must stay there all day," I said. Tabitha agreed. When I shared the message with Evelyn, her bloodshot eyes brightened.

"I think I know the house! It's behind mine, a few houses down! And I think I've even seen that black cat!" I asked Tabitha what direction she went when she ran out: *Around the back of the house.*

Evelyn lamented that she had to go to work and her shift at the hospital would run until ten o'clock that night, which meant she couldn't get home and look for Tabitha until around eleven. I told Tabitha her mother would be in the alley at eleven o'clock that night and she must find the courage to run out to meet her. I suggested Evelyn take an open can of tuna with her so that Tabitha might pick up the scent.

The next morning Evelyn came back to me even more miserable and sleep-deprived than the day before. Her shift had run late at the hospital, and by the time she got home, she had missed the eleven o'clock meeting time. She couldn't find the house with the woodpile, but she did find the Big Wheel, and discovered that the swing set was a jungle gym. She spent over an hour walking up and down the alley calling for Tabitha, but the cat didn't come out. My heart fell. I began to grow discouraged.

Fortunately I was able to reconnect with Tabitha. She said she couldn't wait for Evelyn past eleven and that *he* chased her away. I contacted the bully cat to tell him to leave her alone, but he was very proud and defiant.

She doesn't belong in my yard, he said. Agreeing with him, I promised she would leave his yard that very night if he would let her be. He had nothing more to say about the matter and signed off in a huff. I asked Evelyn:

"What is a safe meeting time for you? What can we realistically say is the best meeting time? Let's make it really late. That's the only time she'll feel safe enough to come out."

"Twelve-thirty," she replied. We decided on it. I delivered the message to Tabitha that her mother would be in the alley at twelve-thirty sharp and her job was to run out from under the house to meet her, meowing at the top of her lungs.

The next day Evelyn came back to me as peaceful as an angel. With tears of relief shining in her eyes, she said she had been calling for Tabitha in front of the *wrong* blue-and-white house. As she walked down the alley at twelve-thirty, she discovered a *different* blue-and-white house, on the other side of the house with the children's toys, this one with a pile of firewood behind it. When Evelyn called for Tabitha, tuna in tow, Tabitha bolted from behind the woodpile, running toward her mother, chirping hysterically all the while: "Mow,

mow, mow, mow . . ."

Evelyn scooped Tabitha up into her arms and took her home. It was a glorious homecoming and one of the most satisfying cases of tracking I've ever experienced.

◾ The Wanderer ◾

Caitlin called me in desperation when her cat had been missing for over a week. The circumstances felt so dire to me that I agreed to make a house call rather than wait for her to send me a picture. I drove to the woman's home way out in the Orange County suburbs to look at photos of a big fat orange cat named Sal. He was a loud-mouthed, needle-nosed redhead—a lady-killer, an indoor-outdoor man who roamed the neighborhood freely looking for love (and food). Sal was a wanderer. Over the many years that he and Caitlin had been together, he had disappeared for a few days at a time, but never for this long. His mother was at her wit's end. Sal was the love of her life.

Caitlin was a charismatic woman with a warm, wide-open face, now tearstained and strained from lack of sleep. The pressure was on. These emotionally charged situations make for very stressful readings. It's not always easy to stay out of the client's fear and see the answers clearly. The dense vibrations that emanate from a panicked client can cast a veil between me and the truth of the situation.

I perched tensely on her cat-hair–covered couch, anxiously milling through stacks of cat photos, looking for the picture of Sal that held the most energy. Focusing on one that captured my attention, I settled in to make contact.

I asked him the usual preliminary question, "What's your favorite food?," before I prepared to ask him the only question that really mattered, which was, "Where the hell are you?"

Pork chops and bacon. The words came in like gangbusters. This was a favorite food I'd never heard before. If this answer was correct, I knew I had Sal on the line. When his mother confirmed, my heart flew up into my throat. I was getting a feel for Sal: If Sal were human, he would be a blue-collar bowling champion, a Fred Flintstone kind of guy who liked to barbecue in his backyard in the suburbs of New Jersey. Laughing, I shared this with Caitlin, who was quick to verify Sal's personality was coming in loud and clear. She lightened up a little, so I tried to relax into the connection. I got the distinct impression that Sal was still in the world of the living, because he was ravenously hungry; this is never a complaint that comes from the Other Side.

I pretended to be casual as I worked my way around the high-voltage question. After a few more mundane questions, I asked him what he could see. Gestalting him, I looked out his eyes, but all I could make out in the shadowy darkness was some clutter. I was worried sick that Sal had gotten himself trapped somewhere he shouldn't be, like someone's attic or garage. I poked around for clues:

"Sal, what do you smell?"

Dust. Car. I'm very thirsty. Afraid he was dying, I tried not to panic.

"Sal, can you tell me what's under your feet?"

I don't know, he answered. Eventually I worked my way up to the really loaded question.

"Sal, do you know where you are?"

I don't know. It's dark. I'm very thirsty. Can you get me some water?

"You've got to help show me where you are so that we can come get you. Then you'll get plenty of water, okay?"

I'll try. I'm getting very weak. I need to eat, and I'm so thirsty. When I Gestalted his body, I felt his life force waning. It's difficult to telepath when you're desperate, so I prayed for guidance and tried to calm myself down. Asking the right questions is 90 percent of the battle. I struggled to think of a strategy that would lead me to him. I scribbled down notes as I fixated on Sal's picture.

"Can you tell me the last thing you saw before you went into the darkness?" I asked. Thank God, that was the million-dollar question. Sal was perfectly willing to describe the last house he saw from the outside. He showed me approximately where the house was from his own house, as if I were looking at the neighborhood from above in an aerial map. I urged him to outline exactly what path he took when he walked out his front door. Gestalting him, I found myself skimming ten inches above the sidewalk. He took me one block south, turned left, went down half a block, and crossed the street. A giant weeping willow stood in the yard of the house next door. He described the house: glass blocks piled on top of each other, white brick, wood with blue-and-white trim, pretty flowers in a garden growing close to the ground.

There's a rainbow in the front yard, he said, displaying the image of beautiful pastel colors lined up in a row. I couldn't make heads or tails of it, so I just wrote it down. Then, with urgency, he showed me the garage door. It was white.

"Sal, are you in there?" I asked. I didn't wait for him to answer. When I shared this information with Caitlin, she pulled me out of my chair. "We've got to walk the neighborhood. Let's go find it!" she cried.

We followed Sal's directions. Caitlin said she thought she knew the house with the weeping willow and the house next door.

Here's what made me love Sal: not the blue-and-white trim he had described perfectly, the glass blocks that were built into the house, or the border of pansies lined with white bricks along the driveway. When I stood in front of the house, I saw something that made me yell out loud. Sal's rainbow was in the front yard! There, before my astonished eyes, was a yard decoration of a donkey pulling a cart. The slats of the cart were painted in multicolored pastels. Each board was a different color.

"The rainbow! There's the rainbow! Can you believe it? This is it! This is it!" I screamed. Caitlin and I beat on the front door. There was no answer. We rang the doorbell over and over. Nothing. We ran to the garage door and called Sal, quietly at first so as not to scare him. "Sal, honey, are you in there?" Nothing. We knocked, then we banged, then we howled and begged. We pounded and cried, both of us refusing to give up. I knew he wasn't dead because all he could see was darkness. On the Other Side, animals always see trees and flowers and people. Sal couldn't see anything but shadows, and he had described clutter and something about a car. He had to be in there! I was confused because I was certain that if Sal were in there, he would answer our call, no matter how weak he was. Utterly bewildered and terribly disappointed, I stood in front of the house, unable to receive any further transmissions. My phone line went dead.

We started ringing doorbells up and down the street. We found some neighbors who told us the owners of the rainbow house had gone on vacation days before. We deliberated about calling the fire department or knocking the door in with a hatchet, but we had nothing to go on—that is, nothing but the hunch of a crazy animal psychic.

Slowly our hearts sank. All of our efforts were in vain. It was well after dark before we finally gave up.

When I went home that night, I couldn't let it go. I was furious to have gotten such clear information that didn't pay off. In my mind I kept hunting for Sal, but I kept seeing the same scene: shadowy darkness, clutter, some kind of car, some grease, and occasionally a whiff of dust or gas fumes. I *knew* he couldn't be dead! I felt him growing more and more thirsty, becoming deathly weak. He *had* to be trapped somewhere, alive! But every time I asked where he was, he'd show me the front of the house with the rainbow in the yard. I knew he was running out of time.

"Hang on, Sal. Hang on, honey," I pleaded with him.

Night and day I tracked Sal, and Caitlin went back to the rainbow house again and again—I begged Sal to meow, but Caitlin never heard a peep through the door. I insisted that Sal was still conscious.

Two nights passed before my tracking transmissions changed dramatically. Sal sent me visions of himself prowling through tall grasses under gargantuan trees. He was frolicking outside in some idyllic forest environment, chasing butterflies. He showed me fresh air, billowy white clouds in the sky, and carefree, laughing people. When I got the scenery, I broke down and cried. It looked too much like the environment cats describe to me when they are on the Other Side. I was certain Sal was dead.

Tearfully, we both wished Sal well and tried to release him. Caitlin was devastated. She called in sick at work and went to bed. I sent Caitlin some flowers to express my sympathy. This case had touched me as deeply as anything I'd ever gone through in my life. I felt like I had lost my own Mr. Jones.

I don't know who was more thrilled and shocked, Caitlin or I, when she received a call the next day from the people in the rainbow house. As she called to tell me the news, I cringed and held my breath. I thought perhaps the people had come home from vacation to find a dead cat in their garage. Guess again. The people were calling from central California, where they had found a live cat in their *trunk!* Cantankerous Sal had been poking around in their garage when they were loading luggage for their vacation and gotten himself trapped in the trunk for a long, long ride. When he finally got released, he really *did* go frolicking in tall grasses under gargantuan trees. The family was in Sequoia National Park! The trees he described to me were sequoias! His hosts found his name and Caitlin's phone number on his tag.

Sal enjoyed a lovely vacation in the country for a week before he came home to his exasperated mother, who was so happy to see him, she forgot to scold him. The little devil had had a great time while he put us through hell. After this ordeal, Caitlin and I were the ones who needed a vacation!

8

Starlight Vision: Entering Dreamtime on the Wings of Love

Sometimes information would come to me at times when I wanted to help someone, and my awareness that I didn't know what to do became like a prayer; it seemed that when I surrendered to my helplessness, the right ideas and words would come. And sometimes, simply being bathed in loving feelings, awash in the energy of the open heart, I'd just seem to get lucky and wisdom would show up, like a bright penny on the sidewalk.

—Belleruth Naparstek,
author of *Health Journeys*
audiocassette series

▓ Sweet Sorrow ▓

"Did I keep him too long?" "Did I let him go too soon?" These are some of the most agonizing decisions we ever have to make. "Should I put him down or let him go on his own? When?" Helping animals cross over is perhaps the most valuable and bittersweet aspect of my work. I try to open my heart and let the ocean of compassion flood through me, but it stings every time like saltwater on a freshly skinned knee. The burning ache, the awe, and the impending ecstasy never diminish with experience.

I've found some guidelines that I hope will be helpful to you. Animals rarely complain that we wait too long to put them down. Those who stay through debilitating diseases, blindness, diabetes, kidney failure—especially when needing daily injections of fluids or insulin—rarely remain for their own best interests. They stay alive for *us*. If I had a nickel for every animal who's told me: *I can't leave yet. My people aren't ready*, I'd be a very rich woman indeed. Rarely do animals complain: *She put me to sleep too soon. I wanted to suffer some more*. They wait until we're ready, until they're *certain* we can survive the pain. They usually hang on much longer than they would prefer. Yes, they can tell you how long they want to stay. They can tell you if they need assistance or if they believe they can ascend on their own, and you can negotiate strategies, creating signs—indications that they are ready to cross over.

I once negotiated these terms for a very wise psychiatrist named Darian; when his dog, Isis, was ready to cross over, Isis would lay her head on a particular pillow. I relayed this message to Isis repeatedly until I was certain she understood. As Isis's days became numbered, Darian would present the special pillow and Isis would shy away from it as if it were a rattlesnake. Finally, in her own time, and during a beautiful ceremony performed by her father, Isis died unassisted. Isis's spirit left her body serenaded by a song Darian played on the stereo: "We all come from the Goddess and to Her we will return."

A horse named Juliet, who was put to sleep in my arms, achieved the most memorable ascension I ever witnessed. Juliet had been suffering from incurable cancer in one of her back legs, forced to stand on three legs for months. Her lovely and enlightened mother, Victoria, sought me out to ask Juliet when she would be ready to go. Juliet told me she was staying *only for her mother,* that if I could prepare Victoria for her departure, Juliet would like to go immediately. I saw Juliet in person, two days in a row. We negotiated that on the day she was ready to die, she would not stand up. To these terms, her mother agreed. While consoling Victoria inside her house, I found framed pictures of her good-looking mentor, a darling old rodeo rider and fanatical horse lover, who was already on the Other Side. I glimpsed her cheerful spirit strutting around the house, fringes flying, spurs jingling—waiting.

The following morning Victoria found Juliet in her stall, unwilling to stand. She summoned the vet and me to the house, where I stood in for Victoria, hugging Juliet's head, as Victoria was too heartbroken to watch. What a gift Juliet gave me! Through eyes blurred with tears, I got to witness Juliet spring out of her body. From the body of the languished horse bounded a frisky white spirit, met immediately by Victoria's mentor—dancing, prancing, whinnying, and laughing merrily around the backyard. They performed several laps of a joyous cat-and-mouse chase before they spiraled up into a cloud of white mist. Why can I see these things? Because I want to. And if you really want to learn, I can teach you.

▓ Mediumship: Starlight Vision ▓

In my experience, I've found that our departed friends spend part of their time on the Other Side with our human ancestors and part of their time with us here on earth, so some of the information that filters in may describe current situations in your own life. (*I like your new haircut, your new red-flowered dress, and the way you rearranged the living room furniture,* or, God forbid, *Your new roommate is a real jerk!*)

Many of the most celebrated psychics of the twentieth century, including the legendary Edgar Cayce, whom *the Journal of the American Medical Association* named the "father of holistic medicine," held the notion that animals have some sort of collective consciousness where they dissolve after death. These psychics attest that only the human species retains its autonomy of spirit after death and returns to earth in the reincarnational wheel. To that I say, Yes! And the moon is made of cheese! (Alpine Swiss, I believe.) What arrogance to assume we are so different from our brothers and sisters: the dolphins, the lions, the eagles, the elephants, and our close kindred, the other primates. Every creature living on this planet has an immortal soul. Our bodies are our *automobiles,* but our souls are the *drivers.* I actually swallowed the collective consciousness belief all my life until I began doing this kind of work. The animals proved me wrong.

The soul of every living creature remains intact, individual, unique, conscious, and observant long after death. Our souls are not just vague energy impressions of what we were on earth; they are more vividly alive than ever. Ten years ago I would have had no grounds to make such a statement. I was as skeptical as you may be now, but after years of conversing with beings on the Other Side, both animal and human, they have convinced me of their autonomy. The spirits have described to me the current affairs in their guardians' lives in such colorful and meticulous detail, as well as their own lives on the Other Side—with grandmothers who cook pie crust, grandfathers who smoke pipe tobacco (which I can actually smell during the readings), great-aunts who play the violin—there is no way for me to deny the fact that our spirits and all spirits everywhere are *eternally conscious.*

Do animals always live with humans on the Other Side? No. I have glimpsed in trance and in dreams vast sanctuaries, entire dimensions populated with nothing but animals. Here in these blissful sanctuaries, I've spotted an occasional human who functions as nothing more than a steward whose only job is to care for and oversee the animals. St. Francis of Assisi may have been one of these animal angels, visiting earth for a short time (I also suspect the two-time Nobel Prize winner, Albert Schweitzer). In the following three stories, I will describe where animal spirits go when they stay with us, where they go when they leave us, and how we can call other human or animal spirits to guide them over to the Other Side.

■ The Armchair Critic: Nagging from the Other Side ■

This story describes my first encounter with Monnica Sepulveda, a gifted intuitive who is also featured in *The 100 Top Psychics in America* (Simon & Schuster) and who instantly became an inspirational friend. At the time of this reading, I had no idea what she did for a living. I received a letter from Northern California containing photos of Monnica's three beautiful cats: Lady, Rocky, and Nikki. Although Monnica had written about the cats in her letter and on the backs of their pictures, I ignored all the notes to focus on the photos alone for several days. When it was time for my phone appointment, I explained to Monnica that I try not to let any conscious information filter in when I do a reading. The spokescat, Lady—a gorgeous long-haired white cat—spoke to me in a voice that matched her body: rich, full, and aristocratic.

Tell Mother I never left her. Sometimes I go to Grandmother Lala's, but mostly I stay with Mother.

Had Lady run away from home? I wondered.

"What is Grandmother's name?" I asked. "Lady, where do you sit in Grandmother's house?" Lady displayed a soft, overstuffed couch where she sat in Grandmother's lap while Grandmother knitted or crocheted. There she had Lala all to herself away from all the other cats. Given this message, Monnica answered:

"Yes, Lala did crochet. And of course there are other cats. I asked my grandmother in spirit to look after all my cats." This was when it finally dawned on me that Lady was on the Other Side. Her voice had come to me so strongly, it took me by surprise. I'd been talking to this cat for days, and I never realized she was *dead!*

"She does have all your cats," I said. "Yes, your grandmother has quite a brood." I saw cats sitting everywhere in the house, on the back of everything. Monnica asked:

"How is she? Ask her what happened to her the morning she was put to sleep. She woke up paralyzed."

Those silly teenage boys! Always going so fast! She reenacted a car accident, bumping her hip, fracturing a vertebrae, and throwing her lower spine out of alignment. *Billy hit me, or a friend of Billy's. One of those rowdy teenagers down the street. Two days before I was paralyzed.*

"That's impossible!" Monnica answered. "She never went out! She fell from a bookcase two days before she was paralyzed, but it couldn't have been a car."

"She says it was a car." I asked the cat to clarify the issue. "Lady, was it the bookcase or a car?"

"Yes. Those teenage boys always going too fast!" She showed me a delayed reaction. The fall from the bookcase exacerbated the damage already done years ago by the car, causing the previous hairline fracture to break away completely. I shared the message.

"She says the accident happened when she was younger, and her lower back always hurt when she tried to use her box. That's why she had so little control," I said.

Monnica answered, "Well, now that you mention it, it's true. She did always have a problem with incontinence. I tried to cure the problem, but finally, I just gave up. I didn't know what else to do, and in the first few years we had her she did go outside and there were some teenage boys living down the street."

"That was it," I told her. "She's showing me impact. The accident could actually have happened when she dodged the car and hit the curb."

We went on to another cat. I read from Monnica's letter, "I had a cat named Sunny who I loved so much. He passed away 6-10-1980. How is he?"

"Lady, is Sunny with you?" I asked.

With Grandma, but Grandpa loves him, she answered. I saw the man with the cat in his lap.

I asked Monnica, "Your grandfather is on the Other Side?"

"Yes," she answered.

"He loves Sunny. Sunny lives with him."

I read on from the letter, "I took care of a stray cat named Oliver until he died. Does he have anything to say to me?" I asked Oliver to come forth and even though I didn't have a picture of him, soon I heard another voice.

Tell her thanks. Tell her I love her. Tell her I miss her . . . and I miss her slippers. He laughed, revealing cat poop in a pair of sheepskin house shoes. I shared.

"I made him a bed out of sheepskin," Monnica said, no longer holding in all the emotion.

"He was a stray that I took in just for the last few months of his life. Oh, he was so sick." Immediately he showed himself to me. He was a teenage needle-nosed redhead, not a bit sick anymore, but spry and cocky.

Tell her I'm my old self again, Oliver said.

I did and tried to comfort her: "He's so young and playful! What a sense of humor! What a character!" I went back to Lady to talk about the two other cats in the photos, Rocky and Nikki, to give Monnica some time to pull herself together.

"Lady, what is your cat name?" I asked.

Queeny, she answered.

"I always called her the Queen!" Monnica whispered between sobs.

"What is Nikki's?" I asked.

Bullet or Dart, Lady said.

"What is Rocky's?" I asked. At this point Nikki interrupted.

I call him Squish. He laughed heartily. It was obviously an insult, one of those private jokes between cats.

"Nikki, pal, how do you get along with Rocky?" I asked.

Rocky's lazy and spoiled. Instantly Rocky jumped in to defend himself.

Nikki gets totally out of control. He tears up Mother's plants, Rocky said.

Nikki retaliated, *Rocky's Mommy's baby—a real mama's boy.* Monnica confirmed: "Oh yes, Nikki eats my plants. I guess he needs the chlorophyll. And Rocky's pet name is Baby Rocko, and I suppose he is a bit spoiled and lazy—"

I saw a flash of Lady, perched in the window next to the kitchen where she regulated the boys' activities from her lofty throne. She interrupted like a referee:

I make Nikki behave himself. Nikki's a food thief! He hunts birds and brings them in. I say, "No, Nikki! Mother doesn't like this! Mother hates this!" But Nikki only laughs. Nikki antagonizes Rocky.

I was just amazed that a dead cat was sitting in the same window she occupied in life, barking orders at the boy cats like a drill sergeant. Even from the Other Side, she spends all her time playing the armchair critic and bossing around the two living cats!

Monnica confirmed that Nikki used to hunt but she won't allow it, and yes, she did have a new boyfriend. Nikki felt compelled to defend himself:

I fight off all the negativity in the house. Tell Mother I keep her channels clear and chase away any spirits that linger around the house when she finishes a reading.

"A reading?" I asked him. "What does Mother do?"

She's a clairvoyant like you, Nikki said.

"Monnica, did you know that Nikki is your psychic police?" I asked.

"It doesn't surprise me," she answered.

Those of you who are hoping to steer clear of some nagging relative on the Other Side might need to think twice about opening your psychic senses. Apparently co-dependency survives the grave.

▓ Heaven in Oklahoma ▓

Sometimes bad things happen to our animals despite our best intentions. Whenever we have to relocate our animals for whatever reason, even temporarily, we put them at great risk. This is a sad story, but one I will include because I think it is important to see the consequences of abandoning your animals even when you think you're acting in their best interest. You will also bear witness to the depths of compassion and love our animals have for us.

A radiant meditation teacher, Beth, taught me much of what I now know about opening the heart chakra. Beth called when she heard I could communicate with animals that had crossed over, and her story poured out. She had lost a dog three years prior and the situation was never really resolved. I immediately got the image of a dog—huge, white, fluffy, blue-eyed, and longhaired. Beth confirmed that Asia was a giant English sheep dog—white and blue-eyed. Beth was forced to relocate Asia because Beth was moving to Los Angeles and couldn't keep a dog in her new home. Beth hoped that the new home would be temporary, but in the meantime, she was forced to leave Asia with some relatives. In Beth's absence, Asia developed unexplainable convulsions that the vets couldn't diagnose. The condition became so acute, Beth had to have Asia euthanized. Of course, Beth was devastated and had never made peace with her guilty conscience.

When I contacted Asia, I heard her voice distinctly. Maybe Asia's urgency to contact Beth helped me hear her. Asia opened the conversation:

I died of a broken heart. If I could not live with Mother, I did not want to live at all.

I explained to Beth that even though animals are as afraid of feeling pain as we are, they are not afraid of death itself the way humans are. They have a much more conscious relationship with their bodies. Now, I'm not referring to animals fighting for survival in the wild or animals in slaughterhouses—I'm referring to domestic animals who often have a more reflective attitude toward death. Some animals can die at will—they can cause organs to shut off. Asia showed me a congenital heart defect; she felt the malfunctioning of the heart valve caused the convulsions. I told Beth, "She felt that you would no longer let her into your heart, so she fell prey to this trauma in her own heart." The dog *literally* died of a broken heart.

Asia showed me Beth's grandmother and an inviting farmhouse on a prairie on the Other Side. She showed me frolicking through tall grasses and butterflies from her own eye level. Translating for Beth, I told her:

"Asia says she is very happy here and she will wait for you. The terrain looks like fields of wheat, like the Oklahoma prairies—"

"My grandmother was from Oklahoma!" Beth cried. If there had been any doubt in Beth's mind that I had found her dog, it disappeared in an instant. I saw her grandmother in spirit, waving at me. Inundated with a wave of loving impressions, I told Beth:

"Your grandmother was an animal lover—a dog lover."

"Yes," Beth confirmed, "she had one dog for years that she adored."

"She has Asia now. Your grandmother liked to cook. She is still baking pies."

"My grandmother was a wonderful cook—loved to bake!"

"Asia is yipping around the kitchen, toenails on the tiles, very hyperactive—"

"Asia was very hyperactive until she got older."

"How old did she live to be?" I asked.

"Eleven," Beth answered.

"Asia is very proud of living so long. Your grandmother lived to be very old, too."

We're very old, you know. We're very old ladies!

"My grandmother lived to be ninety-nine—almost one hundred!" Beth said. "Tell her I'm sorry," Beth whispered. "Tell her I just couldn't bring her with me."

Asia's answer brought tears to my eyes.

I love her, miss her, and I forgive her completely. I don't want her to feel guilty anymore, Asia said. She showed me the scenario of being euthanized, then finding herself somewhat disoriented on the astral plane, like a person who dies of a drug overdose; but Beth's grandmother found her and guided her into the light.

Tell her I love her grandmother, but Beth is my chosen human. I have followed her for many many years. Tell her that by putting me to sleep, she saved me the discomfort of losing control of many of my organs. I had other medical problems beginning to plague me. Hip dysplasia, problems with my kidneys and bladder. If she hadn't helped me cross over, I would have ended up incontinent and crippled. I wouldn't have wanted that. Tell her I lived a long, happy life, and I want her to stop feeling guilty. I sleep with her at nights—between her feet. Ask her if she knows I'm there.

"Yes! She always slept at my feet, between my legs. Sometimes, I still feel the warmth of her body—"

Tell her I'm with her in the morning hours, said Asia.

"Yes!" Beth affirmed. "The morning was always our special time together!"

Tell her I'm still with her. I'm around her most of the time, said Asia. I did and assured her:

"Sometimes it's good to have our friends on the Other Side, where they can function like angels. You can call on her for help or to invoke her strength."

Beth called me later to thank me for helping bridge the gap and appease the guilt that had haunted her for three years. She finally resolved her grief knowing that Asia was in good hands.

▓ The Spirit on the Stairs ▓

One of my first house calls was for two lovely women, Bette and Julie, roommates who asked me to talk to their cats, Titania and Persephone. Especially concerned about Titania, the twelve-year-old diabetic, the women wanted to know what they could do to make Titania more comfortable in her final years. The women told me over the phone that Titania had been treated for skin cancer, and the medication had damaged her pancreas, which triggered the diabetes.

As soon as I made the appointment, I could hear Titania's voice in my head. I ran for a pen.

Needles! Needles! Needles! I'm so tired. My skin hurts all over where I've been pricked! I'm so tired inside.

"You're getting ready to go, aren't you?" I asked her.

Yes. But I'm very worried about my parents. They love me so. It will be very difficult for them. Especially the dark-haired one. She sent a warm feeling of love to accompany the shadow image of this woman.

"Are you going to die soon?" I asked.

Yes. That's why I directed my mothers to you. Her words gave me a jolt.

If this power of divine intervention was possible, who could master it better than an old Siamese cat? Titania spoke as if she were wisdom itself, as if I were talking to a female Buddha, a feline Kuan Yin. I knew Titania had drawn me to her parents to make her transition easier—not for *her*, but for *them*.

I didn't speak to her again until our appointment, when I met her in person. After Titania welcomed me into her home, she sat curled in a bun three feet from my right knee, just out of reach. I sat cross-legged on the floor, respecting her space. But Persephone climbed into my lap and feverishly kneaded my tummy, making biscuits throughout the entire session.

Titania didn't wait for me to question her. She again offered up her lament, *I'm so tired of needles.*

I replied, "I know, sweetheart. I'm so sorry." I asked her parents how long she had been diabetic, but I heard Titania's voice in my head before her parents could answer: *Two years.*

"Neither of you has blood sugar problems?" I asked Bette and Julie. Since neither of them did, I asked Titania if her blood sugar problems had any psychological roots.

"Titania, what is the meaning of your diabetes?"

Sugar is love. I give so much love, all the love to my humans all the time. There is not enough love left for myself, so my body makes sugar. Too much sugar.

I began my Gestalt with Titania. "Her internal organs feel very fatigued." Titania interjected, *Tell them the shots are upsetting my stomach.*

"She throws up all the time," Bette agreed.

I told Titania I was shocked and sorry that nothing better has been developed for diabetes. She said she understood what these shots were meant to do and that they worked, but for her, they had nasty side effects.

Bette asked the dreaded question: "Is she preparing to die?"

"Yes, but she is not upset about it. Animals don't connote the negative with it that we humans do."

I have been with Julie the longest. Ten years, Titania said. When I repeated Titania's words, Julie replied, "Yes, ten years."

"Boy, this cat sure is good with numbers," I said, and sighed. "Most animals aren't this good."

Tell her I love her very much and that I'm worried how she will take it, said Titania. When I did, Julie started to cry. Bette stepped in: "Ask her what we can do to make her more comfortable."

I'd like a bed in that spot made of my mothers' sweatshirts that smell like them; and I'd like a catnip sock to sleep with.

I sleep at Bette's feet, Persephone interrupted.

"Yes! That's right!" said Bette. Then Persephone made a joke: she showed me some shoes with the rich smell of leather; then she showed me herself wetting the shoes.

"Oh no, Bette!" Julie cried. "Your boots! Is Persephone feeling neglected?"

Persephone answered for herself. *Yes! If they don't start giving me more attention, I will ruin her new shoes. Tell them I want a boyfriend when Titania is gone. Titania and I have agreed upon this.* I got the impression that Titania and Persephone had discussed this many times. Persephone, still young and feisty, insisted that the new cat be male.

"But we swore we wouldn't get any more cats!" Bette whined.

"Oh, come on," I said. "You have to! It wouldn't be fair to Persephone. She will be so lonely! And besides, they've already decided." I told them how strongly I advocate keeping animals in twos: even a cat and a dog are usually better together than keeping one animal all alone. A single animal becomes a hostage in your house, with no members of his own species to relate to. It's not fair to isolate them outside their natural environments and force them to live a life where they're bored out of their minds. They must relate to creatures of their own kind and have relationships other than human-animal relationships. I assured them that just because they couldn't hear the cats talking to one another did not mean the cats didn't talk all day. I've even known cats and dogs who talked to caged birds, and these odd-couple friendships were a million times better than no friendships at all. Of course there are exceptions, but most animals are social creatures.

Julie whispered to Bette, "Well, there is that cat your friend told you about. . . ."

Bette nodded knowingly. "You're right," Bette conceded. "We'll get another cat." I cheered silently. My conviction may have changed Persephone's life. These were the moments that gave me the most satisfaction.

"Titania says you've also had pain in your heart. Heart trouble?" I asked Bette.

"No."

Heartache. Heartbreak. Titania sent the words.

"Oh, that kind of heart trouble. She is exactly right!" said Bette. Titania continued:

I'd like to sleep on her chest. I could heal her heart with my heart. Her heart was the one thing that this decrepit old cat had intact; that heart was so filled with love, it was just astounding. She was still in her bun a few feet from me, smiling, purring, and slipping into a deep trance.

"Amelia, you can hear her voice in your head, right? What does her voice sound like?" Bette asked.

"Very, very old!" We all had a good laugh. Whereupon, Titania sat up, stretched her legs, and laughed, then settled back down, paws tucked under.

"She's a wise old soul, isn't she?" asked Bette. Titania answered for herself:

There are few experiences in life that I haven't observed. I've seen much of the outside world, and I know everything about human nature. I've had a long, happy life, and I love my parents very much. Tell them that for me, would you, please? I was happy to.

"Is she in any pain?" Julie asked.

"She says if you could regulate her stomach problem, that's all she could ask from you. She is a very happy old lady and a very powerful crone. She says she has tremendous healing powers. That's why she'd like to sleep on your chest, Bette."

"She is very wise, like she's magical . . . I don't know how to say it," Bette said, sighing.

"Yes, she's quite a shaman," I agreed.

Bette changed the subject, excited:

"Something happened last week. We wrote down the time: March 22 at four-forty-five. Titania usually only meows out loud to us, but she was meowing frantically on the staircase at something we couldn't see. Was it you that she saw?" I asked her if she saw me on the astral plane.

No. I saw a big light fluffy dog with a large fluffy tail. I asked the women which of them had a dog on the Other Side.

"It's about three feet long, floppy ears, longhaired, light-colored, and has a fluffy tail," I explained.

"It's my golden retriever!" Bette cried. "I have been praying for him to come for Titania when it's her time to go! How long does she have?"

Weeks. A few weeks, Titania said.

"How will we know when Titania's ready to go?" Bette asked. "Tell her not to go when I'm not home! Or when either of us is not home!"

Titania sent me the image of pawing at the floor and crying loudly to announce her intent. I asked her if she could wait until they were both home so they could say good-bye to her. I conveyed the message and added, "She'll let you know."

The dog had already come to guide Titania into the spirit world. I received a lovely letter and a present from the women shortly after the reading. They wrote to say Titania had crossed over peacefully when they both were home. Having the opportunity to talk to her before she left was one of the most treasured gifts they had ever been given.

▓ Reincarnation ▓

I had no idea that animals reincarnated when I began doing this work. The animals proved it to me. The rottweiler that belonged to Stacy, a TV actress, told me he had been with his mother *before,* when she was only a child. (Stacy was the only person I've ever lunched with in a swanky Beverly Hills restaurant who offered a housefly his own plate of Chinese chicken salad; and I must say, her generosity worked like a charm—he immediately abandoned her plate for his own.) Stacy's trim rottweiler identified himself as her previous small shaggy golden terrier and went on to describe Stacy's brothers, the house she grew up in, and the nature of his death. Stacy authenticated every word he said and claimed she had always had a sneaking suspicion that this was her old childhood dog.

Another dog told me he liked his *old vet better*. He even elaborated on the tall man's gray hair and glasses. His owner was shocked and thrilled to report that *this* dog had never seen *that* vet. The gray-haired vet was the vet of her *prior* dog, the dog who had died before she found this one. Not only have I discovered reincarnation through my own research, I've heard hundreds of stories of animal owners who were unshakably certain their former animals had come back to them. I've been surrounded backstage by crowds of talk-show audiences, each one waving the picture of an animal and asking, "Is this the same dog? I just *know* my new dog is my old dog! You see, my old dog used to do a special dance when I sang a special song. . . ."

Oh, the peculiarities are endless, the coincidences undeniable, and the similarities so darn exact: the same traits, the same games, the same kisses, the same habits, the same tastes, the same passion for asparagus.

"Could it be that we just project our wishes upon them?" you may ask. "Could they see the pictures in our minds and just act them out?" Sure, but then they act out similarities we've quite forgotten. Oscar, one of my four kittens, "still" shares dozens of habits and talents with his predecessor: He still appears out of nowhere when I make the bed and attacks the sheets, he can still open a turbo-locked cat door, he still nibbles my necklaces, he still wakes me with a kiss, he still strip-mines the flower boxes, he still sleeps with his tongue sticking out, and he is still an accomplished masseur. No matter what part of my body aches—be it neck, shoulder, lower back, or knee, even—Oscar will zero in on the painful spot and massage it furiously. None of the other kittens share any of these idiosyncrasies . . . but one of my old pals did.

People often ask me if animals change species, and although other animal communicators swear they do, this has rarely been my experience. Although animals *can* incarnate in various forms, I've found that animals seem to have a preference for a particular form and stick with it. Nor have I discovered, as others believe, that animals are human spirits in training. I don't deny that it's possible for animals to incarnate as humans—I wouldn't put it past Rodney and Mr. Jones (who both also claim to have been lions in Egypt)—but I simply haven't come across it often in my travels. Horses usually come back as horses, swans as swans, and so on. The following is one of my most

memorable stories starring a miraculous little cat . . . who promised
to come back.

※ Shakespeare Watches Surgery ※

A vet named Dr. Eileen Nichols contacted me when her gorgeous
Norwegian Forest cat, Shakespeare, had been missing for five days in
Beverly Hills. Every day since, Dr. Nichols had called roadside services, pounds, animal shelters, and other vets, but could get no word
on Shakespeare's whereabouts.

The morning after I received the photograph of Shakespeare in the
mail. I was still in bed when the shadow form of a beautiful gray
striped cat appeared standing on my chest.

"Shakespeare, are you on the Other Side?" I asked.

Yes.

"How did it happen?"

He propelled images of a violent car accident.

"Why did you leave home?" I asked.

*I went out the night before and I was safe, so I tried it again on my
own. But on the second night, a dog chased me, a big dirty white dog.* I
saw a violent film sequence: a cat trapped between a dog and a car; he
took the risk and ran out in front of the car. *Tell Mama I love her. Tell
her I'm sorry. I'm so sorry.*

I drove out to Dr. Nichols's home the next day to break the news.
As I watched this young vet weep, there was no doubt in my mind
that her capacity to love animals was vast and she loved this particular cat more than she had ever loved anyone in her life. I knew the
feeling exactly: Shakespeare was her Mr. Jones. He was her sun,
moon, and stars. We decided to contact Shakespeare again. The
beloved cat chimed in:

*Now I'm free in the car and I go with her to Palm Springs every time
she goes. I go to work with her. Tell her I go with her everywhere now.*
(The vet had two practices—one in town and one in Palm Springs
where she spent two days a week.) Silently, I asked Shakespeare for
some evidence.

*Tell her the day before yesterday she performed an operation on a big
black female Doberman. She sliced right down the dog's torso. Seeing*

the surgery in lurid detail, I described the incision that spanned the length of the dog's torso. Dr. Nichols answered in choked sobs:

"It was a necropsy . . . day before yesterday on a female black Dobe—"

Tell her I was there. I watched the whole thing, Shakespeare insisted. With this, I saw a remarkable sight: a longhaired striped kitty stood on the operating table next to the dog!

"Shakespeare! Give me something else!" I begged.

Her dress! She got a new white dress with pink flowers. Tell her it looks good on her. Tell her not to give it away! When I did, Dr. Nichols's tears stopped flowing the moment she made the connection.

"Oh, my God!" she cried out. "A friend of mine just gave me two dresses! A black one and *a white one with pink flowers on it!* I gave the black one away, but I kept the pink and white one!"

Tell her to keep it. I like it on her, Shakespeare said.

"Will Shakespeare come back to me?" Dr. Nichols asked.

Yes. Maybe as soon as October. Tell her it will be through her practice in Palm Springs. Someone will abandon a kitten or I will come through someone she knows there. I will be a fluffy black-and-white tuxedo cat. (He proudly showed me his adorable new black-and-white boots.)

"How will I know him?" the doctor asked.

A funny image appeared in my mind: "He will lick your eyelashes and eyebrows," I said.

"Shakespeare used to do that!" Dr. Nichols gasped.

Tell her I will nuzzle her ear and say Ma-ma, Ma-ma—

"Yes! Shakespeare has always done that. Tell him I've always wanted a black-and-white kitten!" The doctor's tears of anguish turned into tears of joy. Shakespeare suddenly showed me his front paws. He had six toes on each.

"He'll be polydactyl," I said.

"I've always wanted a polydactyl kitty! Tell him that's *exactly* what I want!" I didn't need to tell Shakespeare. He already knew!

※ Healing Indoor Cats ※

Despite the tragedies that can occur with cats and cars, I am a big believer that cats need to have earth under their feet. I know I am at odds with all the no-kill shelters that prevent cats from adoption if in their new homes they will be allowed outside. I understand the logic of this restriction, especially in urban communities where there is considerable traffic, as well as the risk of exposure to infectious diseases carried by other cats. Here in Los Angeles, we have the additional threat of attacks by starving coyotes. Believe me when I tell you, I understand the human perspective. But the human perspective is not my main concern—my main concern is the perspective of the *cats*.

Once in a blue moon, I meet a cat who doesn't want to go outside: these are usually ex-strays who got traumatized outside early in their lives. They have had their fill of the outside world and are perfectly content to sit on a soft couch and look out the window, but those are the exceptions. All animals were designed to have earth under their feet, wind in their hair, sunshine on their faces, trees to enjoy, dirt to dig in, flowers to sniff, other animals to play with, insects to investigate.

I've found a connection to indoor animals and disease—attributed to, in part, by all the indoor toxins a house cat is exposed to: from formaldehyde in the carpets to paint, plaster, varnish, and airborne toxins blown around by air conditioners. Of course, the quality of their food and water is a factor, as is the amount of human emotional strife they absorb, but the most common complaint I hear from indoor cats is that they are painfully bored. Some say if they can't go outside, there's no reason for them to live.

First of all, in holding cats hostage in houses, we impede their learning processes. Their lives have meaning and purpose, too, apart from the lives of their human owners. Having relationships with other cats is essential to them, even if they get in an occasional fight. Can you imagine being isolated from your entire species and being trapped in, say, a cave of bears for your whole life? Even if you were one of *two* humans trapped in a cave of bears, wouldn't you get powerfully tired of each other and crave some other human companionship? Curiosity is the very essence of the cat, and investigating other life forms and the world around her is not only what keeps the cat occupied, it keeps her *well*. Cats must have interesting environments in order to stay healthy, and this means environments jam-packed with other *living things*.

A number of sick or dying house cats have begged me to ask their owners for them, *Can't I go sit outside in the grass for a while? Tell Mother I can't get well until I can sit in the grass.* Which leads me to another theory: in addition to all the creatures that crawl and fly that cats need to interact with, there is a relationship between the cat *and the earth itself* that defies description. As the old adage goes, cats have nine lives; their powers of healing are nothing short of supernatural. These powers of healing are present in a cat's body even when the cat is cooped up in a human house, but the magic flourishes outside, when the cat is allowed to have earth under her feet. I always meditate outside, visualizing two polarities—energy entering from above in the heavens and energy from below that I draw up from the earth—energizing me, polarizing me, and grounding me to the planet. I learned this from my cats. Often, when cats have been medically tampered with by humans, they tell me they could heal *all by themselves* if only they were allowed to sit alone on the grass . . . and I *believe* them.

I lived in an apartment for over a year where Mr. Jones had no earth whatsoever, not even a square foot of dirt in a courtyard. With only a boxed herb garden to tend that he loved very much, and a daily patrol where he'd rub his cheek on every single potted plant in the courtyard—it wasn't enough. In this concrete jungle, his kidneys started to deteriorate at an alarming rate. Complaining incessantly about the lack of nature, he was quite convinced if we moved to a house with a yard, he would be able to recover. I tried a new vet who told me two years ago that Mr. Jones would not live another three months without daily injections of fluids. Mr. Jones insisted he would rather not live if he had to receive daily injections, so fluids were simply not an option for us. If he reached the point where he couldn't live without the injections, I would have to let him go. My life stopped once Mr. Jones got his death sentence. Even my knowledge of reincarnation and the sacredness of death did not ease my anguish. It *couldn't* be his time. It simply did not *feel right.*

Soon enough, I found a house with a big backyard in the suburbs, well out of coyote territory, and we all moved in. Mr. Jones made a miraculous recovery, just as he said he would. Twenty-nine months have passed since his predicted D-day. So busy is he patrolling his new territory, he's as alert as a kitten. Never roaming far, keeping his promise to stay out of the street and return home when called, he spends most of his time blissfully snoozing in the backyard on the lawn. He assures me the move saved his life.

I highly recommend that cat owners who simply can't let their cats outside for some unavoidable reason, like living in a high-rise in Manhattan, simulate an outside space as best they can. Some marvelous companies are manufacturing outdoor cat pens for high-rise balconies so city cats won't fall to their deaths hunting pigeons. Cats love flowers (Rodney adored roses) and pungent herbs, and consider themselves consummate gardeners, even of houseplants. Any kind of balcony garden will be life-giving to your cat, as will all the houseplants your home can accommodate. Please understand that cats derive some sort of energy from other living things that they simply shouldn't have to live without. The more time they spend outside, the more content they will be.

▦ Cats and Hunting ▦

I had a very interesting conversation with Jake, a chiropractor who works on animals. Jake had come over to adjust Mr. Jones's neck and tailbone. Incidentally, the two extremes of the spine seem to have trouble in tandem. When the coccyx goes out, so does the axis at the base of the skull. When animals are limping slightly or seem to be favoring one back paw, the problem is often not the foot or the hip, but the coccyx, which is the last vertebra where the tail connects. Cats who have been abused or picked up by the tail sometimes have this alignment problem. The neck is not easy to diagnose on sight. I find the problem only when animals are complaining of headaches.

Jake was telling me that although he likes cats (and they certainly like him, which says more to me than anything he could say), he prefers birds, so he has always been wary of cats. He asked how I could reconcile the issue of hunting. I've discussed this topic with hundreds of cat owners, and everyone has the same beef: what to do? How can it be stopped? My stance is not very sympathetic.

"Don't" is my answer. I do have moral dilemmas with animals who do not kill their prey quickly, but that is not usually the case with cats. I told Jake, "Stop identifying with the victim. If you identify with the *cat*, you'll understand everything instantly." Then I shared with him this story.

⚔ The Flight of the Dove ⚔

I also identified with nothing but the victim every time one of my cats made a kill or while watching one of those amazing animal documentary programs that feature big cats hunting in the wild—until one experience changed my entire outlook forever.

One day, while admiring a row of a dozen doves on a retaining wall behind my house, I glimpsed out of the corner of my eye a flash of gray fur. Mr. Jones was climbing up the hill behind the wall. As I watched the row of birds, one suddenly disappeared like a duck knocked down in a carnival shooting gallery. The bird went down so quickly, the two birds on either side of him didn't even fly away. After a few seconds they looked at each other curiously as if to say, "Marge, have you seen Bob? I thought he was right there—"

Mr. Jones appeared in front of me with the dove in his mouth. I Gestalted him. The bird had died instantaneously of a broken neck. What I experienced inside my cat was one of the most transcendental states I've ever felt, but what I felt inside *the bird* was even more amazing. My consciousness ricocheted back and forth between cat and bird. I felt and saw the white spirit of the bird flap up out of the body and enter the head of the cat, lingering there in the most divine ecstasy I've ever imagined. For a fraction of an instant, the bird and cat were one—communing in a state of ecstatic union.

There was no animosity in the bird, which had had almost no time to fear pain before its spirit was released. Moving from one form of nature into another, the bird felt no pain or fear about the crossover. It was not trauma that the bird experienced; it was rapture, an energetic communication between the animals. I don't mean to say that animals don't feel fear when they're being hunted. Of course they do. This is what has kept every species of animal fighting for its survival, but I have spoken to so many domestic animals over the years about their impending deaths, and they share a greater sense of tranquillity about death than humans I have known.

I stayed with the cat as he ate the bird. In a matter of moments, the entire bird had been consumed, with not a single feather left. Gestalting Mr. Jones, I tasted the bird as he tasted it and I don't believe we even have anything in the human range of experience that can compare with this brand of deliciousness—certainly a far cry from canned or dried cat food. (I've often wondered why cat food isn't sparrow- or mouse-flavored.) So, a divine exchange occurs, an energetic transaction, that is primary to the existence of the hunter, but I had never dreamed that the prey would share in the transcendental bliss. There seems to be love not only in the *takeover* but love in the *surrender*.

Joseph Campbell says life feeds on life. It's a fact we may not be comfortable with, but it is a law whose jurisdiction we cannot escape as long as we are alive on earth. Even when we eat lettuce and carrots, it may not be the *mass* of the object per se—the vitamins, the minerals—that nourish us, but the *life* in the food, *the spirit itself* that becomes a part of us. This must be equally true, if not even more so, for cats. I believe we're here not to change Mother Nature's world, but to learn from it, including the unpleasant experiences we'd rather not see. In fact, what creates the feelings of unpleasantness is our lack of understanding. We often don't see what's really going on. From the day I Gestalted Mr. Jones, I stopped condemning cats for hunting. Granted, I want them to make quick, clean kills and not play with their prey, but I think the quick kill is the norm, not the exception.

Don't put a bell on your cat for any reason. There's nothing cats despise more than bells announcing their every move. What could be more sadistic than to put a bell on the creature with the world's most sensitive ears? "But I want to know where he is!" people argue. To these people I reply, If your cat wants you to know where he is, he'll let you know where he is. Cats are not toys or slaves. They have a right to their dignity and their own free will.

The cat's design and construction so exceeds our own, I think it leaves many humans feeling jealous and inadequate. Can you imagine being able to bend your knees and jump to a pinnacle eight times your height? That would mean that with only a slight plié, you could jump to the roof of a four-story building. From there you could fly from rooftop to rooftop and take down prey five times your size, using no weapons but your bare hands and teeth. Have you seen films of cheetahs running sixty-five miles an hour to capture an antelope towering over them? Hunting is what cats were created for. It is what they live for. To deny them that pleasure is to bore them to death. I entertain my cats with as many furry and feathery toy substitutes as I possibly can. But when the inevitable kill occasionally happens, I let the cat be. I wasn't thrilled when Billie caught my only woodpecker, nor was

I thrilled when Oscar took down one of my squirrels and dragged it into the den; but they're *cats,* and that's life.

※ Animals and Karma ※

Edgar Cayce, the infamous psychic known as the "Sleeping Prophet", believed humans who perform violence toward *any* animal, including painful laboratory experiments, would accumulate bad karma. Over time I've come to agree with Cayce.

Karma accumulates when we harm other living beings—even indirectly, as when people eat animals that have suffered needlessly, or when women wear fur and buy cosmetics and household products tested on lab animals. When we turn our backs on the reality of violence in our culture, we disassociate, and when we disassociate, we turn our backs on *ourselves.* When we disassociate, we give our power away: to the media, the meat industry, the slaughterhouses, the cosmetic tycoons, the rendering plants. This is precisely why most people are not clairsentient and clairvoyant. This is why most people cannot use Gestalt, remote viewing, and their starlight vision. There are too many aspects of ourselves we don't *want* to see and don't *want* to feel. When we disassociate, we shut out the truth in an attempt to shut out the pain. We become numb, powerless nobodies and further lose ourselves in the pretty flickering of our TV sets. "But I can't help it," you've heard people argue. "Tortured meat is everywhere. All our products have been tested on animals! *I* can't change the world." I used to think this way, too. I've spent a month of Sundays crying in bed over the plight of animals but, as I've said before, crying in bed is not going to save one single little furry head.

We are all born into a world where heinous crimes against animals are the norm and seemingly beyond our control. In my thirty-plus years on this planet, I've never gotten to vote on how animals should be treated. All crimes against animals—farming them for food under miserable conditions, experimenting on them for cosmetic or medical research, slaughtering them in the name of fashion—have never appeared on a ballot in my lifetime. I feel like my hands were tied before I was even born. I hear the message loud and clear: "No one cares what *you* think. *Your vote doesn't count!*"

Bullied by soulless conglomerates, we buy into the illusion of powerlessness. We are brainwashed and confused by the advertising we receive from every direction telling us in one way or another "You are helpless. You are outnumbered. You might as well buy me. What's one more dead rabbit, chicken, cow, cat, or fox? You had steak for dinner. You're wearing leather shoes. You're a hypocrite! What's one more tortured mouse or monkey? What does it matter, anyway? Give up!"

I'm going to let you in on a secret: it matters. *You* matter. No, we can't be perfect, but we can try as hard as we possibly can.

Of course, it's tempting to buy only what's most convenient, all the while rationalizing, *it's too much. I can't help it.* But you can, and if you do, you will add to the momentum of salvation. Help is coming for the animals. The world is evolving ever so slowly, but it *is* evolving. Only a few years ago, the search for cruelty-free shampoo took a good deal of effort. Now, thanks to courageous groups like People for the Ethical Treatment of Animals, and animal-loving consumers like you, the cruelty-free products are gradually overtaking the shelves of drugstores. We are all already consumers. Take back your power of choice.

Many cruelty-free products are still difficult to find, and many more products are unmarked and therefore suspect—for instance, bleach, silver polish, fabric softener, wood polish, tile cleaner, and all forms of household cleansers and disinfectants. A good rule of thumb is that if the boxes don't clearly state "Not tested on animals," assume they are. Many health food stores now carry cruelty-free laundry detergent, fabric softener, and household cleansers. For a complete directory of cosmetic companies that do not test on animals, check the resource section at the back of this book.

The atrocities performed on animals in the name of medical science pose another ethical dilemma. I consulted the National Anti-Vivisection Society about the most intricate surgery I could think of: corneal transplants. Is there any surgery in existence that can justify animal experimentation? No. Corneal transplants were delayed by 90 years because of misleading results on wasteful and heinous animal experiments. The good news is that scientists are finding viable alternatives. For example, Canadian scientists have built "an anatomically complete human corneal equivalent" out of "immortalized human cells and an artificial matrix." They're already planning to use this artificial cornea for drug testing without sacrificing a single animal.

Today's fantasies are tomorrow's science. If corneal transplants could be developed in vitro without the usage of animal experimentation, could the rest of modern research be far behind? According to the summary of current research projects sponsored by the Lord Dowding Fund, "Slowly but surely, universities and research establishments are realizing the true worth of non-animal research, not only on moral grounds but because of its superiority over animal research in terms of accuracy and validity. The life-saving, practical and cost benefits of replacing traditional animal-based practicals with computer simulations are tremendous."

Thanks to the geniuses at Apple Computers, multimedia software programs are achieving exciting cruelty-free victories. The encouraging summary shares the good news:

A pilot study funded by the Lord Dowding Fund, back in 1989–90, and carried out at Liverpool John Moore's University, made use of computer simulations to save the lives of animals during the teaching of cardiovascular physiology and pharmacology. This success inspired Dr. Stevens and colleagues of the University of Wales, School of Pharmacy, to reduce the number of animals' lives wasted in teaching of pharmacology at degree level.

Following the installation of a computer suite and the purchase of software from Sheffield Bioscience, funded by the Lord Dowding Fund, Dr. Stevens has been able to develop practical replacement computer software packages advanced enough to reduce the use of animals permanently, by 80 percent during the first two years of the undergraduate course. The use of "multimedia" software has made this possible, combining animation, sound and video footage in an interactive display. Simulations have consequently become more realistic than has been achieved in the past.

Subsequent simulations have continued to be developed to this date, including an attempt to reduce the number of rats killed specifically for dissection in schools for which "The Rat Stack" (Apple Macintosh) was released in late 1989. It is a simulation in which parts of the rat anatomy can be peeled away or replaced, labeled with descriptive information, or amplified for closer study of the tissues.

So there is hope. With the continued success of multimedia software programs in the next few decades, computer simulations can and should replace animal torture completely. Apple Computers certainly does not misrepresent itself with the slogan *Think differently!*

※ Keep the Balance: Tithe ※

No one can dictate your choices, such as whether or not you wear perfume that was tested on animals, but I can suggest you live within the boundaries of your own integrity. You must come to terms with your own conscience, which may be very different from mine or from that of your best friend. To *make conscious choices* may be your first step. In this way, we no longer live on automatic pilot, eating what our mothers fed us or buying makeup we see advertised on TV. We take back our power by becoming *conscious enough to choose.* If we do what we can, little by little, day by day, there stands some hope that our children will not be exposed to the violence and atrocities of their parents' world.

I admit, as a Texan, I ate steak most of my life. I've always boycotted milk-fed veal because of the deplorable torture of the animals, but it wasn't until after I became an animal communicator that I completely gave up steak. I'll never forget the moment I made that decision. A friend was watching the news one night, and I came in to catch the tail end of a segment about contaminated meat in slaughterhouses. Just as I walked into the room, I locked eyes with a baby calf on the screen, so sick and weak he couldn't stand up, yet he was about to be slaughtered for consumption—my consumption. I took one look into those big brown terrified eyes, pleading into the camera *Somebody help me. Why won't you help me?* and my knees came out from under me. I crumpled onto the couch and dissolved in a sea of tears. For years, I'd been resistant to giving up meat, but when that baby's eyes cut through me, something in me snapped. "That's it," I told God. "No more cows, no more pigs, no more lambs, no more ducks . . . ever, ever again." If you're a vegetarian, you may also be able to identify that moment of clarity—the moment you "woke up" and something deep inside you made a dramatic and permanent shift.

Brochures for PETA gave me the shock treatment necessary to forgo cosmetics tested on animals. I only needed to see one bunny with half her hair burned off her body before I agreed to boycott certain brands of makeup. They didn't need to tell me twice. Education about these matters is a painful initiation, a rude awakening to the heartlessness of our society, but education is our only hope. Of course, many issues arise where I find myself caught between a rock and a hard place. Sometimes I can't find plastic shoes to match my new pink skirt-suit. I, too, fall prey to the convenience of the soulless market-place; then I struggle with the dilemma: How do I balance the scales?

Sometimes the best way to get your prayers answered is to answer the prayers of others. If you have conflicts about your behavior, as we all do, tithing is a great way to balance the scales. If you feel lousy about some hypocrisy in your diet, tithe to a charity like the National Anti-Vivisection Society, People for the Ethical Treatment of Animals, the ARK Trust, Friends of Animals, the Gorilla Foundation, the National Humane Society, or Fauna & Flora International. If you have whittled the furry animals out of your diet, but you still eat feathered ones, volunteer once a week at your local wildlife rehabilitation cen-ter. If you feel guilty about the leather trim on your new purse, volun-teer to walk the dogs at your local no-kill shelter.

We all suffer *now* in our day-to-day lives just by our inability to commune with our furry friends. Only if we cherish and protect them can they bring the endless joy they want to bring us. Everything is a *choice*. We have the power to direct or debilitate whole industries.

Clairvoyance, this higher state of perception, allows us to perceive our choices more clearly, the light and the dark. Clairsentience allows us to feel acutely and intensely both the pleasure and the suffering. The height and depth of your psychic ability will be determined by your willingness to see the truth clearly, no matter how unpleasant. If our innocence is the price of admission into the psychic Shangri-La, our *honesty* buys the ticket and *courage* is our seat belt.

Exercise
Getting Unstuck, an Exercise in Gratitude

What do you do if you feel stuck in any of your telepathic communications? Thank God . . . literally. There are four methods to reach this higher plane where all living beings have access to all other living beings. The first is to enter the silence in meditation, which we've covered extensively. The second technique is to turn off your left brain by engaging in some sort of right-brain activity: dancing, drumming, swimming, painting, practicing piano, playing tennis, and so forth. The third way is to raise your vibration through laughter, to dwell on something that makes you laugh out loud. And the fourth and perhaps most important method is to adopt an attitude of gratitude, which automatically opens your heart. Humility is the key to the magic kingdom. Be patient, worship and adore animals, and they will let you hear them. The dimension of clairaudience is fueled by silent reverence. Impatience is rendered useless in this state of grace. I always tell the animals, "I can wait forever until you answer me." Without this profound reverence—this all-encompassing silent gratitude—I don't think clairaudience is attainable. To truly love the Goddess is to worship her creations; clairaudience is a silent prayer where the Goddess's creations actually *talk back!*

There are times, though, when I am too mentally agitated to slip into that higher plane, times when my worries and concerns are having a rodeo in my cerebral corral and I can't find my heart. These are the times when gratitude works wonders. If I sit to meditate and read an animal, but I can't stop stewing in my own juice, I take my focus off the animal and list at least twenty things I'm grateful for. If you mean it, your heart will open instantly to telepathic communication. When I say "mean it," I'm not talking about being "kinda sorta" grateful. I'm talking about clenching your eyelids together and chanting, "Thank God for running water! Thank God for running water! Thank you! Thank you! Thank you!" until tears stream down your cheeks. You think I'm kidding? Have you ever tried to live without running water? The things for which you're grateful may not be that monumental. I learned this technique from Reverend Beverly Gaard, my third eye meditation teacher, whose list included "An ant, a leaf, a twig . . ." My list this morning looks something like this.

Twenty-three Things to Be Grateful For

a hot cup of coffee

a good pair of tweezers

garden clogs

earplugs

cinnamon rolls

indoor plumbing

toenail clippers

Winsor & Newton paint

two working legs

gardenias in bloom

that the United States is not at war

that women have the vote

that corsets are out of style

that foot binding is out of style *(really)*

antibiotics

air-conditioning

frankincense

jazz

a clothes dryer

a sharp razor

corncob holders

Vivaldi's *Four Seasons*

warm socks

I'd like to remind you that you *are* your attention. Gratitude causes a paradigm shift. Count your blessings, and voilà! Suddenly your glass is not half-empty anymore. After I'd listed my twenty-three things to be grateful for today, I picked up Kurt Vonnegut's *Timequake,* where I found this passage:

> My uncle Alex Vonnegut, a Harvard-educated life insurance sales-man . . . taught me something very important. He said that when things were really going well we should be sure to *notice it.*
>
> He was talking about simple occasions, not great victories: maybe drinking lemonade on a hot afternoon in the shade, or smelling the aroma of a nearby bakery, or hearing somebody all alone playing a piano really well in the house next door.
>
> Uncle Alex urged me to say this out loud during such epiphanies: "If this isn't nice, what is?"

Later Vonnegut elaborates on his favorite scene of his favorite play, also my favorite scene of my favorite play, *Our Town* by the late Thornton Wilder.

> What hit me really hard that night, though, was the character Emily's farewell in the last scene, after the mourners have gone back down the hill to their village, having buried her. She says, "Good-bye, good-bye, world. Good-bye, Grover's Corners . . . Mama and Papa. Good-bye to clocks ticking . . . and Mama's sunflowers. And food and coffee. And new-ironed dresses and hot baths . . . and sleeping and waking up! Oh, earth, you're too wonderful for anybody to realize you!
>
> "Do any human beings ever realize life while they live it?—every, every minute?"

I once worked with an enormous orange cat named Uncle Henry. His mother, Layla, sent me a picture of His Majesty lying on his back on a lawn chair by a swimming pool, like Rodney Dangerfield poolside at the Flamingo Hotel. I worked with Uncle Henry often for a year or so, only because he was a Calamity Jane—perpetually in trouble for one shenanigan or another—constantly infuriating his mother. He was curious, ornery, cantankerous, selfish, and stubborn—everything a cat should be. I was madly in love with him. Then came the call that ripped my heart out. Layla had just pulled her car out of the driveway. She hadn't realized Uncle Henry was sleeping behind one of the wheels. She had backed over him and killed him. I'll never forget that phone call and the agony in the poor woman's voice. Layla was inconsolable, crying so hard I could barely understand a word she said. She felt all the more guilty because she had been mad at him, scolding him harshly earlier that same day.

If there is only one piece of wisdom you glean from this book, let this be it: we are fragile. Our time here is short. We must take the time to cherish every tender, fleeting moment we share together.

After you've listed at least twenty things you're grateful for, bring your focus back to the animal you want to contact. From this identification with universal gratitude, look at your animal's magnificent face and say this out loud: "I love you. I love you. I love you. I am so grateful to have this opportunity to love you. I am so grateful you have this opportunity to love me. Life has brought us together to learn how to communicate with each other. If this isn't nice, what is?"

While imbibing all those loving vibrations and reveling in the expanding glow of your heart, try your communication techniques again.

■ Perceiving Stardust: Seeing "Ghosts" ■

We human beings are nothing but vibration. Animals are nothing but vibration. Plants are nothing but vibration. Your coffee table, your house, your car, are nothing but billions of kinetic electrons, which are primarily space—space between one atom and another, space inside each atom, between the nucleus and the electron. These atoms are grouped so closely together that they form the illusion of dense mass, but in reality what appears as matter is largely nothing but invisible spinning vibrating points of light. And what is an atom made out of? What is the nucleus made out of? What are the electrons made out of? We don't know. We pretend to know. Our scientists have given a name to God incarnate: they call it *energy*. I call it *stardust*.

Are the atoms in your body any more alive than the atoms in your coffee table, which might even have once been the atoms in a living tree? No, the atoms are equally alive. The energy is interchangeable. You may argue, "We're alive and the table is not." The difference between the collection of spinning atoms you call your coffee table and the collection of spinning atoms you call your body is that your body has an additional layer of consciousness, a pilot in the cockpit— the *you* that you call *you*. So the physical bodies that we are all driving around are God incarnate in their own right, but we have yet another dimension of life at work inside us, a dimension that no scientist on earth has ever been able to explain. The physical body is mind-boggling in and of itself. But the inner pilot—the spirit, the Speaker— almost completely eludes us. The ability to see and hear the astral body is the ability to converse with the pilot, whether or not he is currently flying an airplane.

Or, to put it another way, our bodies are radios, picking up frequencies and responding with health or disease depending on what vibrational rates they engage in, but the spirit within the body functions as the radio station capable of transmitting and receiving dozens, maybe hundreds, of different frequencies a day. Most people are comfortable with one or two programs they've selected on their mental dials, but we can change the dial.

The difference between human beings and coffee tables is that human beings have the ability to *choose* what they will play, what they will listen to, and what they will be.

Astral bodies are invisible to the naked eye. Why? Just as we can't see fluorescent lights moving because they vibrate at the rate of 60 hertz, astral bodies surpass the speed that the human eye can follow, but they are only "invisible" in one sense. We can sense these energy vibrations in other ways.

You may get chewed out by your boss, allowing her to flip your channel to a negative (slower) vibration for the rest of the day. Fortunately the opposite is also true: you may be around a friend who really amps you up, who is happy, cheerful, empowered, vibrating at a higher frequency. And it's contagious. Some people make you feel like a drained battery while others make you feel recharged. So the ability to perceive disembodied spirits hinges upon your learning to vibrate at a higher frequency. Astral bodies reside in a dimension of higher frequency, and you can learn to raise your vibration to meet theirs. Both the heart and the third eye work in this dimension, but here in this dreamtime, your eyes are rendered useless. In this final exercise, you will learn to *step up* your frequency to meet animals on the Other Side, including human animals. I call this phenomenon starlight vision, the ability to see stardust.

Exercise in Starlight Vision
Your Internal Rainbow

Sit quietly with the photo of the departed animal you wish to contact. Our human relatives on the Other Side almost always keep our animals for us, so our past animals are usually easy to locate. If our animals do not choose to live with our ancestors, or vice versa, the animals may be spending time with a friend of the family, or they may inhabit one of the astral animal sanctuaries. No matter where they are, you can locate them and explore new territory.

Once you have mastered this exercise with your own departed animals, you may try a more advanced exercise where you swap pictures with one of your friends. But for now, work with an animal who once lived with you, an old friend with whom you feel particularly connected. In this instance, strong emotions will help rather than hinder your initial attempts. In this exercise, the love between you and this animal is a bridge across the universe.

If you can sit comfortably outdoors, the earth will embrace, support, and center you, while the open sky above you will lure your upper chakras open and entice your spirit to soar.

Relax any tension in your body and focus on your breath. Put your attention in the bottom of your feet. Feel your feet reaching down into the earth like roots. Branches of light shoot down your spine, through your legs, and deep within the surface of the earth. Take a moment to enjoy feeling grounded. Your roots of light hold you safely and gently against Mother Earth. Quickly feel each chakra as we climb up through the body. Each chakra is an energy wheel spinning with light, singing with sound. Give each wheel a push. From the outside of a human body, the chakras spin counter-clockwise. From your own internal position behind your own chakras, you will spin them clockwise, from left to right. As they spin, they emit beautiful bell-like music.

The base chakra is red, humming with life. The tone is low and rich. See the color of a ripe tomato. If you see gray or black shades in the red, spin it until the tone clears into a dazzling, vibrant red. If the color is dim, add more paint. Visualize roses, freshly picked apples, poppies. If the sound is faint, turn up the volume. Tune the key until it resonates deeply. This is the first note of your scale. Mine corresponds to middle C on the piano.

The navel chakra is orange, glowing with joy. The sound steps up one key. Give it a little push and let the fear roll out. Spin out any stuck emotion, any old hurts and pain you no longer need to carry in your stomach. Visualize pumpkins, oranges, and bright orange geraniums. Feel the vibration of the key D.

The spleen chakra is yellow, spinning with light. The note rises in tone. As you give it a gentle spin, let go of any limiting beliefs you have about yourself. Let go of any "I should have" and "If only I weren't so" thoughts. Free the guilt and spin it out of your bowl like chocolate cake batter slung off a cake mixer's beaters. The fears go flying. See yellow buttercups, butterflies, and fields of wheat. Hear the note E.

The heart chakra is green, bubbling with love. Like a waterfall of emerald light, it overflows in a chorus of love, peace, the quiet song of being. Give the wheel a push and bask in the life-giving green. Think of tall, wet grass, rain forests, spinach, asparagus, and baby peas. Let the heaviness in your heart lift off. Let the shadows fly away. Silently sing the note F.

The throat chakra is blue, mellow with serenity. Like the bluest skies after a summer rain, the blue is not contained inside you, but expands to include the sky above you, the air drifting around you, and the deep blue sea. If you wish, open your eyes, look up, and drink in the sky. Think of bluebells, forget-me-nots, and cobalt waters. With every breath, breathe in the blue. Enter the blue. The note is G.

The third eye chakra is violet, shimmering in space. With your eyes closed, gently look up. You may see a white ball like a star circling a lavender canvas. You might spy the tiny lavender ball circling like a carousel horse. If the ball is spinning in the wrong direction, direct the strength of your will to stop the ball. Firmly push it the other way and set it back on course. If the trajectory is off and its orbit is wobbly or uneven, patiently see it forming perfect circles. Think of purple grapes on the vine, amethysts, African violets, and orchids. The note is high, strong, and piercing. Vibrate the note A.

The crown chakra is white, glowing with wisdom. The note is higher still, crystal-clear, and bell-like. Reach for it. Hum it or sing it and hold the high frequency. From the top of your head glows a white light. The crown opens like a lotus, unfurling its petals in the sunshine. If flowers could sing, this is the music they would make. There is no longing here, no suffering, and no striving to attain. There is only having and knowing and gratitude. Eternal gratitude. Thank the Goddess for the life she has bestowed in you. You are one of her most precious and beloved creations. Emanate the note B.

Now we're going to go higher still, out of the traditional chakra system and out of the body. Above the crown we locate the first satellite, floating above your head like a shining moon. Picture a white sphere orbiting about a foot above your head. It can move up and down freely as if on a cord, reaching out into the universe. The next chakra is your connection with the stars.

The moon chakra is white, tingling with anticipation. You are being watched over. You are loved. Feel the buzz of activity filled with light, ricocheting with prisms of color, like sunlight on freshly fallen snow. The white snowflakes sparkle with every color of the rainbow. This chakra has wings. From here we can take flight. The tone rises like the piping of a piccolo. Hear the high C. This is the fourth dimension, a reality where there are no boundaries.

Higher still is another chakra, an orbiting star, singing in the night sky like a coloratura soprano. Three feet above your head, it's still a part of you, connecting you to the cosmos by a beam of starlight. This is the doorway to the fifth dimension. Hear the high D ringing like a clear bell, piercing the darkness, and finally catapult yourself higher still. *From here you can go anywhere.*

Vibrating high in the galaxy above the earth is your highest chakra, connecting you to your eternal essence. This is the sixth dimension, virtual domain, and the world between worlds, in a realm beyond space and time, in the peace that passeth all understanding. Yet you are here. It is a part of you. Hear the high E boldly opening up as voices of angels rejoice in a choir far above your head. The tones blaze with vibrant sound, singing out across the universe. You have just entered dreamtime on the wings of love.

Now, with the awareness of these three open energy vortexes above your head, bring your focus back down to your physical body and look out your eyes. You may feel different: dizzy or light-headed, prickling with electricity, mysteriously peaceful or buzzing with elation. You didn't know you were that big, did you? Every being on this planet extends deep into the earth and far out into the stars.

Now look at the picture of your animal. Pick up your pen.

Ask this question: "Where are you?"

Close your eyes. Clear your mind. Focus on your heart. When you're ready, pretend you *are* the animal.

What does the world look like around you?

What does the ground feel like beneath your feet?

Do you smell anything in particular?

What temperature is the air?

What colors do you see?

What textures do you feel?

Who is with you?

Enter the silence and listen for words. You may get a name. You may see or hear an initial in your mind's eye. You may see something that was indicative of one of your relatives, for example your grandfather's watch, your grandmother's glasses, a piece of jewelry or china your departed aunt gave you. You may get sounds that come later in the name. You may hear a nick-name you were called as a child. You may get a word that means many things: the name June, the month June. You might hear a word that rhymes with one of your relative's names. You may see a color. You may feel or smell your animal. You might hear her voice, a faint bark, meow, chirp, or whinny. She still loves you. She's still here. Nothing ever dies.

If you did this meditation indoors, open your eyes and let your attention float around the room. If your eyes settle on the piano, you might have a quick memory flash of a relative sitting at her piano. If your eyes settle on your easy chair, you might for an instant see your departed uncle in his rock-ing chair with your beloved animal in his lap. Let them use your brain to filter in their messages. This is the way you learn to identify objects and make associations.

Ask your animal: What does your house look like?

You will probably see more than one human milling around in their "house." Often, the houses resemble not the homes your ancestors died in, but the homes where they grew up as children. The humans will holographi-cally create the happiest, most comfortable environments they experienced on earth. Sometimes they even manifest fantasies of what they hoped to experience and never achieved.

Dogs will sometimes go to the spirit who was the biggest dog lover, cats to the cat lover. Sometimes, but not always. Sometimes they go to an unlikely person to teach that spirit how to love them (just as they do here on earth) or so they can be the "only cat in the house." Usually human spirits find increased compassion for animals once they arrive at the Other Side.

When you are doing a reading with a departed animal, trying to discern which relative they're with, ask specific questions: In the house, is there music playing? Is the music live or is it a phonograph? What instruments do you hear? Do you hear singing? What style of music is playing? What era? Can you make out the words?

Now ask your animal friend:

What form have you taken?

Where do you sleep? In someone's lap? What does she do while you sleep? Crochet? Embroider? Read?

What are the people doing?

Do they have jobs?

What other animals are with you?

If this is not your animal, you may like to ask, What did you die of? If it is yours, you may want to ask, Were you in pain? Now is the opportunity to clear up any old heartbreaking issues. Ask the questions you need to ask:

Are you mad at me?

Did I let you go too soon?

Did I keep you too long?

These are the times when the tears flow. The animals are so forgiving, so benevolent; I've never seen a person who didn't walk away from these sessions relieved. It will take the weight of the world off your shoulders to know that you're forgiven, to know that you're still loved. Now, feel free to ask:

Do you still spend time with me?

When?

Where do you like to sleep in my house?

The animals frequently visit in the wee hours of the morning, sleeping on our beds, but they leave as soon as we wake. The best time to get a glimpse of your old friend is just as you nod off to sleep or the second you wake, before you move or make a sound.

How do you get along with my living animals?

Who else is with you?

Are you coming back to me? If so, when?

Here's where the negotiating process starts. You can't coax animals back to earth until they're good and ready, but you may be able to negotiate; for example, they'll come back only after the new dog dies; after the children are grown; when you move to a house with a bigger yard. You may even be able to agree on certain signs so you can identify your reincarnated animal.

How will I know it's you?

Where will I find you, or will you find me?

You can continue your questioning any way you like, but here are some popular questions:

What does your world look like on the Other Side?

Can you tell me a secret so I know it's really you?

Do you have a message for me?

Do you have advice for any of my living animals?

If you have a clear connection, this is an excellent way to get behavioral and medical advice. When you've finished with your session, leave out a treat for your friend. They might not be able to eat the food, but they sure appreciate the smell. Leave out a plate of your old friend's favorite food. If one of your living animals gulps it down, that's okay, too. Your spirit animal can enjoy the tastes through the living animal, via Gestalt. Or put down a special bed for your visitor. Clear off your departed cat's favorite windowsill or bring out your dog's old blanket.

For the next few days keep your awareness open. You may get messages later to reaffirm your contact. You may open a magazine and see a replica of your friend. You might see a commercial or billboard as you drive by that has a special message for you. One of your human friends may blurt out something that had a special meaning to you and your animal friend. You may hear a song on the radio in your car that reaffirms the presence of your friend. Stay alert. Become acutely observant. Let your senses fine-tune themselves and your frequency *step up*. Remember, your friend can manipulate the world around you only if you are open and observant. The messages are everywhere, and the animals send their love. It's always about love. And if you get a call out of the blue by someone who says, "You've just *got* to take one of these kittens [or puppies or this horse]," don't think about it! Just say "yes!" It's probably your friend who just crossed the universe for you.

☒ Aurora's Protest ☒

I'm not going to lie to you. I don't know anything about hands-on healing. I don't know why it works, but here is the story of the first time I tried it, and it's a humdinger. I had been invited to perform some experiments with the masterful Dr. John Craige, God rest his soul, a vet light-years ahead of his time. At his holistic clinic I met Aurora, an adorable miniature collie with a cancer the size of an apple protruding from her tummy. Dr. Craige informed me that even after the cancer had been removed from one organ, it moved to another. It was now in her pancreas. Of all the sick animals I'd ever seen, this case seemed to have the most obvious psychological base. The phenomenon of osmosis illness is such a mystery; it may be difficult to define, but it is impossible to ignore. Aurora was involved in and acting out many psychological dynamics she had absorbed from her mother, Erica. I spoke to her as she lay listless on the cold metal table in front of me, Erica by her side.

"What is causing this cancer, Aurora?" I asked.

I am Erica's mother, so I have to have this, she replied.

"Erica, how old were you when your mother died?" I asked.

"Three," Erica said.

I am her father, too.

"How old were you when your father died?" I asked Erica.

"Nine," she said.

One of her parents died of cancer, Aurora said.

"Which one of your parents did you lose to cancer?" I asked.

"My father," Erica said.

"I get that one of them was an alcoholic. What did your mother die of?" I asked.

"Alcoholism," Erica said.

"The pancreas controls the blood sugar," I said. "So your mother's situation may be connected to Aurora. She seems to be mirroring your parents' illnesses because she believes *she is* your parent. I know it may sound crazy, but our animals mirror so much of what goes on inside of us."

"Aurora, why are you acting this out?" I asked.

I am both her parents. Her parents got sick like this, so I have to get sick, too.

"How can we help you give this up?" I asked.

Erica is dating a dark-haired man who hates me. He is a cold, insensitive man. He doesn't treat her well, and I know she can do much better than that.

"How long have you been with your boyfriend?" I asked.

"My fiancé? Four years," Erica said.

"Aurora says that the man hates her."

"Oh, he does! He's very jealous," Erica agreed.

"Aurora says you can do better than him, that this man isn't very sensitive toward you," I told her.

"Oh, I've heard that a lot. Several of my friends tell me that." Erica tried to brush it off.

"It's amazing how frequently our animals are really mirroring our emotional problems," I said.

To make her see, Aurora said.

"Aurora thinks your boyfriend has to carry your childhood trauma until you address it. She says this boyfriend is acting out some of the psychological problems you haven't dealt with from your childhood. I firmly believe that people who do not love animals are not worthy of our love, because that's all animals are—receptacles of unconditional love. I know you're spending a fortune on Aurora's medical bills, but if you spend a little bit more on your own recovery, whether it's positive thinking seminars or support groups or self-help books, I believe it will help Aurora's recuperation," I said.

"Aurora, is there someone else out there for your mother?" I asked.

Yes! He's got blond hair, and he's a teacher. Aurora sent me a picture of a man who was lecturing in front of a classroom and I described him to Erica.

"Aurora says he's got sandy blond hair, he wears glasses, has a stocky build, and is some sort of teacher or lecturer," I said.

"I dreamed about a blond man last night who was a teacher!" Erica gasped. Her eyes filled with stunned tears. "I woke up this morning thinking for the first time in my life, *Maybe there really is someone else out there for me!* I've never thought there was, but the dream of this blond man was so strong! Please ask Aurora if she will get better."

Only if she leaves her boyfriend. If she marries him, I will die. If she gives him up, I will give up the cancer, Aurora said.

The vet came into the room just then to talk to us about the limp little dog. Erica said that she had hardly moved for days. She couldn't even stand up. Erica was desperate, but the vet's prognosis was grim. There seemed to be little hope for this adorable dog. When Erica and the vet had finished conferring, I asked them if I could be alone for a few moments with Aurora.

What happened next sounds like a story from the *National Enquirer.* It was an incredible event I have never experienced before or since.

As I stood over this dying dog, beyond hope, I put my hands on her back and began to pray. Suddenly I was reminded of a picture I had seen in Geoffrey Hodson's book *Kingdom of the Gods:* an illustration of how a healing angel might appear. Mr. Hodson, a British clairvoyant, saw myriad magnificent spirits and devas, claiming that if you pray for healing, you can call to your aid a healing angel. The painting depicted a tremendous angel standing over the sickbed of a child, totally enfolding the child in the rays of light that burst forth from its eyes, throat, and heart.

I decided to give it a shot. What did I have to lose? If such things can be seen by one man, what keeps them from being available to all of us?

I pictured an angel floating above the examination table. I imagined it as clearly as I possibly could and begged it to heal this precious dog. A few minutes later I felt the darkness lift off our hearts. The air around us began to glow, and I felt fingers of light reaching down from above. A change occurred in the atmosphere, as if a window were suddenly cast open in a dark, stuffy room, filling it gently with a spring breeze. I took a few peaceful breaths, drinking in this calm. I asked the angel to use my hands to funnel energy into Aurora. Instantly my hands began to tingle. I found myself smiling for no reason except that this sensation felt so good.

Beaming down from the celestial being, streams of light poured into the dog. With every passing moment, the angel made her presence more and more concrete, pouring rainbows down out of her heart and into the dog. Splashed in the aftermath, I basked in the periphery. I became very aware of her wings—two giant wings completely encompassed the room, from the table to the ceiling.

Suddenly Aurora jumped up, barking excitedly. Of her own accord, she leaped off the high table and tore out of the open door. Aurora ran down the hallway of the vet's office, barking joyfully!

When she reached the end of the hallway, she turned around and ran back. Erica and Dr. Craige dashed into the room when they heard the hubbub. They stood with openmouthed stares as the little dog raced up and down the hallway, barking like a healthy puppy hot for a game of fetch.

"Sheesh. Look at her go!" Erica said incredulously. "Did she jump off that table all by herself?" I nodded yes, no less amazed than they.

Dr. Craige boomed at me, "My God, woman! When she brought her in, she couldn't walk! *What the hell did you do to that dog?"*

"I dunno, I guess I scared the shit out of her!" I whispered. I told Erica later about the angel, but I never let the vet in on our secret.

Erica stayed in touch with me for a few more years to give me progress reports. Aurora's condition was holding and Erica's marriage to the man Aurora disliked was postponed. Finally, she called to tell me that two weeks before her wedding day to that same man, Aurora died. She had held out for two years from the time we stirred up mischief with the angel.

Erica reported that throughout the outdoor ceremony, a very persistent white dove stalked her. She felt that Aurora had sent the dove. Aurora confided that, yes, the dove was her magic touch to the ceremony. She requested I ask her who she was with now. So I asked her which of Erica's relatives was keeping her on the Other Side.

Tell her I'm with Anthony Thomas, she said.

"She is with the spirit of a man named Anthony Thomas. Do you have a relative named Anthony Thomas?" I asked her.

"No, not yet," she answered with a gasp. "That's the name I've picked out for my baby. I've always wanted a little boy, and when he comes, I'm going to name him Anthony Thomas." Evidently the spirit of the little dog was waiting on the Other Side with the spirit of her *unborn child.*

Epilogue

Rodney's Command Performance

That morning in June when Rodney left, he almost took me with him. He had been battling a form of colitis for years. Finally he could hold nothing down. He grew so weak that he could barely stand, and a whole team of L.A.'s finest vets couldn't save him. Rodney and I had agreed that he wouldn't be "put down." He assured me he could "go on his own" with dignity. He had been my best friend and assistant for eight years. I had learned to trust his judgment.

The morning he died, we lay together side by side on the living room floor—waiting. As Rodney's breath grew more hoarse and labored, I held him, crying like a baby. He had been unconscious for almost three hours while I prayed continuously, desperately, for his release. I lay with my hand over his heart.

My eyes were clenched tight, still burning with tears, as I saw this vision. A doorway opened in the air above us, just under the ceiling. A door swung open and a river of light cascaded into the room. Through this doorway stepped my grandmother Rheau Nell, who in her life on earth had cared for a vast menagerie of animals. Her presence did not astonish me half as much as the company she brought with her. Out of the light bounded Gus and Gretel, my childhood dogs, a silver German shepherd and my beloved Rhodesian Ridgeback! I hadn't seen them in over twenty years. They danced around me in a furious frenzy of love and kisses. My grandmother was as she ever was, complete with red beehive and cat-eyed glasses. (Rheau Nell was one of the first women in Ardmore, Oklahoma, to own her own business in the 1940s. She was a hairdresser and what you might have called "a stunner.")

Suddenly my grandmother reached her arms toward me, and it wasn't to embrace me. The gesture was not without compassion, but it was strong and demanding. I knew what she wanted, and I knew I couldn't say no. I "stood up" out of my physical body and found myself holding the spirit of my cat. Trembling and wracked with sobs, I handed Rodney's spirit to Rheau Nell. The very instant she took him from my arms, his "real" heart stopped beating under my hand. Rheau Nell turned around and slowly disappeared into the light, this time with Rodney's spirit in her arms. The two dogs bounded after her. The door snapped shut. The vision disappeared, and when I opened my eyes, my dear friend was dead.

I stacked a hundred pictures around him, of all his happiest moments, and a bouquet of roses (his favorite) at his feet. At his head I put my statue of Sekhmet, the Egyptian lion goddess. Then I went across the street to get him a piece of Popeye's fried chicken. (With his stomach problem, he hadn't been able to eat anything spicy for years, so I thought he could at least indulge now.) I'll never forget stepping out into traffic on L.A.'s busiest thoroughfare, Ventura Boulevard, daring the cars to hit me. I was crying so deliriously, I didn't care if I lived or died. That night I found a spot on a mountaintop with a panoramic view of the luminous San Fernando Valley. Like most cats, Rodney had always had a penchant for high places. The twinkling lights seemed to go on forever. There, I wrapped Rodney in his favorite thermal blanket and buried him with a piece of Popeye's fried chicken.

When I walked away from that grave, I turned my back on animal communication. I stubbornly refused to read animals for almost two years—until Oscar was born. I just didn't want to do it without Rodney.

■ Rodney's Return: An Unexpected Party ■

My emotional uproar started the Saturday before, on April 4. Tearful tantrums plagued me all day for no apparent reason, accompanied by sudden bouts of anger and panic. I also was stricken with inexplicable abdominal cramping. I prayed that night that the suffering would leave me, but I woke up Sunday morning worse, not better. Even a trip to church did not soothe the anxiety. Throughout the service I had an odd sensation of panic in my stomach and, dare I say, er, womb. My uterus ached so badly, I had to get up during the sermon to find a water fountain where I could wolf down an aspirin. It had no effect on me whatsoever. (Drugs never work on feelings that are not your own.)

On the way home, the panic attack was so severe, I began to pray for my sanity. I cursed at God and my spirit guides, "Where are you guys? I feel totally abandoned down here! For crying out loud, I need some help! Give me a sign that you hear me!"

When I pulled up into the driveway and climbed out of my car, doubled over with pain, my *sign* was waiting for me in the front yard. I hadn't seen her for some time. From the day we'd moved in to this house, Gidget, the neighbor's little black cat, had insisted on living with me. Mr. Jones would not tolerate her, but she was so persistent, I fed her outside. When we first met, she told me she didn't have a home, she didn't like the people next door, and she wanted to live with me. She spent the majority of her time in my yard, waiting to flirt with Mr. Jones.

This particular Sunday morning, she dashed toward me and climbed into my lap as I collapsed on the sidewalk to greet her. Immediately I saw she was pregnant—*extremely* pregnant—and out of her mind with panic. I told her I'd help her in any way I could: I'd midwife the babies. Instantly she ran into our garage, singing in a chorus of desperate chirps. (Mother cats have a special frantic meow when they are going into labor.) I tried to coax her into the house, but she would have none of it. She ran back into the garage to poke around in a pile of cardboard boxes, looking for a place to give birth. I let her pick a box, which I lined with clean towels and a heating pad. Gidget told me she would have four kittens. Although she appeared to be on the verge of exploding at that very moment, she settled into her chosen box and said she didn't think the babies would come until later that night.

After an hour of careful monitoring, she dozed off to sleep, so I decided to abandon the vigil and grab a quick lunch. I cut an exit door in the box and left her with food and water, then ducked out to a local vegetarian restaurant. No sooner had the salad come than my abdominal cramps became so severe that I quivered on my barstool. I ordered the food to go and raced home in a mindless frenzy.

Just as I lifted the lid to Gidget's box, she let out a cry and the first kitten's head appeared. Gidget delivered the first three kittens slowly under my supervision. My faith was renewed. My prayers were answered; I took back all my confused curses. I fawned over the three kittens and wept. That cardboard box in my garage became my temple —it might as well have housed all the stained glass in Notre Dame.

But there was still the matter of the fourth kitten. The first three kittens were gray-striped tabbies. "The fourth one will be orange," I told myself. Of this, I was absolutely convinced. I didn't know why. When the fourth one finally emerged and was gray like the others, I was bewildered. By this time Gidget was exhausted and failed to cut the fourth kitten's umbilical cord. I clipped it with sterile scissors and tied it off with dental floss. This fourth tike was a boy—the loudest and most cantankerous of the clan.

The next morning, when I hurried out to see my new family, one kitten inched away from the pack and caressed my thumb with his cheek. I rolled him over to see he was the one I had tied off with dental floss. The kitten spoke to me. *Good morning,* he said. Hmm. Sounds familiar, I thought. "Which of you have been with me before?" I asked the children. A tiny female voice became audible inside my head. *There aren't any of us who haven't been with you before,* she said. I was stupefied, but I supposed it *was* possible, what with all my childhood cats. I looked at number four suspiciously. He was by far the most aggressive, socking his sisters in the face, struggling for tit and squealing loudly if I turned him over on his back like a turtle.

But there was something familiar about him: he had a certain *je ne sais quois.*

That night I prayed to get some clarity about Rodney. I dreamed I was admiring the kittens: three gray and one orange. Well, I have to keep the *orange one,* no matter which of the others we keep, I told myself. In this dream, the fourth newborn was a soft honey-yellow color.

The next night the dream was more distinct. Once again, I was admiring the kittens, preparing to select only two to keep. Again there were three grays and one orange; but this time they were older, as if we had flashed forward in time. The orange kitten had bold caramel stripes. I lay down eye-level with him to get a closer look. He grew larger before my eyes, and his nose elongated like a feline Pinocchio. His head morphed into Rodney's! His nose was immense! He looked at me and smiled. I woke up with a start.

Over the course of the next five weeks, the fourth kitten began to turn orange. Don't get me wrong, he was still a gray-striped cat, but his stomach took on a luscious golden hue, as if he'd waded through a bowl of honey. His underbelly grew more yellow every day until he was identifiably *more orange* than the others. Since the neighbors claimed they "forgot" to get Gidget spayed, I "forgot" to give the kittens back. I decided to keep all four kittens and name them after jazz masters: Billie Holiday, Ella Fitzgerald, Cyrus Chestnut, and this suspiciously orange one I named Oscar Peterson.

Now Rodney and I had had a secret ritual. If you remember, at the moment of our first meeting, he reached his little pipe cleaner arms around my neck and kissed me on the lips, giving me the most deliberate kiss of my life. We agreed it would be our sign if ever he were to return to me. I wasn't thinking about it or projecting it on my new clan the morning I lay down in the garage to pet my five-week-old family. But out of the blue I felt Oscar traversing the length of my body with his tiny piston paws. He was on a mission. He shimmied up my chest and, without faltering, wrapped his tiny arms around my throat and kissed me on the lips. He pulled back, looked me in the eye, and kissed me again with all his might. Then he winked!

"Rodney!" I gasped. "Where have you been?!"

Suddenly, I was filled with an extraordinary feeling of speed and motion, of dizzying flight through streaking comets and spinning stars. At the speed of light, the cat had whooshed through light-years and solar systems of color and sound. In the same distinguished voice I'd always heard, he said only this:

I crossed the galaxy for you, Mother.

You see, it's true. Love never dies. No matter where or when, we will be in love forever—together.

Man and Creature

(From *The Teaching of Reverence for Life*)

by Albert Schweitzer

The ethics of reverence for life makes no distinction between higher and lower, more precious and less precious lives. It has good reasons for this omission. For what are we doing, when we establish hard and fast gradations in value between living organisms, but judging them in relation to ourselves, by whether they seem to stand closer to us or farther from us. This is a wholly subjective standard. How can we know what importance other living organisms have in themselves and in terms of the universe?

In making such distinctions, we are apt to decide that there are forms of life which are worthless and may be stamped out without its mattering at all. This category may include anything from insects to primitive peoples, depending on circumstances.

To the truly ethical man, all life is sacred, including forms of life that from the human point of view may seem to be lower than ours. He makes distinctions only from case to case, and under pressure of necessity, when he is forced to decide which life he will sacrifice in order to preserve other lives. In this deciding from case to case, he is aware that he is proceeding subjectively and arbitrarily, and that he is accountable for the lives thus sacrificed.

The man who is guided by the ethics of reverence for life stamps out life only from inescapable necessity, never from thoughtlessness. He seizes every occasion to feel the happiness of helping living things and shielding them from suffering and annihilation.

Whenever we harm any form of life, we must be clear about whether it was really necessary to do so. We must not go beyond the truly unavoidable harm, not even in seemingly insignificant matters. The farmer who mows down a thousand flowers in his meadow, in order to feed his cows, should be on guard, as he turns homeward, not to decapitate some flower by the roadside, just by way of thoughtlessly passing the time. For then he sins against life without being under the compulsion of necessity.

Those who carry out scientific experiments with animals, in order to apply the knowledge gained to the alleviation of human ills, should never reassure themselves with the generality that their cruel acts serve a useful purpose. In each individual case they must ask themselves whether there is a real necessity for imposing such a sacrifice upon a living creature. They must try to reduce the suffering insofar as they are able. It is inexcusable for a scientific institution to omit anesthesia in order to save time and trouble. It is horrible to subject animals to torment merely in order to demonstrate to students phenomena that are already familiar.

The very fact that animals, by the pain they endure in experiments, contribute so much to suffering humanity, should forge a new and unique kind of solidarity between them and us. For that reason alone it is incumbent upon each and every one of us to do all possible good to nonhuman life.

When we help an insect out of a difficulty, we are only trying to compensate for man's ever-renewed sins against other creatures. Wherever animals are impressed into the service of man, every one of us should be mindful of the toll we are exacting. We cannot stand idly by and see an animal subjected to unnecessary harshness or deliberate mistreatment. We cannot say it is not our business to inter-fere. On the contrary, it is our duty to intervene in the animal's behalf.

No one may close his eyes and pretend that the suffering that he does not see has not occurred. We must not take the burden of our responsibility lightly. When abuse of animals is widespread, when the bellowing of thirsty animals in cattle cars is heard and ignored, when cruelty still prevails in many slaughterhouses, when animals are clum-sily and painfully butchered in our kitchens, when brutish people inflict unimaginable torments upon animals and when some animals are exposed to the cruel games of children, all of us share in the guilt.

As the housewife who has scrubbed the floor sees to it that the door is shut, so that the dog does not come in and undo all her work with his muddy paws, so religious and philosophical thinkers have gone to some pains to see that no animals enter and upset their sys-tems of ethics.

It would seem as if Descartes, with his theory that animals have no souls and are mere machines which only seem to feel pain, had bewitched all of modern philosophy. Philosophy has totally evaded the problem of man's conduct toward other organisms. We might say that philosophy has played a piano of which a whole series of keys were considered untouchable.

To the universal ethics of reverence for life, pity for animals, so often smilingly dismissed as sentimentality, becomes a mandate no thinking person can escape.

The time will come when public opinion will no longer tolerate amusements based on the mistreatment and killing of animals. The time will come, but when? When will we reach the point that hunt-ing, the pleasure in killing animals for sport, will be regarded as a mental aberration? When will all the killing that necessity imposes upon us be undertaken with sorrow?

Suggested Reading

Beck, Martha, Ph.D. *Expecting Adam*. New York: Times Books, 1999.

Blake, Henry. *Horse Wisdom Trilogy—Talking With Horses: A Study of Communication Between Man and Horse, Thinking With Horses,* and *Horse Sense: How to Develop Your Horse's Intelligence*. London: Trafalgar Square, 1991, 1993, and 1994, respectively.

Campbell, Joseph. *The Power of Myth*. New York: Bantam Doubleday Dell Publishing Group, Inc., 1988.

Cooper, Paulette. *The 100 Top Psychics in America*. New York: Pocket Books, 1996.

Covey, Stephen R. *The 7 Habits of Highly Effective People*. New York: Simon & Schuster, 1989.

Day, Laura. *Practical Intuition*. New York: Broadway Books, 1996.

Edwards, Betty. *Drawing on the Right Side of the Brain*. Boston: Houghton Mifflin, 1979.

Estes, Clarissa Pinkola, Ph.D. *Women Who Run with the Wolves*. New York: Ballantine Books, 1992.

Fitzpatrick, Sonya. *What the Animals Tell Me*. New York: Hyperion, 1997.

Frost, April. *Beyond Obedience: Training with Awareness for You and Your Dog*. New York: Harmony Books, 1998.

Gallwey, Timothy. *The Inner Game of Tennis*. New York: Random House, 1997.

Grant, Joan. *Winged Pharaoh*. London: Arthur Baker Ltd., 1997.

Mackay, Nicci. *Spoken in Whispers: The Autobiography of a Horse Whisperer*. New York: Fireside, 1997.

McKinnon, Helen. *It's for the Animals*. Fairview, N.C.: Helen L. McKinnon, 1995.

Mariechild, Diane. *Mother Wit*. Santa Cruz, Calif.: The Crossing Press, Inc., 1981.

Myss, Caroline, Ph.D. *Anatomy of Spirit*. New York: Three River's Press, 1996.

Naparstek, Belleruth. *Your Sixth Sense: Unlocking the Power of Your Intuition*. San Francisco: HarperSanFrancisco, 1997.

Orloff, Judith, M.D. *Second Sight*. New York: Warner Books, 1996.

Robbins, Tom. *Skinny Legs and All*. New York: Bantam Books, 1990.

Roberts, Monty. *The Man Who Listens to Horses*. New York: Ballantine Books, 1996.

Schoen, Allen M., D.V.M., M.S., and Pam Proctor. *Love, Miracles, and Animal Healing*. New York: Fireside, 1996.

Schweitzer, Albert. *The Teaching of Reverence for Life*. New York: Holt, Rinehart and Winston, 1965.

Teish, Luisah. *Jambalaya*. San Francisco: HarperSanFrancisco, 1985.

Ueland, Brenda. *If You Want to Write*. Saint Paul, Minn.: Graywolf Press, 1987.

Vonnegut, Kurt. *Timequake*. New York: The Berkley Publishing Group, 1997.

Zukav, Gary. *The Dancing Wi Li Masters*. New York: William Morrow and Co., Inc., 1979.

Resources

Recommended Animal Foods

Artemis
21720 Sherman Way
Canoga Park, CA 91303
(818) 348-3018

Felidae
Canidae Corporation
P.O. Box 3610
San Luis Obispo, CA 93403
(800) 398-1600
(909) 599-5190

Flint River Ranch
Super Premium Health Food
   for Pets
1243 Columbia Avenue B6
Riverside, CA 92507
(877) 354-6874

Innova
Natura Pet Products
P.O. Box 271
Santa Clara, CA 95052
(800) 532-7261

It's for the Animals
Natural Care & Resources
Helen L. McKinnon Holistic
   Consultant/author
(888) 339-IFTA
http://members.aol.com/IFTA2

Nature's Recipe Pet Foods
Corona, CA 91720
www.naturesrecipe.com

**Solid Gold Health Products
for Pets, Inc.**
Katz-n-flocken
1483 N. Cuyamaca
El Cajon, CA 92020

Animal Advocacy Organizations and Charities

Action for Animals Network
523 N. Paxton Street
P.O. Box 9039
Alexandria, VA 22304
(703) 261-3283 (fax same)
anmintxk@erols.com
www.enviroweb.org/aan

**Activist Civil Liberties
Committee**
P.O. Box 19515
Sacramento, CA 95819
(916) 452-7179

**Advocates for Moral
Reevaluation of Animal
Experimentation**
10830 S.W. 85 Court
Gainesville, FL 32601

**African Anti-Poaching
Foundation**
Box 2357
Dingley Island, Brunswick, MD
    04011
(207) 784-3332
Fax: (207) 784-6937

Alaska Wildlife Alliance
P.O. Box 202022
Anchorage, AK 99520
(907) 277-0897
Fax: (907) 277-7423
awa@ascache.com

Alaskans Against Snaring Wolves
608 W. 4th Avenue, Ste. 31
Anchorage, AK 99501
(907) 276-WOLF

Alley Animals, Inc.
P.O. Box 27487
Towson, MD 21285-7487
(410) 823-0899

Alley Cat Allies
1801 Belmont Road N.W., Ste. 201
Washington, DC 20009
(202) 667-3630
Fax: (202) 667-3640
alleycat@alleycat.org

Alliance for Animals
122 State Street, #406
Madison, WI 53703
(608) 257-6333
Fax: (608) 257-6400
alliance@allanimals.org
www.allanimals.org

**Alternative Research and
Development Foundation**
14280 Gold View Drive
Eden Prairie, MN 55346
(612) 949-2409
ardfijmc@aol.com

**American Anti-Vivisection
Society**
801 Old York Road, Ste. 204
Jenkintown, PA 19046-1685
(215) 887-0816
Fax: (215) 887-2088
aavonline@aol.com
www.aavs.org

**American Equine Rescue
Organization**
P.O. Box 7159
Beverly Hills, CA 90210-7159
(310) 285-8955
Fax: (310) 278-9009

**American Fund for Alternatives
to Animal Research**
175 West 12th Street, Ste. 16-G
New York, NY 10011
(212) 989-8073 (fax same)

American Humane Association (headquarters)
63 Inverness Drive E.
Englewood, CO 80112
(303) 792-9900/(800) 227-4645
Fax: (303) 792-5333
www.amerhumane.org

American Society for the Prevention of Cruelty to Animals (ASPCA)
424 East 92nd Street
New York, NY 10128-6804
(212) 876-7700
Fax: (212) 410-7658
website @aspca.org
www.aspca.org

The American Society for the Welfare of Cats
123 Lakeview Drive, Box 594
Alloway, NJ 08001
(609) 935-2870
Fax: (609) 935-8413
magic@snakebite.com
www.accsyst.com/~magic/cats.html

American Tortoise Rescue
23852 Pacific Coast Highway, #928
Malibu, CA 90265
(800) 938-3553
Fax: (310) 589-6101
Turtleserq@aol.com

Animal Defense League/ Coalition to Abolish the Fur Trade—Boston
P.O. Box 381855
Cambridge, MA 02238-1855
(617) 623-8243
caftboston@juno.com

Animal Liberation Action Group
Campus Connection, Reeve
 Memorial Union, University of
 Wisconsin—Oshkosh
748 Algoma Boulevard
Oshkosh, WI 54901-3512
(920) 424-0265
Fax: (920) 424-7317
AnimalLib@uwosh.edu
www.uwosh.edu/organizations/alag

The ARK Trust, Inc.
5551 Balboa Boulevard
Encino, CA 91316
(818) 501-2ARK
Fax: (818) 501-2226
genesis@arktrust.org
www.arktrust.org

Association for the Protection of Fur-bearing Animals/The Fur Bearers
2235 Commercial Drive
Vancouver, BC VSN 4B6, Canada
(604) 255-0411
Fax: (604) 897-4589
taosanctuaries@itexas.net
www.primate.wisc.edu/pin/idp/org/
 sanct/023.html

Association of Veterinarians for Animal Rights
P.O. Box 208
Davis, CA 95617-0208
(530) 759-8106
Fax: (530) 759-8116
AVAR@igc.org
www.avar.org

Australian Association for Humane Research
P.O. Box 779, Darlinghurst
New South Wales 1300, Australia
61-2-9360-1144
Fax: 61-2-9361-6448
humane@aahr.asn.au
www.aahr.asn.au

Bat Conservation International
P.O. Box 162603
Austin, TX 78716
(512) 327-9721
Fax: (512) 327-9724
www.batcon.org

Bear Watch Society
1850 Commercial Drive, Box 21598
Vancouver, BC V5N 4AO, Canada
(416) 462-7541
Fax: (416) 462-6092
bears@bearwatch.org
www.bearwatch.org

Beavers: Wetlands & Wildlife
146 Van Dyke Road
Dolgeville, NY 13329
(518) 568-6046 (fax same)
beavers@telenet.net
www.telenet.net/~beavers

Best Friends Animal Sanctuary
5001 Angel Canyon Drive
Kanab, UT 84741-5001
(435) 644-2001
Fax: (435) 644-2078
info@bestfriends.org
www.bestfriends.org

Born Free Foundation
3 Grove House, Foundry Lane
Horsham, West Sussex KH13 5PL
United Kingdom
44-1403-240-170
Fax: 44-1403-327-838
wildlife@bornfree.org
www.bornfree.org.uk

**California Animal Defense &
Antivivisection League, Inc.**
P.O. Box 3047
Gardena, CA 90247
(310) 549-9196
Fax: (310) 768-7744

**California Equine Retirement
Foundation, Inc.**
34033 Kooden Road
Winchester, CA 92596
(909) 926-4190 (fax same)
savethehorse@earthlink.net

**Canadians for Ethical Treatment
of Food Animals**
Box 18024, 2225 West 41st Avenue
Vancouver, BC V6M 4L3, Canada
(604) 261-3801 (fax same)

Cheetah Action Trust
P.O. Box 32328, Camps Bay 8040
South Africa
27-21-439-0597
Fax: 27-21-405-9650

Chimp Haven
702 Richland Hills, P.O. Box 760081
San Antonio, TX 78245
(888) 98Chimp
Fax: (718) 884-4008
chimphaven@aol.com
www.chimphaven.org

**Create-A-Smile Animal-Assisted
Therapy Team**
1140 Westwood Boulevard, Ste. 207
Los Angeles, CA 90024
(310) 208-3631
Fax: (310) 208-2779
therapy@aat.org
www.aat.org

**DELTA Rescue (Devotion and
Everlasting Love to Animals)**
P.O. Box 9
Glendale, CA 91209
(818) 241-6282

The Delta Society
P.O. Box 1080
Renton, WA 95057

The Elephant Sanctuary in Hohenwald
P.O. Box 393
Hohenwald, TN 38462
www.elephants.com

Fauna & Flora International
Great Eastern House
Tenison Road
Cambridge CB1 2TT
United Kingdom
44 (0) 1223 571000
44 (0) 1223 461481
e-mail: info@fauna-flora.org

Fauna & Flora International—U.S.A.
3490 California Street
Suite 201
San Francisco, CA 94118
(800) 221-9524
(415) 346-7612
e-mail: Faunaflora@earthlink.net

Feminists for Animal Rights
P.O. Box 41355
Tucson, AZ 85717
(520) 825-6852
far@envirolink.org
www.enviroweb.org/far

Friends of Animals
777 Post Road, Ste. 205
Darien, CT 06820
(203) 656-1522
Fax: (203) 656-0267
foa@igc.org
www.friendsofanimals.org

The Gentle Barn Foundation
6050 Corbin Avenue
Tarzana, CA 91356
(818) 705-5477
www.gentlebarn.org

The Gorilla Foundation
Box 620-640
Woodside, CA 94062
(650) 851-8505/MEGOAPE
Fax: (650) 365-7906
hanabiko@earthlink.net
www.gorilla.org

Harvard Law School Student Animal Legal Defense Fund
1563 Massachusetts Avenue
Pound Hall, Room 103
Cambridge, MA 02138

Home for Unwanted and Abandoned Guinea Pigs
3772 Pin Oak Circle
Doraville, GA 30340
http://members.aol.com/
　homeforgps/advice2/home.htm

The Humane Society of the United States
2100 L Street NW
Washington, DC 20037
(202) 452-1100
Fax: (202) 778-6132
www.hsus.org

International Donkey Protection Trust
Sidmouth, Devon EX10, UK
44-1395-578-222
Fax: 44-1395-579-266
thedonkeysanctuary@cs.com

International Society for the Protection of Mustangs and Burros
P.O. Box 14194
Scottsdale, AZ 85267
(480) 502-7900
Fax: (480) 502-2205
103053.1112@cs.com

International Wolf Center
5930 Brooklyn Boulevard
Minneapolis, MN 55429-2418
1-800-ELY-WOLF
wolfinfo@wolf.org
www.wolf.org

Last Chance for Animals
8033 Sunset Boulevard #835
Los Angeles, CA 90046
(310) 271-6096
(310) 271-1890
www.lcanimal.org

Mountain Lion Foundation
P.O. Box 1896
Sacramento, CA 95812
(916) 442-2666
Fax: (916) 442-2871
MLF@mountainlion.org
www.mountainlion.org

National Anti-Vivisection Society Limited UK
261 Goldhawk Road
London W12 9PE
020 8846-9777
info@navs.org.uk

National Antivivisection Society U.S.
53 W. Jackson Street, Ste. 1552
Chicago, IL 60604
(800) 888-NAVS
navs@navs.org

National Federation of Badger Groups
2 Cloister Business Centre,
8 Battersea Park Road
London SW8 4BG, United Kingdom
44-171-498-3220
Fax: 44-171-627-4212
www.geocities.com/RainForest/
   Canopy/2626

National Greyhound Adoption Program
8301 Torresdale Avenue
Philadelphia, PA 19136
(215) 331-7918
www.ngap.org

National Opossum Society
P.O. Box 3091
Orange, CA 92857-001
www.opossum.org

National Wild Horse Rescue and Sanctuary
1354 East Avenue, #252
Chico, CA 95926
(530) 343-2498 (fax same)
wildmestengo@aol.com

The Nature of Wildworks
P.O. Box 109
Topanga, CA 90290
(310) 455-0550
wildworks1@aol.com
www.wildworks.com

New England Anti-Vivisection Society
333 Washington S., Ste. 850
Boston, MA 02108-5100
(617) 523-6020
Fax: (617) 523-7925
info@ma.neavs.com
www.neavs.org

Orangutan Foundation International
822 Wellesley Avenue
Los Angeles, CA 90049
(310) 207-1655
Fax: (310) 207-1556
ofi@orangutan.org
www.orangutan.org

People for the Ethical Treatment of Animals
501 Front Street
Norfolk, VA 23510
(757) 622-PETA (7382)
peta@peta-online.org
www.peta-online.org

PIGS, a sanctuary
P.O. Box 629
Charles Town, WV 25414
(304) 725-PIGS (7447) (fax same)
PIGSANCT@aol.com
www.pigs.org

Psychologists for the Ethical Treatment of Animals
403 McCauley Street
P.O. Box 1297
Washington Grove, MD 20882
(301) 963-4751 (fax same)
drea@cove.com
www.northshore1.com/animalhell/

Rabbit Lady's Rabbit Rescue
P.O. Box 140317
Brooklyn, NY 11214-0137
(718) 331-8918

Rainforest Action Network
221 Pine Street, Ste. 500
San Francisco, CA 94104
(415) 398-4404
Fax: (415) 398-2732
rainforest@ran.org
www.ran.org

Rainforest Relief
P.O. Box 150566
Brooklyn, NY 11215
(718) 398-3760
relief@igc.apc.org

Rat Allies
P.O. Box 3453
Portland, OR 97208
(503) 287-7894

Retirement Home for Horses
P.O. Box 2100
Alachua, FL 32616-2100
(904) 462-1001
Fax: (904) 462-1002

Save a Turtle
P.O. Box 361
Islamorada, FL 33036
(305) 743-6056

Save Our Swans
8242 Lake Pine Drive
Commerce Township, MI 48382
(248) 360-6585

Save the Whales
P.O. Box 2397, Venice, CA 90291
(800) WHALE-65
Fax: (831) 394-5555
savethewhales@interworld.net
www.savethewhales.org

SKUNKS (Society of Kind Understanding for Not Killing Skunks)
P.O. Box 82
Topanga, CA 90290
(310) 724-9643
Fax: (818) 779-7915
Skunks1@aol.com

Tiger Haven
237 Harvey Road
Kingston, TN 37763
(423) 376-4100
Fax: (423)376-0284
IndiaB@tigerhaven.org

Winged Iguana Hotline
contact: Joleen Lutz
(818) 842-6084

World Wildlife Fund
1250 24th Street NW
Washington, DC 20037-1175A
http://www.wwf.org

Companies That Don't Test on Animals

(An asterisk indicates companies with products that contain no animal ingredients.)

A.J. Funk & Company
ABBA products, Inc.*
Abracadabra, Inc.*
Adrien Arpel
Advanced Research Labs
AFM Enterprises*
Alba Botanica Cosmetics
Alexandra Avery/Purely Natural
    Body Care
Alexia Alexander*
Allens Naturally*
Almay Hypo-Allergenic
Aloe Creme Laboratories
Aloe Up, Inc.
Aloe Vera of America, Inc.
Amberwood
American International Inc.
American Merfluan, Inc.*
American Safety Razor*
America's Finest Products
Amway Corporation
Ananda Country Products*
Andalina
Animals Love Us
Aphrodite's Garden
Aramis Inc.
Arbonne Int'l*
Archangel Trading Co., Inc.
Arixona Natural Resources
Aroma Lamp, Inc.
Aromavera Company
Attar Bazaar/Chishti Co.
Aubrey Organics
Aura Cacia, Inc.*
Auro Trading Company
Auromere Ayurvedic Imports*
Aurora Henna Company
Autumn Harp, Inc.

Aveda Corp.
Avigal Henna*
Avon Products, Inc.
Aware Diaper, Inc.
Ayagutag
Ayurveda Holistic Center*
Aztex Secret*
Banana Boat Products
Barbers Hairstyling for Men and
    Women, Inc.
Barbizon, Int'l, Inc.
Basically Natural
Bath and Body Works
Baudelaire, Inc.
Beauty without Cruelty*
Beehive Botanicals, Inc.
Belle Star, Inc.
Belle's Secret Garden
Benekiser Consumer Products
Benetton Cosmetics Corp.
Bio-Botanica, Inc.
Biogime*
Bi-O-Kleen Industries*
Bio-Pac
Bio-Tec Cosmetics, Inc.
Blackmores, Ltd.
Blessed Herbs
Blue Cross Beauty Products
Blue Ribbons Pet Care
Body & Soul
Body Drench
Body Love Natural Cosmetics
Body Suite
Bodyography
BodyTime
Bonne Bell, Inc.
Borlind of Germany, Inc.
Botanical Products, Inc.

Botanicus, Inc.
Bouhon Cosmetics, Inc.
Brocato International Hair*
Bronson Pharmaceuticals
Brookside Soap Co.*
California Skin Therapy
California Tan
Camo Care
Candy Kisses Natural Lip Balm
Carina Supply, Inc.
Carma Laboratories, Inc.
Carme
Caswell-Massey
Celestial Body
Chanel, Inc.
Chempoint Products Company
Chenti Products, Inc.
CHIP Distribution Company*
Christian Dior Perfumes, Inc.
Citre Shine
Clarins of Paris
Clean and Easy
Clear Vue Products, Inc. *
Clearly Natural Products, Inc.
Clientele, Inc.
Clinique
Color Me Beautiful
Colourings
Columbia Cosmetics Mfg., Inc.
Comfort Manufacturing Co.
Common Scents
Compassionate Consumer
Conair Corporation
Concept Now Cosmetics
Co-op America
Cosmyl, Inc.
Country Comfort
Country Save Corporation
Crabtree & Evelyn, Ltd.
Creme de la Terre
Crystalline Cosmetics, Inc.
CSA/IQ
Decleor USA, Inc.
Del Laboratories

Deodorant Stones of America*
Dep Corporation
Derma-Life Corp.
Dermatologic Cosmetics Labs
Dermatone Lab, Inc.
Desert Essence
Desert Naturels*
DeSoto-Prescott, Inc.
Don't Be Cruel, Inc.
Dr. Bronner's "All-One" Products*
Dr. Hauschka Cosmetics
E. Burnham Cosmetic Co., Inc.
Earth Friendly Products
Earth Naturals
Earth Science, Inc.
Ecco Bella
EcoSafe
Ecover Products
Eden Botanicals
Epilady Int'l, Inc.
Essential Products of America,
    Inc.*
Estee Lauder Cos.
European Touch
Faultless Starch Bon Ami
Flex (Revlon)
Focus 21 International, Inc.
Forever New*
Four (IV) Trail*
Fragrance Impressions Ltd.
Framesi
Frank T. Ross & Sons, Ltd.*
Free Spirit Enterprises*
Freeman Cosmetics Corp.
Frontier Cooperative Herbs
Fruit of the Earth, Inc.
Gena Labs
General Nutrition Corp.
Georgette Klinger, Inc.
Giorgio
Giovanni Hair Care Products
Golden Lotus*
Golden Prise-Rawleigh Enterprises
Goodbodies, USA, Inc.*

Green Ban*
Gucci Parfums
h.e.r.c. Inc.*
H20 Plus L.P.
Healthy Times*
Heavenly Soap
Heritage Store, Inc.
Hobe Laboratories, Inc.
Holloway House, Inc.
Home Health Products Co.
Home Service Products Co.*
Huish Detergents, Inc.
Human Kind
Humane Alternative Products
II-Makiage, Inc.
Internatural
J.R. Liggett Ltd.
Jacki's Magic Lotion
Jaclyn Cares
Jafra Cosmetics, Inc.
James Austin Company
Jason Natural Cosmetics
Jeanne Naté
Jeanne Rose New Age – Creations
    Herbal Body Works
Jessica McClintock Inc.
John Paul Mitchell Systems*
Joico Labs, Inc.
Jojoba Resources, Inc.
Jolen, Inc.
Kallima International, Inc.
Key West Fragrances & Cos.
Kiss My Face
Kleen Brite Labs, Inc.
KMS Research, Inc.
Kneipp Corp of America
KSA Jojoba*
La Naturals, Inc.
LaCosta Products, Int'l
LaCrista, Inc.*
Lady Bird Exclusive Private
Lady of the Lake Company
Lancôme (Cosmair)
L'anza Research Lab*

Levlad, Inc.
Liberty Natural Products, Inc.
Life Brand
Life Tree Products*
Lightning Products
Lily of Colorado
Lion & Lamb Products
Liz Claiborne Cosmetics
Logona USA, Inc.
Lotions & Potions
Lotus Light Enterprises*
Louise Bianco Skin Care, Inc.*
Magic of Alow, Inc.
Magick Botanicals/Magick Mud
Marcal Paper Mills, Inc.
Marchemco Corp.
Martin von Myering*
Mastey De Paris, Inc.
Maybelline, Inc. (Yardley)
Melaleuca, Inc.
MEN by Geoff Thompson
Merle Norman Cosmetics
Metrin International*
Mia Rose Products, Inc.
Micro Balanced Products
Mill Creek
Modafini, Inc.
Mountain Ocean, Ltd.
Murphy-Phoenix Co.
Narwhale of High Tor, Ltd.
National Home Care Products, Inc.
Naturade
Natural Bodycare*
Natural Childcare, Inc.
Natural Research People, Inc.
Naturally yours, Alex*
Nature Cosmetics, Inc.*
Nature de France, Ltd.*
Nature Food Centers, Inc.
Nature's Choice
Nature's Colors Cosmetics, Ltd.
Nature's Elements Int'l
Nature's Gate Herbal Cosmetics
Nature's Plus

Naturistics

Natus

Nectarine

Nemesis, Inc.

New Age Creations/Jeanne Rose

New Age Products*

New Earth Cosmetics

New Methods

New Moon Extracts, Inc.*

New Ways

Nexxus Products Company

Nirvana Inc.*

Nivea (Beiersdorf)

No Common Scents

Noah's Ark Cosmetic & Household, Inc.

Nordstrom Cosmetics

Norelco*

North Country Glycerin Soap

NuSkin International, Inc.

Nutri-Metics Int'l Inc.

Nylynn Cosmetics, Inc.

Oasis Brand Products

Ocyfresh USA, Inc.*

Only Natural, Inc.

Orange-Mate, Inc.*

Oriflame International

Orjene Cosmetics Co., Inc.

Orlane

Orly International

Palm Beach Beauty Products

Para Labs, Inc.

Parfums Houbigant Paris

Parfums Nina Ricci, US

Park-Rand Enterprises

Pathmark

Patricia Allison

Paul Penders

P-Bee Products

Peaceable Kingdom

Peelu Products, Inc.

Pet Connection

PetGuard

Pets 'N People, Inc.*

Potions & Lotions – Body & Soul

Premier One Products

Prescriptives

Prestige Cosmetics

Princess Marcella Borghese, Inc.

Pro Finish

Prof. & Tech. Servs., Inc.

Professional Choice Hair Pds.

Pro-Ma Systems, Inc.

Rachel Perry, Inc.

Rainbow Concepts

Rainbow Research Corp.

Rainforest Essentials

Ralph Lauren Fragrances

Ranir/DCP Corp.

Rathdowney, Ltd.

Ravenwood

RC International

Real Aloe, Co.

Redken Laboratories, Inc.

Redmond Products, Inc.

Reviva Labs, Inc.

Revlon, Inc.

Rialto

Riviera Concepts, Inc.

Royal Labs Natural Cosmetics*

Russ Kalvin's Hair Care

Safer Chemical Co.

Safeway, Inc. (housebrands only)

Sally Hansen

San Francisco Soap Company

Sanofi

Santa Fe Fragrance, Inc.*

Sappo Hill Soapworks

Scandinavian Natural Health & Beauty Products, Inc.

Schiff

Schroeder & Tremayne, Inc.

Schwarzkoph, Inc.

Sebastian International, Inc.

SerVaas Labs, Inc.*

Seventh Generation

Shahin Soap*

Shaklee U.S., Inc.

Shikai Products
Shirley Price Aromatherapy
Siddha International
Sierra Dawn*
Simple Wisdom, Inc.
Simplers Botanical Co.*
Sinclair & Valentine*
Skedaddle, The Natural Alternative
Sleepy Hollow
Smith & Vandiver, Inc.
Soap Factory
SoapBerry Shop
Soujourner Farms
Spa Natural Beauty
StarBrite
Stiefel Labs, Inc.
Strong Skin Savvy, Inc.
Studio Magic, Inc.
Sukesha Haircare
Sumeru Garden Herbals*
Sunfeather Herbal Soap Co.*
Sunshine Natural Products*
Sunshine Products Group
Super Nature Cruelty Free
   Products
Tanning Research Labs
TAUT by Leonard Engleman
Terra Flora Herbal Body Care
Terra Nova
Terry Labs
The Principle Secret

Third Millennium Science
Tom Fields, Ltd.
Tom's of Maine
Trader Joe's Company
Traditional Products
Tressa, Inc.
Ultima II
Uncommon Scents, Inc.
United Colors of Benetton Tribu*
Val-Chem Co., Inc.
Vapor Products
Veg Essentials
Vegelatum*
Venus & Apollo
Vermont Soapworks*
Victoria Jackson Cosmetics, Inc.
Victoria's Secret
Virginia's Soap, Ltd.
Visage Beauté Cosmetics, Inc.
Warm EArth Cosmetics*
Watcher's Organic Sea Prd.
Weleda, Inc.
Wella Corporation
Wellington Labs, Inc.
Winter White*
Wisdom Toothbrush, Co.
WiseWays Herbals
Wysong Corp.
Yves Rocher, Inc.
Zia Cosmetics
Zinzare International Ltd.

Companies That Do Test on Animals

Alberto-Culver Co. (TRESemme)
Alcon Labs
Allergan, Inc.
Andrew Jergens Co.
Aziza
Bausch & Lomb
Boyle-Midway
Bristol-Myers Squibb Co.
Carter-Wallace (Arrid, Lady's Choice)
Chesebrough-Ponds (Oil of Olay)
Church & Dwight (Arm & Hammer)
Clairol
Clarion
Clorox
Colgate-Palmolive
Commerce Drug Co.
Consumer Value Stores
Coty
Cover Girl
DowBrands
Drackett Products Co.
EcoLab
El Sanofi Inc.
Eli Lilly & Co.
Elizabeth Arden
Fabergé
Fendi
Givaudan-Roure
Glame Glow
Helene Curtis Industries (Helene Curtis)
ISO
Jhirmack
Johnson & Johnson
S.C. Johnson & Son
Johnson Products Co.
Jovan (Quintessence)

Kimberly-Clark Corp. (Kleenex)
Kiwi Brands
Lever Brothers
Max Factor
Mead
Melaleuca, Inc.
Mennan Co.
Naturelle
Neotoric Cos. (Alpha Hydrox)
Neutrogena
Neutron Industries, Inc.
Pantene
Parfums Int'l (White Shoulders)
Pennex
Pfizer
Physicians Formula Cosmetics
Playtex Corporation
Prince Machiavelli
Proctor & Gamble Co. (Crest, Tide)
Quintessence
Reckitt & Colman
Richardon-Vicks
Schering-Plough (Coppertone)
Schick
Scott Paper Co.
SmithKlineBeecham
St. Ives Labs, Inc.
Stanhome Inc.
Sterling Drug
Sun Star
Sunshine Makers
3M
Unilever
Vidal Sassoon
Warner-Lambert
Westwood Pharmaceuticals
Whitehall Laboratories

Reprint Acknowledgments

Grateful acknowledgment is made to the following for permission to reprint previously published material:

The Crossing Press, Inc.: Excerpts reprinted with permission from MOTHER WIT by Diane Mariechild, copyright 1981. Published by the Crossing Press, Freedom, California.

Doubleday: Excerpt from THE POWER OF MYTH by Joseph Campbell. Copyright © 1988 by Alfred Van Der Marck Editions and Apostrophe S Productions, Inc. Reprinted by permission of Doubleday, a division of Random House, Inc.

Graywolf Press: Excerpt from IF YOU WANT TO WRITE copyright 1987 by the Estate of Brenda Ueland. Reprinted from IF YOU WANT TO WRITE with the permission of Graywolf Press, Saint Paul, Minnesota.

HarperCollins Publishers: Excerpts from THE DANCING WU LI MASTERS by Gary Zukav. Copyright © 1979 by Gary Zukav. Reprinted by permission of HarperCollins Publishers.

Henry Holt and Company: "Man and Creature" from THE TEACHING OF REVERENCE FOR LIFE by Albert Schweitzer, © 1965 by Henry Holt and Company. Reprinted by permission of Henry Holt and Company, LLC.

Helen L. McKinnon: Excerpt from IT'S FOR THE *ANIMALS!* NATURAL CARE AND RESOURCES by Helen L. McKinnon. Reprinted by permission of the author.

National Anti-Vivisection Society, UK: Excerpts from "A Technical Report" by the National Anti-Vivisection Society; excerpts from the "Summary of Current Research Projects" sponsored by the Lord Dowding Fund. Used by permission of the National Anti-Vivisection Society, UK.

Paul Simon Music: Lyrics from "Tenderness" by Paul Simon. Copyright © 1973 Paul Simon. Used by permission of the Publisher: Paul Simon Music.

Penguin Putnam Inc.: Excerpts from TIMEQUAKE by Kurt Vonnegut, copyright © 1997 by Kurt Vonnegut. Used by permission of G.P. Putnam's Sons, a division of Penguin Putnam Inc.

Thinking Allowed Productions: Excerpt from THE HALOGRAPHIC BRAIN, a Thinking Allowed videotape. © 1988, Thinking Allowed Productions.

Index

About the Author

Amelia Kinkade wrote her first how-to book at the age of six. Although "Treat Your Hamster with Care" never made it to publication, thirty years later Amelia accomplished her life-long mission: to champion the thoughts and feelings of animals through her writing. She also enjoyed a career as a professional jazz dancer, choreographer, and actress before coming back to her true love—animals. Passionate about her work, she maintains a private practice in Southern California where she counsels every species of animal from elephants to gorillas, show horses to seeing-eye dogs, lions, and house cats. She also enjoys teaching workshops in animal communication all over the country. In her leisure time, Amelia writes and illustrates children's books with the assistance of her own feline family: Billie Holliday, Ella Fitzgerald, Cyrus Chestnut, and the infamous Oscar Peterson. They model for free.